Our Earth, Ourselves

———————•———————

ENVIRONMENTAL ACTION STAFF

Bill Asp

Thomas Atkins

Rose Marie L. Audette

Margaret Brault

Lynne Capehart

Ruth Caplan

Lisa Collaton

Carol Dansereau

Robert Dewey

Mary Dresser

Nicholas Fedoruk

David Goeller

Morgan Gopnik

Scott Hempling

Nancy Hirsh

Leon Lowery

Casey Padgett

Jim Pierce

Drusilla Schmidt-Perkins

David Simmons

Hawley Truax

Bayard Williams

Jeanne Wirka

Our Earth, Ourselves

The Action-Oriented Guide
to Help You Protect and Preserve Our Planet

RUTH CAPLAN
EXECUTIVE DIRECTOR

and the staff of
ENVIRONMENTAL ACTION

FOREWORD BY PETE SEEGER

A Philip Lief Group Book

Riverside Community College
BANTAM BOOKS
NEW YORK · TORONTO · LONDON · SYDNEY · AUCKLAND

This book is dedicated to grassroots environmental activists—
past, present and future.

OUR EARTH, OURSELVES
A Bantam Book / April 1990

A Philip Lief Group Book
6 West 20th Street, 11th floor, New York, NY 10011

Book design and composition by The Sarabande Press
Graphics by Visual Solutions

Library of Congress Cataloging-in-Publication Data
Caplan, Ruth.
Our earth, ourselves / by Ruth Caplan and the staff of
Environmental Action; foreword by Pete Seeger; produced by the
Philip Lief Group.
p.   cm.
Includes bibliographical references.
ISBN 0-553-34857-4
1. Pollution.   2. Pollution—United States.   3. Environmental
protection—Citizen participation   4. Environmental protection—
United States—Citizen participation.   I. Environmental Action
(Organization)   II. Philip Lief Group.   III. Title.
TD175.C37   1990
363.7'00973—dc20   89-18379 CIP

Published simultaneously in the United States and Canada

PRINTED IN THE UNITED STATES OF AMERICA
0 9 8 7 6 5 4 3 2

CONTENTS

ACKNOWLEDGEMENTS

This book has been a cooperative effort in the truest sense of the word. From the Environmental Action staff who shaped the book's approach and wrote the chapters, to the activists who told their stories, to the outside reviewers who gave helpful suggestions, and to the many who refined the final text, we all worked together to produce *Our Earth, Ourselves*.

Without three people, however, the book could never have been written. Hawley Truax, co-editor of *Environmental Action Magazine*, coordinated the many elements of the project, played a large role in the writing effort, and with good cheer kept us all on schedule. EA's media coordinator, David Goeller, took major responsibility for editing and polishing the book and writing the profiles, "People Making a Difference." And special thanks also go to Patty Leasure, with The Philip Lief Group in New York, whose help, ideas and vision were invaluable.

Our Earth, Ourselves draws on the expertise of our staff—present and past. Every staff member contributed directly or indirectly to the project, with major research and writing efforts by Lynne Capehart, Lisa Collaton, Morgan Gopnik, Nancy Hirsh, Leon Lowery, Casey Padgett and Jeanne Wirka. Considerable help also came from Thomas Atkins, Nicholas Fedoruk, Jim Pierce, Carol Dansereau and Robert Dewey. Thanks to Rose Marie Audette, the other editor of our magazine, for her exceptional effort to keep the magazine going during the course of the book project. Daniel Becker, a former staffer, remained with us in spirit and contributed valuable suggestions, expertise and general wisdom to several chapters. Portions of Chapter 9 are drawn from *Making Polluters Pay*, an activist handbook written by Andrew Moore and published by EA. This chapter reflects the toxics organizing experience of Adrienne Anderson.

We are extremely grateful to those outside of our organization for their expertise, advice and support. Special thanks to chapter reviewers Steve Anderson and Liz Cook. Others who helped move this book from concept to reality include Anne-Marie Amantia, Hal Burdett, Sara Freedheim, Erica Guttman, Allen Rosenfeld, Dianne Russell, Steve Schwartzman and Jay Townsend.

Finally, we thank the New York crew. The Philip Lief Group guided the book's development and production from start to finish. Linda Loewenthal, our editor at Bantam, provided insightful suggestions and expeditious editing. And thanks to Tim Frew for digesting vast amounts of research materials and writing assistance; Scott Corngold for writing assistance; and Susan Davis for copyediting.

Ruth Caplan

FOREWORD

BY PETE SEEGER

If there is a human race on this planet a few hundred years from now, it will be because millions of people found ways to become active in their home communities, and through their actions persuaded their neighbors to change their outlook and, in part, change their way of life. This book points the way.

Words are convenient tools. I'm using them now. But if we depend on them too much, we can fool ourselves. We also need action. For me and my family, it's been food and festivals, pictures, songs, sailing, picking up litter, recycling and voting, as well as, I'll confess, a lot of committee meetings, messages and phone calls. At least we've helped win a few victories. The Hudson River, which was an open sewer 20 years ago, is now swimmable in the middle part. In 5 to 10 years, it should be swimmable near New York City.

Friends, the following song was written long ago but it could have been written for this book. Can we work together? Can we sing together? Let's try.

MY RAINBOW RACE

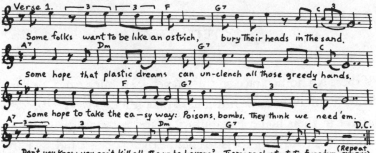

Verse 1.

Some folks want to be like an ostrich, bury Their heads in the sand.

Some hope that plastic dreams can un-clench all those greedy hands.

Some hope to take the ea—sy way: Poisons, bombs, They think we need 'em.

Don't you know you can't kill all The un-be-lievers? There's no shortcut to freedom. (Repeat CHORUS)

Verse 2.

Go tell, go tell all the lit-tle children. Tell all The mothers and fathers Too.

Now's our last chance to learn to share what's been given——to me and you. ONE BLUE SKY A— (Repeat CHORUS 1½ times).

(Note: Altos and baritones will find This a lot easier to sing in the Key of G or A)

Words and Music by Pete Seeger ©1967 Sanga Music, N.Y., N.Y.

Our Earth, Ourselves

CHAPTER ONE

Our Earth, Our Mission

BY RUTH CAPLAN

This book is about the serious disease that is afflicting our Earth and what we can do to improve the planet's health.

By now, we are all familiar with the symptoms of this global illness. They include ozone smog choking our cities. Oil soaking our beaches. Radon filling our basements. Summers becoming hotter and hotter. Garbage barges looking for a place to unload. Toxic chemicals contaminating our drinking water.

3

Pesticides tainting our fruits and vegetables. Global population outstripping food production. Skin cancer rates rising from increased exposure to the sun's harmful ultraviolet rays.

Humans are the carriers of this disease. We are also the ones who must administer the cure.

Our Earth, Ourselves is a call to action. Some books tell you how to fix a house. This book tells you how you can help fix our planet. We have chosen to focus on problems that are most likely to affect your health and welfare—increased flooding and loss of productive farmland from global warming, increased risk of cancer from ozone depletion, toxic chemicals, unhealthy air, unsafe energy—where taking personal action and organizing in your local community *can* make a difference. We are convinced that as people become more sensitive to how their everyday lives contribute to environmental problems, they will take corrective action and choose new paths.

In each chapter you will find concise descriptions of major environmental threats facing us today. For each problem, we outline the kinds of actions that will have concrete results. You will find a variety of ways you can get involved: as an individual, as a member of your community, as a voter. You will also find in each chapter vignettes of people who refused to take "no" for an answer—people who responded to environmental challenges with actions that have made a real difference.

You may also find that a particular problem is of special concern to you: This book will show you how to get more involved. And in addition to the specific suggestions for action at the end of each chapter, we have included a chapter on "Becoming an Environmental Activist" to give you some tools that we have found especially helpful.

Just as there is an ecological niche for countless varieties of species, there is also a niche in the environmental movement for a broad array of actions. Some actions we can take as individuals; some are best done by informal groups; some require the cooperation of our communities; some need the leverage of national environmental organizations; and some demand the leadership of our elected officials in state capitals and Washington, D.C. There is an important niche in the environmental movement for you. Whether you decide to bring your aluminum cans and newspapers to a recycling center, or help start a local environmental group in your community to protect your drinking water, or write your state representative in support of energy efficiency legislation, you can become part of the solution.

You undoubtedly decided to read this book because you care about the environment and want to get involved. Environmental Action decided to write this book because we believe citizen action is the most important part of the prescription to cure our planet. While each of us alone may bring about a small change, all of us together can make a tremendous difference.

The good news is that you are not alone. Millions of Americans care. When you take any one of the steps outlined in this book, you can do so knowing that Americans across the country are concerned about the environment just as you are. A 1988 Gallup Poll found that 84 percent of Americans are very concerned about pollution of fresh water, up from 48 percent in 1970; 73 percent are very concerned about air pollution, up from 46 percent in 1970. And in 1988, 65 percent of Americans said the United States is spending too little to protect the environment, according to the National Opinion Research Center. These findings are confirmed by poll after poll.

Given the global nature of many of our environmental problems, recent evidence of growing public concern around the world is heartening. When Louis Harris conducted the first international poll on the environment in 1988, he found overwhelming support for environmental protection: In 15 countries spread over five continents, 80 percent of the respondents considered water pollution a major problem; 71 percent supported higher taxes to prevent pollution of our air, land, and water.

In many cases, pollution and other problems in our environment know neither state nor national boundaries. The smokestacks of coal-burning power plants in our Midwest are the sources of acid rain falling in Canada. Our Southwest gets fallout from smelters in Mexico. Dangerous ozone smog travels thousands of miles from traffic-clogged cities to remote wilderness areas. Our fruit may contain dangerous pesticides that were applied in South America, but made in the U.S.A. — pesticides that U.S. companies are forbidden to market here, but are free to sell overseas.

Unless we think globally, some threats to our Earth may prove irreversible: global warming, desertification, deforestation, loss of species, destruction of the stratospheric ozone layer. Not just America, but the world must change the way it does business. This means that industrialized nations must make major cutbacks in their production of global warming gases. Newly industrializing nations must be helped to finance nonpolluting energy sources. Nations with rain forests must find ways to have a viable economy without cutting down their forests for short-term profits. We have a global economy. How it operates will set the course either for future environmental devastation or for our being able to live within the bounds of our sustainable resources.

When you think about the global problems that we face, you should keep in mind a well-used axiom in the environmental movement: Think globally and act locally. You are part of the global economy, which means your actions here at home can become a part of the solution, no matter on what level you choose to act.

At the local level, environmentalists have been termed NIMBYs—"Not In My Backyard"—by the industries they fight. Sure, nobody wants a toxic waste dump in their backyard. Now the time has come to redefine our backyard. It extends beyond the boundaries of our property, our town, our country. It is everywhere. Once we each grasp this concept, the polluters will have nowhere to run.

It is this need for increased awareness of how all of us around the world are part of the problem and part of the solution that makes the challenges of the next two decades significantly different than the challenges of the last two decades since the first Earth Day in 1970. Today we know that the industrial pollutants released from smokestacks in one nation cause forest loss in nations downwind. We see that our discarded plastic containers no longer just litter our roadsides; they are washed up on remote island shores. We are aware that the chemicals used in refrigerators to keep our food cold contribute to global problems of climate change and threaten to increase skin cancer throughout the world. We know that the car is a major contributor not only to the smog shrouding our cities, but to the accumulation of greenhouse gases that cause global warming.

When we act locally to address our global problems, we can often help solve more than one problem at once. Energy efficiency is a good example. If we make our homes more energy-efficient, we reduce the amount of electricity needed from burning fossil fuels and from nuclear power plants. This means less acid rain; less carbon dioxide, which is a major contributor to global warming; and more time to develop renewable energy sources for our future energy needs. And, similarly, if we drive cars that are more fuel-efficient than today's vehicles, we will help clear our air of smog, reduce toxic air emissions, and slow global warming.

Can we do it? Yes. This country has already proven that it

can decrease its energy use without decreasing its productivity, as indicated by the Gross National Product (GNP). Since Earth Day 1970, the United States has reduced the amount of energy needed for each unit of GNP by more than 25 percent. While the GNP increased almost 50 percent, our total energy use increased less than 8 percent during this period.

We have also significantly improved the efficiency of our automobiles. In 1976, just after the federal fuel-efficiency law was passed, our new domestic automobile fleet averaged 16 miles per gallon. By 1988, the new domestic auto fleet averaged 28 miles per gallon. This 75 percent improvement was a result of Detroit having to comply with federal law.

But we can and must do much more, as our pollution problems are far greater than we realized on Earth Day 1970. The carbon dioxide released from U.S. cars and light trucks contributes 1 of every 20 tons of carbon dioxide released worldwide by the burning of fossil fuels. Carbon dioxide is the major contributor to global warming. If we increase the efficiency of our auto fleet to 45 miles per gallon, we will reduce carbon dioxide emissions from each new car by 40 percent. If we start today, we will be able to celebrate our achievements together when Earth Day 2000 arrives.

This book will show you how your individual choices, combined with organized pressure, will lead us toward a future that can sustain our life-giving resources. One of our major challenges is to use fewer resources on a per capita basis. Another is to reduce our use of hazardous materials. This means using energy more efficiently. It means being able to buy durable products that can be repaired. It means growing our food and manufacturing our goods in ways that minimize the use of toxic chemicals.

Organized pressure is important. Time and again, big business interests succeed in weakening or delaying environmental regulations the American public supports. Moreover, we are being deprived of environmental choices because of economic decisions being made by corporations. Environmental products are often priced too high for us to afford. If agribusiness shifted to growing pesticide-free produce, the economies of mass production would lead to lower prices for organic fruits and vegetables.

Our choices are further limited because environmentally sound products are often not even put on the market. Nontoxic paints are nonexistent, not because of technological problems, but because of corporate economic decisions. Nor are corporations investing the research-and-development money required to make such products available. Consumer pressure *can* make a difference. Without it, corporations will continue to offer polluting products and then claim they are just following consumer demand, as Detroit is doing with its gas guzzlers.

We also need our local, state, and federal governments to be our partners. Without government regulations requiring products that do not pollute, we, as consumers, will be robbed of important opportunities to make environmental selections. Without government assistance, many Americans will not be able to afford energy-efficient housing and transportation. Without government research funding, we will not be able to develop advanced nonpolluting technologies.

The challenge ahead for all of us is very great. It calls on us to change the way we go about our daily lives, both individually and collectively. Can we do it? Stop for a moment to think about all the projects we have begun, wondering whether we could ever finish them: painting our houses, packing to move, feeding and clothing our families. But stroke by stroke and day by day, millions of us accomplish these tasks. Now our challenge is to start doing all these things with a new environmental awareness.

Environmental Action has always believed in the effectiveness of grassroots and political action. We all need to recognize that across the country, activists have already made significant strides in protecting our environment. Today, in the face of even more far-reaching threats, many more people are ready and willing to act. *Our Earth, Ourselves* is a blueprint for action. It is designed to help us work toward a future where we are no longer polluting the very resources we need for our survival.

As we mobilize to make the 1990s the environmental decade, we can look ahead with confidence, knowing that we are building on the work of many others. Starting in the late 19th century, John Muir wrote about his deep love of the wilderness that later led him to spearhead the first efforts to protect these magnificent areas from development. In 1949, Aldo Leopold broadened our environmental vision in *A Sand County Almanac* to include an understanding that humans must function as members of the natural world, not as conquerors of it, if we are to survive.

With the publication of *Silent Spring* in 1962, Rachel Carson awakened us to the devastating effect of pesticides on wildlife and their potential harm to humans. And in 1972, U.S. Supreme Court Justice William O. Douglas, in his eloquent dissent in *Sierra Club* v. *Morton*, argued that natural objects, such as the trees atop Mineral King Mountain, should have legal standing "to sue for their own preservation." Since the law treats corporations the same as people, wrote Douglas, "so it should be as respects valleys, alpine meadows, rivers, lakes, estuaries, beaches, ridges, groves of trees, swampland or even air that feels the destructive pressures of modern technology and modern life." These and other ecological visionaries have helped shape our thinking about the environment and have helped protect our natural resources from the ravages of unbridled development.

As a political movement, environmentalism was born on April 22, 1970—the first Earth Day. Twenty million people took to the streets. New York's Fifth Avenue was closed down. In communities across the country, people picked up litter, plugged sewer effluents that were contaminating rivers, demonstrated at polluters' factories. Congress recessed for the day so members could return home and show their environmental stripes. Earth Day was the first environmental mass mobilization in our nation's history and reached people from all walks of life.

Environmental Action was founded by the organizers of the first Earth Day because they wanted the momentum of Earth Day to continue. The focus of the environmental movement was broadened significantly. No longer was its scope primarily preservation of wilderness and wildlife. Pollution of urban and suburban areas was seen as a serious threat to human health, and so the new environmentalists targeted polluters. Environmental Action led the way by pointing the finger at polluters and their friends in Congress, using the Dirty Dozen campaign to focus a public spotlight on the members of Congress with the worst environmental records.

Grassroots groups concerned about conditions in their own backyards sprang up in the wake of Earth Day. Some opened recycling centers staffed by volunteers. Others protested the growing pollution problems in communities across America. Whether it was a toxic waste dump, the loss of wetlands to a shopping mall, or a nuclear power plant, citizens were no longer willing to leave their future in the hands of profit seekers, politicians, and detached regulators.

For these groups, pollution was not an abstraction. There were the "ecotage" tactics of "The Fox" in Kane County, Illinois, who posted signs pinpointing a local polluter. When that didn't work, The Fox was finally driven to dumping toxic waste in the company's corporate headquarters. In California, Cesar Chavez organized a grape boycott to protect farmworkers from unsafe exposure to pesticides. Petition drives were initiated in many communities to stop waste incinerators. Environmentalists began running for local offices. In these and myriad other ways, the new wave of environmentalists spawned by Earth Day made their voices heard in their local communities and across the nation.

Back in Washington, D.C., the organized environmental movement, invigorated by Earth Day, played an essential role in keeping pressure on policymakers and regulators. National and grassroots organizations prodded Congress in the 1970s into strengthening two of our basic environmental laws: the Clean Air Act and Clean Water Act. The same pressure resulted in the Resource Conservation and Recovery Act, which is intended to reduce toxic and solid waste, and the superfund law to clean up the nation's worst toxic waste sites.

But passing laws is not enough if they are not properly enforced. So environmentalists put pressure on regulators as well. Consumer pressure turned out to be an effective way to get regulators to change. One major victory was banning the use of chlorofluorocarbons (CFCs) in aerosol cans.

In 1973, two chemists at the University of California-Irvine discovered that CFCs—a class of laboratory-made chemicals with widespread application and growing use worldwide—were able to destroy the stratospheric ozone molecules that shield our Earth from most of the sun's cancer-causing ultraviolet rays. One of the most common uses for CFCs was as the propellant in aerosol spray cans. Publication of the ozone-destruction finding in 1974 produced newspaper headlines such as "Aerosol Spray Cans May Hold Doomsday Threat."

Environmental and consumer organizations urged people to avoid aerosol cans and to push for their outlawing. The federal government was flooded with letters. One survey showed almost 75 percent of the people sampled had heard of the connection between aerosols and ozone depletion and that half of these people had stopped using aerosol products. By June 1975, the heat led Johnson Wax, a major producer of spray-can products, to halt the use of CFCs voluntarily. In 1977, the government, trailing behind consumers and some private-sector giants, finally banned the use of CFCs in spray cans. This is just one example of how consumer pressure can make a difference in cleaning up our environment.

Pressure for change on the local, state, congressional, and regulatory fronts was beginning to pay off in other ways as well. For instance, Lake Erie was coming back to life. With the banning of DDT, the bald eagle and the osprey were reproducing once again. The environmental movement was making a difference.

The oil crisis caused by the Arab oil embargo of 1973 and the growing concern about pollution from nuclear and fossil- fueled power plants provided the impetus for a second national environmental event: Sun Day on May 3, 1978. On campuses and in communities across the country, citizens began celebrating at dawn. Later, they held workshops and demonstrated solar technologies. Practical how-to books appeared in bookstores. From solar cookers and food driers to passive solar homes and solar collectors, the creative imagination of Americans was starting to harness the sun's energy.

At the same time, wind power was being promoted by activists who thought there was a cleaner, better way to produce electricity than by burning polluting fossil fuels such as coal. The utilities laughed at this notion, but less than a decade later, there were windmill farms in California producing commercial amounts of electricity.

Some members of the new environmental wave talked about

going back to the land. Some actually did so, leaving the rat race of successful professions to begin organic farms. You will meet one such person in Chapter 5. For some people, the "back-to-the-land" movement was a passing phase. For others, it became a permanent way of life. For still others, the new environmental consciousness was expressed by staying in the cities and starting food co-ops, bicycling to work, or becoming vegetarians.

In the public's mind, this movement often became inter-twined with the highly publicized hippie counterculture. This blinded many Americans to the underlying vision, a conviction held by Native Americans for centuries, but one that many of us have yet to grasp: We must find a way to live in harmony with the resources of our planet. This is not a question of alternate lifestyle. It's a matter of survival.

In fact, the two movements of environmental activism and back-to-the-land vision overlapped very little. The activists focused on local or very specific campaigns that were winnable. The visionaries didn't care about specific victories; they wanted to change our whole relationship to our Earth.

If we are going to solve our environmental problems, we must combine action and vision. Not only must we change personal lifestyles, we must change the way America does business. We must understand how environmental problems are interconnected, and we must seek solutions that are mutu-ally reinforcing. Only then will each of our individual actions, no matter how seemingly insignificant when taken alone, contribute to the goal of creating a world that can feed, clothe, and house its people today, tomorrow, and into the next millennia.

Earth Day 1990, the twentieth anniversary of Earth Day, is our launching pad for a new era of environmental activism — this time circling not just the country, but the globe. It is an affirmation that we are one people whose first allegiance is to the Earth and a recognition that we must not wait for ecological disasters before we balance our natural resources and our burgeoning population.

If we fulfill the commitments of Earth Day 1990, the day will likely come when our children's children will ask us increduously, "How did you breathe air, drink water, and eat food that was so polluted?" We believe the day will come when our children will take their children to the seashore and thank us because there are clean beaches to enjoy, fresh air to breathe, a sun in a clear sky, and an unpolluted ocean stretching forth to the horizon.

This can be our legacy if we act. But should we fail to develop and act on our respect for the Earth, the day will surely come, as it has in Mexico City, when schools will be closed for a month to protect children from dangerous levels of air pollution and when parents will wait until midnight before daring to open their windows for a few hours.

The choice is ours. If we make the wrong choice, we may be living the scenario presented in the next chapter.

CHAPTER TWO

As the World Warms

·

CURBING GLOBAL WARMING

It's August 14, 2034, smack in the middle of another summer of our discontent on Planet Earth. Hot, steamy summertime—and the living's not easy.

Especially in places like Chicago, where the thermometer records its fifth triple-digit reading in as many days. Heat victims crowd the neighborhood health clinics that were established in 2029 to relieve pressure on the hospitals. The city has imposed staggered 3-hour lunch breaks to prevent the air-conditioning demands of downtown offices from causing power brownouts. During these "sizzling siestas," workers seek relief in the new underground parks or in theaters along The Loop. There are long lines for air-conditioned matinees of "The Karate Kid, Part 17," the summer's big hit. At the Mercantile Exchange, trading is slow on corn and wheat. With shrinking harvests in the Midwest, the high-rollers are betting on temperature futures—how much averages will rise in dust bowl towns like Cedar Rapids and Topeka in 2035.

In New York City, the dikes have fallen into disrepair. Pumps run continually, but streets are still awash from rising tidal waters. Only half the subway system has been converted to overhead power. In the rest, water is a constant source of short circuits of the third rail. Whenever the thermometer passes 95 degrees, which is happening more and more these days, water in the streets is turned into cloying humidity.

The New York City day has flip-flopped. In the world of business and commerce, from Wall Street to Times Square, the workday begins at 4 p.m. All outdoor construction is done at night. Yankee games start at 2 a.m., the same hour Broadway turns on its lights. As always, the fortunate of New York City are able to escape, but they no longer head for the Hamptons, because rising waters have inundated the Long Island coastline.

The situation is much the same for most low-lying areas along America's perimeter. Higher ocean levels have ravaged the Atlantic and Gulf coasts, eroding beaches. Big cities like Miami and New Orleans were able to afford dikes. But Atlantic City is underwater and what's left of Key West is accessible only by air and water.

In the heartland, corn and wheat production is falling victim to heat and drought to the point that experts are warning that in 3 years the United States will be meeting more than half its grain needs with imports. Underground water supplies are disappearing rapidly as agribusiness withdraws increasing amounts for irrigation. The Great Plains is dying as a breadbasket.

Farther west, reduced precipitation in the Rockies and the Sierras continues to have far-reaching effects. The western desert is widening and spreading northward. Fires level millions of acres of dry forests. Redwood groves are a memory. In California, the water wars between the once-fertile Central Valley and the thirsty cities are raging. Around the country, painful economic disruption and increasing food shortages are causing growing despair, with frequent eruptions of urban rioting.

Welcome to "Global Warming: 2034," the massive climate change that scientists were warning about decades before. For people living in 2034, it seemed the most frustrating part of the horrible mess was that for too long the world ignored the danger signals and warnings, deciding instead to wait for irrefutable and possibly irreversible proof.

To find out what these warnings were all about, we'll return from future fantasy to the reality of the late 20th century and the "greenhouse effect"—the name commonly applied to the atmospheric dynamics that create global warming.

THE GREENHOUSE EFFECT

In simplified terms, here's how the process works: The sun's rays penetrate the Earth's atmosphere and reach the planet's surface where they are absorbed by land and water. The Earth's surface in turn radiates infrared energy back into the atmosphere. The bulk of this invisible energy passes through the main components of the atmosphere—nitrogen and oxygen—and escapes into outer space. If the atmosphere contained no other gases, our Earth would be a rather cold place, some 50 degrees colder. But the atmosphere contains a small percentage of molecules that block and absorb some of the escaping energy.

The absorption of this radiation produces significant amounts of heat. Even though the absorbing molecules are relatively few, the result of the process is a warmer atmosphere than would otherwise be the case. This curious atmospheric property of allowing solar radiation to enter freely while partially blocking returning radiation is similar to the heat-trapping role played by the glass in a botanical greenhouse. The atmospheric process has thus gained the convenient yet inaccurate name of the greenhouse effect.

In the context of global warming, the absorbing gases are called "greenhouse gases." They include carbon dioxide—the most significant—chlorofluorocarbons, ground-level ozone, methane, nitrous oxide, and water vapor.

The planet Venus provides a good example of a very strong greenhouse effect. If our sister planet had an atmosphere identical to Earth's, it would be a somewhat hotter place because it is closer to the sun. But the mostly carbon dioxide atmosphere of Venus makes it much hotter—840 degrees on the surface.

The proper amounts of greenhouse gases in our atmosphere are what has made it possible for Earth to sustain life as we know it. Without them, too much of the sun's heat would be radiated directly back into space and the Earth's temperature would be cooler; too high a concentration of greenhouse gases and the Earth becomes warmer.

THE IMPLICATIONS OF GLOBAL WARMING

Since the industrial revolution of the last century, humans have been adding increasing amounts of greenhouse gases to the atmosphere. Scientists say the Earth's average temperature has risen about 1 degree since the 1850s. The planet has experienced a series of natural climatological swings that over millions of years have run the gamut from ice age to extreme heat. In the 1980s, voices from the scientific community began warning that modern civilization was overloading our atmosphere with greenhouse gases and upsetting our planet's climatological balance.

The concluding statement of a major international conference on global warming held in Toronto in July 1988 put it this way: "Humanity is conducting an unintended, globally pervasive experiment whose ultimate consequences could be second only to a global nuclear war. The Earth's atmosphere is being changed at an unprecedented rate by pollutants resulting from human activities, inefficient and wasteful use of fossil fuels, and the effects of rapid population growth in many regions. These changes represent a major threat."

A month earlier, the danger was enunciated much more succinctly by Dr. James Hansen, the physicist who is director of NASA's Goddard Institute of Space Studies and one of the scientific community's foremost authorities on the dangers of global warming. "We're loading the climate dice," Hansen told a hearing by the Senate Energy and Natural Resources Committee.

The hearing was important. But this was not the first time the global warming threat was raised on Capitol Hill. On a number of previous occasions, Hansen and other government scientists had delivered similar messages to other congressional committees.

What they said in June 1988 was a stronger version of what they had shared with the Senate Environment Committee two years earlier: The greenhouse scenario had advanced beyond the stage of theory. Global warming is real. It is occurring *now* and must be confronted before the Earth experiences dangerous climate changes that might be irreversible. ["Global warming is inevitable. It is only a question of magnitude and time," said Robert Watson, also a NASA scientist.] A handful of senators heard this dramatic testimony in 1986, and the regular Capitol Hill coterie of environmental reporters wrote stories that attracted limited interest.

Two years later, when similar warnings were voiced before the Energy Committee, the hearing room was jammed with media, including crews from the television networks. The difference? America was sweltering in the summer of 1988, part of what became the hottest year on record since the government began keeping weather statistics 100 years earlier. Baked urban areas, parched and dying crops, widespread drought, forest fires throughout the West—these and other heat-related problems—coupled with warnings from respected scientists added up to "big news." It marked the day that the media discovered global warming and put it on the front pages and the nightly news.

None of the witnesses could say flatly that the summer of 1988 was caused by global warming. But they said the searing temperatures and related effects were entirely consistent with the greenhouse theory.

Although 1988 was the hottest year on record in the United States, it was not an isolated occurrence. Before 1988, the five hottest years recorded, in descending order, were 1987, 1983, 1981, 1980, and 1986.

Another warning sign comes from Mauna Loa in Hawaii, where scientists have been measuring carbon dioxide concentrations in the atmosphere since 1958. Over 30 years, carbon dioxide levels there have climbed by 25 percent to a point that scientists say is the highest in at least 130,000 years.

Sea levels are rising worldwide. This is consistent with

warnings that global warming will melt glaciers and warm ocean temperatures, thereby increasing the volume of the waters.

Using more sophisticated computer models not available to their predecessors, a growing chorus of scientists is warning of more extreme temperature increases in the early to middle 21st century. The mid-latitudes, a heavily populated belt that includes the United States, the Mediterranean, and much of China, could be hard hit by these changes. These scientists differ on the question of how hot and how soon. Generally, they are predicting average temperature rises of from 3 to 9 degrees over the next century. The last time temperatures were 9 degrees higher, dinosaurs populated the Earth.

These projected higher temperatures deal in averages, not extremes. Different regions would experience varying increases in temperature. Most models project less of an increase in equatorial areas and more of an increase in the mid-latitudes and areas extending to the polar regions. Croplands in the central United States could become too hot and dry for corn and wheat. A warmer northern Canada could become North America's grain belt.

A major question is how oceans will react to rapid climate change. In many respects, science knows more about the solar system than it does about the relationship between the oceans and climate dynamics. Spurred by global warming, researchers now are focusing on this great unknown factor. However, they do know a basic rule of physics: Warm water occupies more space than cold water. The Environmental Protection Agency estimates that the present rate of global warming could cause a sea-level rise of from 5 to 15 inches by 2025. Other projections warn that sea levels could rise as much as 5 feet in the next hundred years.

Some scientists say that warmer oceans could alter current

patterns that generate strange weather. Some predict more frequent, more intense hurricanes. This is not good news for coastal populations and low-lying areas such as river deltas and floodplains.

The Earth's climate has been changing for eons. But as it has swung from warm to icy to warm again, the planet has had centuries to adapt to the changes. Rapid change is another matter. The faster the change, the more unpredictable the results and the harder it will be for society and the natural environment to cope with the situation.

The consequences of global warming are far easier to predict than how rapidly it will occur. Entire species may be unable to adapt to warmer temperatures and drier conditions. Ecological systems could fall out of balance. Vegetation and trees could be especially at risk. The warming of a region, even by a few degrees, could make plants more vulnerable to pests and diseases. Forests in the South, for example, could be replaced by grasslands. If the rate of temperature increase is too rapid, it could outstrip a forest's natural ability to migrate successfully in the direction of its preferred temperature range.

Farmers also could be hit hard by global warming. Even at the current rate of warming, farmlands worldwide could be devastated by heat waves, droughts, and chronic dust bowl conditions. During the summer of 1988, U.S. crop yields fell below domestic consumption for the first time in history. We had ample grain reserves to make up the deficit, but repeated droughts of that magnitude could strain the nation's grain supply.

City dwellers can expect to swelter more often. One scenario for 2050 has Washington, D.C., getting 12 days of 100+ temperatures each year. The nation's capital already is noted for its humid summers, but it averages only one 100+ day a year. Denver might have polluted air, but at least it's rather temperate, with the mercury rarely topping 100. The Mile High City could expect 16 days of 100 + readings in 2050.

If you want to visit Elvis Presley's mansion in Memphis, don't wait until the summer of 2050. Memphis now averages four 100 + days. In 60 years the number could soar to 42. That's still better than the scenario for Dallas—78 days when the thermometer tops 100. That's virtually all summer and more than 4 times the number of 100 + days the Texas metropolis now experiences.

Triple-digit temperatures mean more than discomfort. With them come more hospital admissions for heat-related problems. The young and the elderly are the people most at risk. A study conducted for the Environmental Protection Agency said that heat-related deaths in the United States would soar from about 1,200 a year to nearly 7,500, with a doubling of carbon dioxide in the atmosphere which is projected during the next century.

Hansen and other scientists estimate that even if humans halted all emissions of greenhouse gases today, those already loaded into our atmosphere would cause yet another 1 degree increase in the Earth's average temperature.

This is not a pretty picture for ourselves, our children, and their children. There *are* numerous steps that can be taken, locally and internationally, to slow, stabilize, or even reverse the rate of warming. But before looking at remedies, let's take a look at the major natural and manufactured gases that are causing our problems.

THE GREENHOUSE GASES

CARBON DIOXIDE (CO2)

A colorless, odorless substance, carbon dioxide (CO2) is the most prevalent greenhouse gas, accounting for about 49 percent of the human-made warming of the atmosphere. As a natural part of the atmosphere, it comprises only 0.033 percent of dry air at ground level. Thus, it takes a relatively small amount of CO2 released by human activity to increase its noticeable level in the atmosphere. Sources of CO2 include respiration of mammals, decomposition of organic matter, and—most important in the greenhouse equation—burning fossil fuels. These fuels account for as much as 75 percent of the human-made C02 loaded into our atmosphere each year.

Unfortunately, fossil fuels are at the heart of modern civilization. Oil, coal, and natural gas heat and cool our indoor environment throughout the developed world. Fossil fuels are our main source of energy for the cars, trucks, buses, trains, ships, and aircraft that take us to work and play and deliver the products that fill our tables and stock our stores.

Worldwide, there were a record 21.6 billion tons of CO2 released by burning fossil fuel in 1988, an amount equal to about 1 percent of the CO2 already present in our atmosphere. This rate of CO2 production from fossil fuels alone will cause a doubling of CO2 in the atmosphere sometime in the next century. The United States, home of the world's biggest vehicular fleet and just 6 percent of the world's population, accounted for nearly 20 percent of the fossil fuel CO2 in 1988. The United States not only led the world in CO2 loadings from fossil fuel combustion, it was highest in emissions on a per-person basis, followed by Canada.

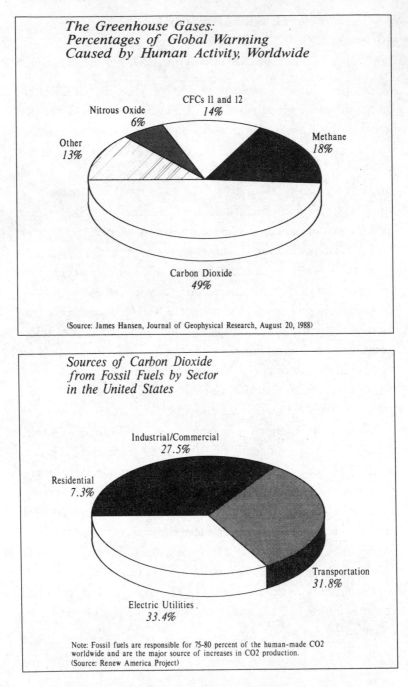

The Greenhouse Gases:
Percentages of Global Warming
Caused by Human Activity, Worldwide

CFCs 11 and 12
14%

Nitrous Oxide
6%

Other
13%

Methane
18%

Carbon Dioxide
49%

(Source: James Hansen, Journal of Geophysical Research, August 20, 1988)

Sources of Carbon Dioxide
from Fossil Fuels by Sector
in the United States

Industrial/Commercial
27.5%

Residential
7.3%

Transportation
31.8%

Electric Utilities
33.4%

Note: Fossil fuels are responsible for 75-80 percent of the human-made CO2
worldwide and are the major source of increases in CO2 production.
(Source: Renew America Project)

After 1971, with industrialization growing around the world, the United States's relative contributions to CO_2 emissions began declining. This trend continued until 1987, when the United State's share of worldwide emissions started rising again, according to the World Resources Institute, a Washington-based research and policy organization.

Other major carbon dioxide sources are the Soviet Union, Western Europe, China, and Japan. Though Japan is a highly industrialized nation, it is far more energy-efficient than the United States, with less than half the per capita emissions of CO_2.

Total global emissions from fossil fuel combustion are rising. Most projections put the increase in fossil fuel consumption at from 1 to 2 percent a year. One estimate says the U.S. CO_2 output could rise by as much as 38 percent by 2010.

The rise is expected to be greater in nations such as China and the Soviet Union if they turn increasingly to their vast deposits of coal to power industrial development and improve standard of living for growing populations. Still further increases in CO_2 emissions can be expected from the developing Third World, where nations are scrambling to grab a share of international markets and where birth rates far exceed those in the developed world.

The Third World's quest for development and increased agricultural production is producing another major and growing source of carbon loadings into the atmosphere: the mass destruction of tropical forests. Worldwide, the destruction of these and other woodlands accounts for an estimated 20 percent of the CO_2 human activity is pumping into the atmosphere each year.

Trees are the natural ally of humans in the battle against global warming. A tree takes in CO_2, returning oxygen to the air and storing carbon. A harvested tree is a double blow to the atmosphere. Not only does it no longer absorb carbon dioxide, if it is burned, the carbons stored in it are released into the atmosphere. Tree by tree, the carbon releases are tiny. Forest acre by forest acre, they are large. And they become immense when millions of acres of tropical rain forest are cut down and burned. By 1989, an estimated one-eighth of the vast Amazon rain forest in Brazil had been slashed and burned. The tragic irony of the destruction of tropical forests in Brazil and other nations is that the cleared land and its fragile soil are able to support farming and ranching for a few short years at best before they are exhausted.

METHANE

Also colorless and odorless, methane accounts for an estimated 18 percent of warming of our atmosphere. Although methane forms a smaller part of the greenhouse-gas volume than does CO_2, it is potentially more dangerous. Each methane molecule is 30 to 40 times more efficient at trapping heat than a CO_2 molecule.

Methane is released from a variety of sources: Natural gas is mostly methane, so natural gas leaks contribute to global warming. Other methane is released during coal mining, oil and gas drilling, and petroleum refining. Burning wood releases methane; garbage dumps emit it. Methane is a by-product of the bacterial decomposition of organic matter in places like rice paddies, swamps, and the intestines of plant-eating creatures such as termites. Methane is contained in the flatulence of cattle and sheep. Methane production worldwide is expected to increase as more cattle are raised and more rice is cultivated to feed increasing numbers of human beings.

Methane levels in our atmosphere have been rising about 1 percent a year for a decade. Normally, methane achieves a stable

AS THE WORLD WARMS

balance in the air. It breaks down through the interaction of sunlight, ozone, and water vapor and is consumed by micro-organisms in water and soil. However, the scientific journal, *Nature*, reported in 1988 that nitrogen fertilizers, which are increasingly used worldwide, interfere with the ability of microbes in the soil to remove methane from the air.

CHLOROFLUOROCARBONS (CFCS)

One of the newer entries in the grim global warming sweepstakes, chlorofluorocarbons (CFCs) have, since their laboratory development in 1928, grown to contribute about 14 percent to the warming of our atmosphere. Odorless and colorless, CFCs are double threats to our Earth, not only contributing to global warming, but also destroying the vital stratospheric ozone layer. (Chapter 3 will discuss this situation in greater detail.)

As greenhouse gases, CFCs are from 10,000 to 20,000 times more effective in trapping heat than CO_2. CFC molecules are also long-lived—from 75 to 100 years. A methane molecule lasts for about 10 years. By contrast, a CO_2 molecule survives for several thousand.

CFCs are all around us. They are coolants in our refrigerators and air conditioners. They are used as solvents for cleaning computer chips, in the manufacture of many plastic foam products, and in aerosol spray cans in much of the world, although this use has been banned in Canada, Sweden, and the United States. Halons, a related chemical, are very effective as fire extinguishers.

Scientists say that atmospheric concentrations of CFCs have been growing about 5 percent a year. In 1987, an international conference settled on a plan to cut CFC production in half by 1999, based on 1986 levels. Some critics of the plan estimate that loopholes will hold the maximum decrease to 30 percent.

Both figures are well below the 85 percent reduction urged by the Reagan administration's Environmental Protection Agency, which was not otherwise known for environmental activism.

NITROUS OXIDE (NOx)

Colorless and sweet-smelling, nitrous oxide (NOx) is known to many people as laughing gas, the mild anesthetic used by dentists. It represents about 6 percent of the global warming produced by greenhouse gases. NOx is a byproduct of fossil fuel combustion, deforestation, bacterial reactions in soil, and the breakdown of widely used nitrogen fertilizers.

OTHER CONTRIBUTORS

A variety of substances produce the remaining 13 percent of atmospheric warming. Naturally occuring water vapor contributes to global warming. So does the human-made problem of ozone smog in lower levels of the atmosphere. This ozone is the major part of our air pollution problems, which will be discussed in detail in Chapter 4.

Dr. James Hansen's warnings about global warming have provoked criticism that he and other scientists are premature in their grim prediction and that they lack definitive proof that we are threatening our Earth and ourselves with massive climate change. Critics like motor vehicle manufacturers are urging a wait-and-see approach. In an editorial in mid-1989, the *New York Times* accused Hansen and his colleagues of crying wolf.

Hansen's response included, in part: "When is the proper time to cry wolf? Must we wait until the prey, in this case, the world's environment, is mangled by the wolf's grip?. . . A greater danger is to wait too long. The climate system has great inertia, so as yet we have only realized a part of the climate change which will be caused by the gases we have already added to the atmosphere. Add to this the inertia of the world's energy, economic and political systems, which will affect any plans to reduce greenhouse gas emissions. Although I am optimistic that we can still avoid the worst case climate scenarios, the time to cry wolf is here."

PEOPLE MAKING A DIFFERENCE

•

ANDY LIPKIS

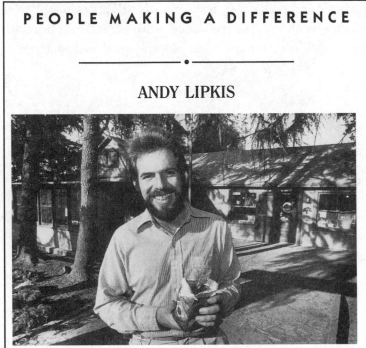

JEFF S. SHARE

Andy Lipkis is a Johnny Appleseed in a world of Paul Bunyans, a tree-planter extraordinaire on a planet where forests are being destroyed at an alarming and dangerous rate.

When Lipkis was 15 years old in 1969, the global warming theory was well-known among scientists but not by the public at large. The spectre of a planet baked by the excesses of industrial pollution and the destruction of rain forests wasn't on Lipkis's mind when he asked officials at a summer camp in California for permission to tear up a camp parking lot so he could plant trees to help offset forest losses from air pollution. He got "no" for an answer and learned the first basic lesson for environmentalists: BE PERSISTENT. He was, and the trees were planted.

As a college sophomore studying ecology, Lipkis learned that the California Division of Forestry had 20,000 surplus smog-resistant seedlings, perfect for replacing trees killed by smog in the San Bernardino National Forest. State foresters said the trees could only be sold, not given away. Lipkis did not have the money to buy the trees, nor the time to raise it. Soon the state would destroy the seedlings to make way for the next year's crop. From this, Lipkis learned another environmentalist lesson: GO PUBLIC. He called newspapers and politicians and generally spread the word. Suddenly, officials were offering him 8,000 free seedlings; the other 12,000 had been plowed under.

Lipkis had only a week to get his seedlings planted. He learned a third lesson: BE CREATIVE. He convinced a dairy to donate 8,000 milk cartons, he spent $60 for a load of topsoil, and he got a developer to donate another load. Enlisting college friends and Boy Scouts, Lipkis got the seedlings planted.

Such were the origins of TreePeople, the nonprofit organization Lipkis formed in Los Angeles to handle the donations citizens sent in after his battle with the Division of Forestry.

Like its trees, TreePeople grew. Although Lipkis doesn't keep a tally of how many trees the group has planted, he reckons during the 1984 push for the Olympics alone his group planted one million trees around Los Angeles. This inspired efforts elsewhere: Australia's 200 Million Tree Campaign and mass plantings in Ireland and London, as well as in Atlanta, Chicago, and Houston. Lipkis and TreePeople closed out the 1980s by aiding plans to plant 5 million more trees in Los Angeles, 20 million in California, and 100 million trees in the American Forestry Association's campaign to break up heat islands in cities.

TreePeople trains citizen foresters and educates people about local and global forest issues. It helped start the Junior Conservation Corps to help divert youth from criminal gangs. TreePeople teaches 50,000 young people a year to recycle, compost, plant seedlings, and identify herbs. It rescued 70,000 surplus fruit trees from nurseries and gave them to low-income families. Some 5,000 such trees were successfully replanted in Africa.

In the beginning, "It was smog and trees," says Lipkis, whose activism has been made even more important by the global warming threat. One of Lipkis's basic tenets is "people taking responsibility for their own lives. Tree planting is our access point to developing stewardship in the general population. We see the tree as a meeting ground for everybody, no matter what their background. Everybody can plant and care for a tree."

WHAT WE CAN DO

INDIVIDUAL ACTIONS

Demand and Practice Auto Efficiency

Efficient use of energy is our most potent, practical weapon in the battle against global warming. Because cars and light trucks account for one-fifth of our CO_2 emissions and are also sources of three other greenhouse gases—CFCs released from air conditioners, ozone smog, and nitrous oxide—our first priority as individuals should be conservation in the transportation sector.

There are more than 135 million cars registered in the United States, and each car emits an average of 5 tons of CO_2 per year. The amount of CO_2 a car produces is related directly to its efficiency. Hence, the more efficient our cars, the less we will be contributing to global warming.

Cars are far more gas-efficient than they were 15 years ago, yet our transportation sector is using a million more barrels of oil per day than it did in 1973. Individuals are driving more miles with fewer people in their cars. More trips are being made in light trucks—jeeps, minivans, and pick-ups—which are subject to lower federal gas mileage standards than passenger cars. Urban driving has increased, as has urban congestion, both of which eat up gasoline.

Buy Efficiency

Buying a fuel-efficient car will decrease your contribution to global warming and help tell auto makers there is a growing demand for these vehicles. Include fuel efficiency in your list of preferred options when you buy a new car. Standard shift cars tend to be more efficient.

Every year, the EPA publishes a gas mileage guide that helps you compare the fuel efficiency and average yearly fuel cost of

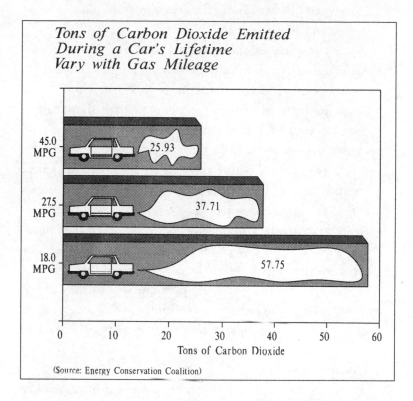

Tons of Carbon Dioxide Emitted During a Car's Lifetime Vary with Gas Mileage

(Source: Energy Conservation Coalition)

similarly sized vehicles. Dealers are required to have free copies in their showrooms. Free copies are also available from the Department of Transportation at (800) 424-9393.

Increase the Efficiency of the Car You Have

Your driving habits can greatly affect the amount of gas your car uses. Here are some steps that will help reduce your car's gas consumption:

- Don't warm up your engine before driving; instead, start out slowly. Avoid racing your engine. Turn off your engine if you have to idle for over one minute. Accelerate and slow down gently; avoid jackrabbit starts or quick braking except for emergencies.

- Obey speed limits. Fuel efficiency generally tapers off at higher and lower speeds.
- Try not to carry extra weight in your car.
- Avoid short trips. Do as little city driving as possible; it consumes twice as much fuel as highway driving.
- Limit your use of air conditioners, as they significantly decrease your car's fuel efficiency. Park your car in the shade to keep it cool. If the car is hot, roll down the windows to cool it before turning on the air conditioner. It's also harmful to engines to turn on the air conditioner before the engine is warmed.
- Keep your car in top operating condition by getting tune-ups regularly, and change oil and filters for both air and oil often. Keep tires inflated to the pressure manufacturers recommend; use radial tires when possible because they add to fuel efficiency. Make sure your wheels are aligned, and use gasoline with the proper octane for your particular model.

Cut Down on Car Use

Our global warming problems can be addressed most quickly and effectively by improving the efficiency of our cars in the ways outlined above. But, ultimately, we must cut down on our car use by creating a society less dependent on cars. Even with more efficient vehicles, their ever-growing number will eventually bring us to the point where the total emission of greenhouse gases will exceed today's. Here are some ways to minimize car use:

- Plan your trips carefully, choosing the shortest, least congested route during nonpeak hours.
- If you live in an urban area, check your public transportation schedules. Buses and subways can be more convenient than you may think. Call your transit agency for information.

- If mass transit won't work, join a car pool. It will cut down on gasoline costs and reduce wear and tear on your car. To hook into an existing car pool, try the index of your yellow pages. Some states have computer networks of commuters who car pool to work in your area. You can also organize a car pool yourself; try posting an announcement at work or in the local paper.

- Consider a bicycle. It's a clean form of transportation. It can be quicker than driving in some congested urban areas. It's also a good form of exercise. Try to create a more bike-friendly environment in your workplace by requesting sturdy bike racks, showers, and changing facilities.

- Work with your local government to make your community more bicycle-friendly. A good first step is to push for your local jurisdiction to acknowledge bicycling as a viable transportation option by assigning someone in its transportation department to deal with bike issues. Push for increased bicycle access to public transit through bike-and-ride stations that have secure storage facilities for bikes. Then get rid of those dangerous drainage grates that trap bike tires. Get your town to create special bike lanes on major thoroughfares. Make sure your roadsides are well-swept. All this can be done without significant financial strain on your town's budget.

For more information on bicyling call the League of American Wheelmen at (301) 944-3399, Bicycle Centennial at (406) 721-1776, or Rails to Trails at (202) 797-5400.

Improve Efficiency in Your Home

More than 7 percent of the CO_2 emissions in the United States comes from homes that burn fossil fuels for cooking, heating, hot water, and other uses.

- Oil furnaces produce more CO_2 than natural gas; opt for the latter if you have the choice.
- If you own an oil furnace, have it thoroughly cleaned and tuned up every year. This cleaning should include vacuuming heat-exchange surfaces and replacing the burner nozzle and all filters. As with cars, a furnace that runs well will be more efficient.
- You should have your furnace periodically checked for efficiency; the CO_2 emission level should be at or below 11 percent.
- Make sure your home is properly insulated. Chapter 4 will provide details.

Plant Some Trees

Another direct action you can take to combat global warming is tree planting. Trees absorb CO_2, and every little bit of CO_2 that is diverted from the atmosphere helps. But trees are not a panacea. To offset current levels of global CO_2 output, we would need to plant some 3 billion acres of trees worldwide. This would require a space that is more than 1 ½ times larger than the continental United States.

Planting trees in the city or around your home can have other more significant benefits. Cities are often 10 degrees warmer than suburbs, partially due to the "heat island effect" caused by the vast expanses of paved areas. Shade from trees can minimize this effect, dramatically reducing the need for air conditioning—an enormous consumer of energy often generated by burning CO_2-producing fossil fuels. Similarly, a few trees placed strategically around your home can reduce air conditioning needs by 10 to 50 percent.

Here are some tips for tree planting from TreePeople, a nonprofit tree-planting organization:

- Before planting, visualize your tree fully grown in that

spot. Can you foresee any problems with driveways, sidewalks, nearby buildings, telephone or power lines?

- Dig a hole 6 to 12 inches wider than the tree's root ball. The depth should be 1½ times the height of the root ball.
- Make sure the root ball doesn't have compacted, self-strangling roots. Loosen them with your fingertips. Keep the roots out of direct sunlight.
- Put some of the loose dirt back in the hole and place the tree so that the top of the root ball is at the soil surface. Pack the soil firmly around the roots with the handle of your shovel to eliminate air pockets. Add more soil and pack again until it is even with the top of the root ball.
- Stake and tie the tree if necessary.
- Use the leftover soil to form a 4-inch deep by 3-foot wide water basin around the tree. Water deeply.

Tree planting is a natural community project. Organize a tree-planting day in your neighborhood. You can get help from neighborhood organizations or local environmental groups. And donations—money from local businesses, corporations, service clubs or even trees themselves from a local nursery— should not be difficult to raise for such a life-affirming activity. Be sure to contact your local Department of Public Works before planting on city property.

For more information contact, The American Forestry Association at (202) 667-3300 or TreePeople at (213) 273-8733.

GETTING POLITICAL

Just as changing individual lifestyles and habits is crucial to reversing the global warming trend, so is political action. We can't afford to wait for market demand to turn the auto industry around. We must pressure our state and federal governments to steer Detroit, Stuttgart, and Tokyo on to a more sustainable path and encourage transportation practices that will help turn our focus away from the car.

Political action can take the form of lobby days, where busloads of people converge on the nation's Capitol for intensive one-on-one contact with legislators and their staffs. This takes some organizing work, but the results are often worth it. Other types of political action include high visibility demonstrations in home districts; letters to the editors of your newspapers; phone calls directly to your legislator's office when you have a specific action to advocate; and, of course, volunteering to work for environmentally oriented candidates at election time.

Finally, don't underestimate the effectiveness of sitting down and writing a personal letter to your elected representatives. Think of it as a 25-cent ticket to a better world. Legislative offices pay attention to the letters they receive, especially when they get a lot of them on the same subject. Get your friends and neighbors involved in the letter-writing.

At the State Level

There are certain areas—such as setting speed limits and providing assistance for local mass transit—where the most appropriate arena for action is at the state level. Take advantage of the leverage you have over legislators in your own state. Urge them to:

- Establish special highway lanes during rush hours for "high-occupancy vehicles" such as car pools.
- Institute road, bridge, and tunnel tolls that favor cars with two or more passengers.
- Increase demand for more efficient vehicles by requiring law enforcement, public works, and state highway vehicles to meet higher fuel-efficiency standards, just as the federal fleet currently does.
- Set automobile registration fees and sales taxes on a sliding

scale that penalizes "gas guzzlers" and rewards "gas sippers."

HOW TO WRITE CONGRESS (AND OTHERS)

A letter can make a tremendous difference. On Capitol Hill, letters are the barometers of political pressure. Legislators' staff members tally up positions on specific issues, report the statistics to their bosses, and respond to each letter.

Few elected officials ignore mail from constituents. Most want to be reelected, and it is recognized in the halls of Congress that those who write also vote. And letters are known to represent the views of many others.

Some letters are more influential than others. Personal letters from constituents stressing their own views in their own words are the most effective. Much of the following advice can be used in writing to your governor, state representative, mayor, city council, or even corporations.

Salutation and Address
   • The Honorable _____
   U.S. Senate
   Washington, DC 20510
   (202) 224-3121
   Dear Senator _____ :

   • The Honorable _____
   U.S. House of Representatives
   Washington, DC 20515
   (202) 224-3121
   Dear Representative _____ :

• The President
The White House
1600 Pennsylvania Ave., N.W.
Washington, DC 20500
(202) 456-1414
Dear Mr. President:

The Basic Format:
• Paragraph One: State what you are writing about and what you want your elected official to do.
• Paragraphs Two and Three: Give your reasons—the bill's impact on you and the district, for example.
• Final Paragraph: Restate your position and the action you're seeking.seeking.

Here are some additional tips that can help make your letter to Congress more effective:
• **Focus on just one subject.** This is better than diluting your key point with others. In addition, since most congressional offices assign different staffers to handle different issues, your letter will more likely reach the appropriate person.
• **Identify the bill.** If applicable and if you can, refer to legislation by its title and bill number, the person who introduced it, and what it will do. Don't assume your representative and senators or their staffs have memorized every bill in the hopper.
• **Be courteous.** Steer away from emotional outrage; use logical persuasion instead. And never threaten politicians. They'll just write you off as a lost vote.
• **Ask for a specific action.** Be clear about the action you want ("Please co-sponsor. . ." or "Please vote for. . .") and ask your lawmaker's position on the issue. Unless your request is focused, you may receive only a vague response. If the answer is not responsive, write again!
• **Give your reasons for taking a stand.** It's not enough to say, "I'm opposed." Give logical, convincing arguments—but not too many.
• **One page is normally sufficient.** Staffers should be able to scan your letter quickly for your position and arguments. You can bolster your point by enclosing magazine articles or other supporting materials, but to avoid looking like a pack rat, refer to these materials in your letter and neatly label them "BACKGROUND."

- **Make it personal.** Use personal stationery. Explain in your own words the bill's impact. If you've written to this elected official before, mention it and refer to his or her response.
- **Offer information they don't have.** If you have expert knowledge, share it. A scientist's expert opinion on an environmental problem or a personal description of key events in the district may move your letter from a lowly staffer's desk right into the lawmaker's hands.
- **Mention the member's voting record.** This says, "I know what you're doing and I vote."
- **Stress the local angle.** The first concern of members of Congress is the well-being of their constituents. They are more likely to agree with your position if you can show how it will benefit the people back home.
- **Concentrate on your own delegation.** If you do write a member from another state, send a copy to your own representative or senators and put "cc: Your member's name" below your signature. Otherwise, your letter may be routed to your legislator for response.
- **Type or handwrite.** Just make sure it's legible.
- **Use the appropriate format.** See box for proper salutation and address. Make sure you type your name and address on the letter itself.
- **Be timely.** Your letter won't be influential if a bill has already passed. A telegram can help. Western Union offers an overnight "Public Opinion Message" to elected officials for $7.95 for 20 words. Call (800) 325-6000.
- **Follow up.** Show you are truly concerned. Praise a positive action, or ask them to change their position if they vote wrong.
- **Give positive reinforcement.** It's important to thank members for voting right, especially if you wrote a letter asking for that action.

In Congress

Citizen pressure on Congress is a key element in the global warming fight. Write your representative and senators and express your concern about global warming. Urge them to support the following measures:

- Increased vehicle efficiency. Since the first oil crisis in 1973, average gas mileage of new cars has doubled. This is thanks in large part to the Corporate Average Fuel Economy (CAFE) standards created by Congress in 1975. It's time to increase these federal fuel efficiency standards from the current ceiling of 27.5 miles per gallon (mpg). Pressure your legislators to increase them to 45 mpg for cars and 35 mpg for light trucks by 2000. These alone would reduce the nation's CO_2 emissions about 4 percent.

- Return the maximum highway speed limit to 55 miles per hour. Traveling at 65 miles per hour instead of 55 mph can lower fuel economy as much as 15 percent. You can also urge your state to maintain the 55 mph speed limit. Nine states have already done so.

- Introduce an equitable federal gas tax of 50 cents per gallon over a 5-year period—10 cents per year—to decrease wasteful use of gasoline. Increase the "gas guzzler" tax for the least-efficient new cars and reestablish the "gas sipper" rebate program to reward the purchase of efficient vehicles.

- Fund stepped-up research into alternative fuels for our vehicles and into the production of electricity through renewables like solar power.

- Federal aid for mass transit decreased from $4.6 billion in 1981 to $3.15 billion in 1989. Urge Congress to increase funding for mass transit, including high-speed and light rail systems and energy-efficient buses.

For more information on fuel efficiency and global warming, contact the Energy Conservation Coalition—a coalition of environmental groups headquartered at Environmental Action Foundation, (202) 745-4874. If you want additional information on public transportation, contact the Association for Commuter Transportation, (202) 659-0602, or the National Association of Railroad Passengers, (202) 546-1550.

HOW ALTERNATE FUELS STACK UP AGAINST GASOLINE

Methanol

Pros: Requires few engine modifications. May have lower NOx emissions than gasoline. Good antiknock fuel. Renewable if produced from biomass—corn or any other organic matter that contains carbon.

Cons: Produces less energy per gallon than gasoline, so more frequent refueling or larger fuel tanks are required. More flammable than gasoline. Embrittles rubber and some plastics; corrodes some metals. Produces formaldehyde, a suspected carcinogen. Natural gas, the cheapest feedstock for methanol, will have to be imported if the United States uses methanol in large volumes.

Global Warming Impact: Produces less CO_2 than gasoline per unit of energy when used as a vehicle fuel, but a switch to methanol could result in more total CO_2 emissions depending on how it is produced. Production from natural gas would mean slightly lower levels than that contributed by gasoline. If produced from coal, CO_2 emissions would double those of gasoline levels. Methanol produced from biomass yields lower total CO_2 emissions, depending on the energy used in growing, harvesting, and processing the feedstocks.

Ethanol

Pros: Requires few engine modifications. Produces less carbon monoxide and NOx than gasoline. Better antiknock fuel. Renewable source of energy.

Cons: Less energy per gallon than gasoline, meaning larger fuel tanks or more frequent fill-ups. Requires large volumes of corn, sugar cane, and other feedstocks. Existing methods of distilling ethanol are energy-intensive.

Global Warming Impact: Produces less CO_2 than gasoline when used in vehicles, but total CO_2 impact depends on energy source for distillation process and whether crop growing is energy-intensive.

Compressed Natural Gas and Liquid Natural Gas

Pros: Requires few engine modifications. Global and U.S. supplies are more plentiful than those of oil.

Cons: Requires cumbersome fuel tank. Domestic and foreign supplies are finite just like oil. Cheaper foreign sources could lead to continued and increased U.S. reliance on imported energy. Higher NOx emissions than gasoline.

Global Warming Impact: Burns 6 to 15 percent more efficiently than gasoline, producing less CO_2 per unit of energy. However, transporting natural gas can release methane.

Electricity

Pros: Efficient. Quiet. No tailpipe emissions.

Cons: Could increase the need for electric power plants. Current battery capacity limits distances between recharges to 50 to 100 miles. Speeds of current generation of electric vehicles limited to 30 to 60 mph.

Global Warming Impact: Virtually no emissions from vehicle. These gains could be lost if the electricity used to recharge vehicles is produced from fossil fuels.

Hydrogen

Pros: Very efficient. Uses the most abundant element on our planet. Exhaust gases consist largely of water vapor. Conventional engines can be modified for hydrogen. Existing supply network for home heating gas and electricity can be used.

Cons: Higher weight and larger size of fuel storage system reduce vehicle's operating range and carrying capacity.

Global Warming Impact: If electricity produced from fossil fuels is used to power the electrolysis stage of hydrogen fuel production, total CO_2 emissions could increase 25 percent.

Our list of what you can do to combat global warming is by no means exhaustive. In fact, many of the steps we advocate in later chapters will also combat global warming, demonstrating how the different facets of the environmental crisis are so often interconnected. For example, increasing energy efficiency in your home will help reduce air pollution from coal-fired electric generating plants *and* help slow global warming. Similarly, recycling programs that are crucial to stemming our wasteful use of resources can also help reduce global warming by reducing our use of energy. And, as the next chapter shows, a total ban on chlorofluorocarbons, which represent 14 percent of global greenhouse gas emissions, is a crucial step in facing the dire threat of stratospheric ozone depletion.

PEOPLE MAKING A DIFFERENCE

—————— • ——————

WES BIRDSALL

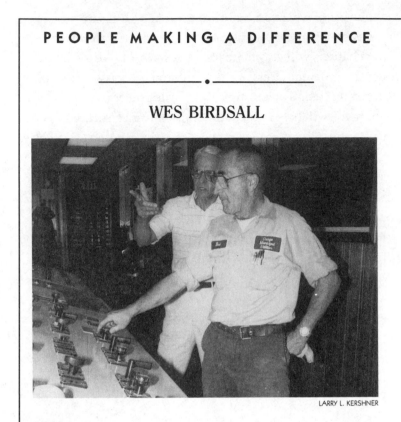

LARRY L. KERSHNER

When the United States was reeling from the Arab oil embargo and soaring energy prices in 1974, Wes Birdsall hit the streets in Osage, Iowa, extolling the virtues of improved home insulation as a means of conserving energy. Judging from his message, Birdsall could have been a save-the-world environmental activist. Surprisingly, he was, and still is, a utility executive, a member of an entrepreneurial class that generally puts consumption ahead of conservation.

Since 1974, Birdsall has gained worldwide attention as the energy-saving general manager of Osage Municipal Utilities, Inc., a supplier of electricity and natural gas to residential, commercial, and industrial users in the northeastern Iowa town of 3,800 people.

Birdsall's first energy efficiency efforts were strictly business. Osage Municipal buys most of its electricity from a coal-fired plant in

Wisconsin and has a diesel generator to add power during peak demand. Natural gas is also purchased from out of state. With power demand growing at 7.2 percent a year, increasing amounts of money were leaving Osage to pay for wholesale power, and the utility was facing expenditures of up to $7 million for new generating gear by 1984.

Birdsall responded by setting a power growth target of 3 percent a year and began preaching *energy conservation* through company ads and mailings. Birdsall spoke to groups about weatherization, and the utility began a weatherization program for low-income homeowners. The utility set strict building insulation standards that new customers had to meet to get service, and Osage Municipal took infrared scans of buildings to pinpoint where heat was escaping. It checked its own facilities and lines to detect power losses. And the town installed more efficient street lights. Devices were even installed on air conditioners so Osage Municipal could switch off compressors during peak demand.

Utilities aren't known as gift-givers, but Birdsall's is: 95 percent of Osage's homes use water-heater insulation jackets that were handed out by the utility. It also gave away compact fluorescent light bulbs, which save money for the customer. In fact, over the life of one such bulb, 400 pounds less coal need to be burned than with a standard bulb. And less coal burned means less carbon dioxide contributing to global warming.

Birdsall's results are impressive: Improved efficiency saved Osage an estimated $1.2 million in 1988. Because most of the money stays in the area instead of buying power from out-of-state wholesalers, these efforts have aided the economic development of the community. Electricity demand has risen less than 3 percent a year since 1974, even though Osage's population and commercial activity have grown. Natural gas use for heating has fallen some 37 percent. Osage Municipal's savings are passed along to customers through lower bills; rates were cut 5 times for a total of 19 percent from 1982 through 1987.

Reflecting on this, Birdsall says: "Our first thought was to keep the money in our community. Helping the environment was an offshoot of it." Is he an environmentalist? "Yeah, I guess I am. We should all be looking out for the environment. I'm proud to be called an environmentalist."

CHAPTER THREE

Saving Our Skins

PROTECTING THE OZONE LAYER

When the British Antarctic Survey turned its atmospheric sampling devices skyward over our Earth's largest and coldest continent in 1984, scientists were surprised by what they found. The stratosphere above Antarctica was marked by a huge hole in the ozone layer. The ominous void in the skies was unexpected. When similar measurements were taken in 1987, the hole had increased and was estimated to be larger than the continental United States and higher than Mount Everest. The ozone hole appears from August through November, which is springtime at the South Pole; it is now known to extend beyond Antarctica.

In the years after 1985, scientists from the United States and other nations returned to the Antarctic to study the ozone hole that appears during the August-November period. For at least a few weeks each year, before ozone returns with the onset of summer, there's a reduction of this vital gas over the extreme southern regions of Argentina, Australia, Brazil, Chile, New Zealand, and Uruguay.

Why should we be concerned about the seasonal absence of ozone molecules so high above the coldest place on our Earth? Think of the ozone hole as a danger signal, a warning that modern chemistry is upsetting one of our atmosphere's many vital and delicate balances, one that is considered vital to life as it has evolved on our planet.

The stratospheric ozone layer is essential to all life—plants, animals, humans. Its job in the balance of nature and the environment is to shield our Earth from the destructive ultraviolet rays of the sun. But every day, in fact every minute, we are pumping into the air tons of synthetic chemicals that are efficient and long-lasting destroyers of stratospheric ozone. These are chlorofluorocarbons, the CFCs that we already know contribute to global warming. In the greenhouse equation, CFCs are secondary players. In the depletion of stratospheric ozone, they are the stars of the horror show.

With less ozone in the atmosphere, increasing amounts of ultraviolet radiation reach the Earth's surface. For humans, increased exposure to ultraviolet rays means more cases of skin cancer and cataracts on the eyes. Additionally, increased levels of ultraviolet radiation are harmful to crops, and scientists warn that higher amounts threaten the very existence of the delicate microorganisms at the base of the marine food chain. In 1974,

46 years after CFCs were created in a DuPont laboratory, the scientific community began publicly questioning the danger of CFCs to the planet. In an article published in *Nature* magazine, University of California-Irvine chemistry professor F. Sherwood Rowland and Dr. Mario J. Molina, his postdoctoral student, warned that CFCs released into the atmosphere would destroy ozone in the stratosphere. They estimated that if CFC emissions continued at the then-present rate (they are now higher), as much as 13 percent of the ozone layer would be destroyed within the coming century. Their findings were initially met with skepticism.

In March 1988, the Ozone Trends Panel convened by the U.S. government estimated that in the areas of the northern hemisphere where most people live, the ozone layer decreased by 2 to 3 percent between 1969 and 1986. Reductions as high as 6 percent, however, were recorded during the winter months in far northern areas such as Alaska and Scandinavia.

Like global warming, ozone depletion seems to be happening at a much faster pace than was originally forecast. In fact, we have already experienced more ozone loss than scientists previously predicted would occur by the year 2020. Some estimates translate a 1 percent reduction in stratospheric ozone into a 2 percent increase in the amount of ultraviolet radiation striking the planet's surface. And certain scientists estimate that ozone loss could mean a 5 to 20 percent rise in ultraviolet radiation reaching our Earth's most populated areas by 2030. Another study estimated that a 2.5 percent loss of ozone could translate into a 10 percent increase in skin cancer.

WHAT IS OZONE?

Ozone is a photochemically altered form of oxygen that comprises only 0.005 percent of our atmosphere. It is found everywhere in the atmosphere, from ground level to the top of the stratosphere, where it is most abundant. And depending on where it is found, its effects are comparable to Dr. Jekyll and Mr. Hyde.

At ground level, ozone—much of it human-made—is a key component of smog and one of our most serious air pollution and public health menaces. (Chapter 4 details this problem.) But high in the stratosphere, between 12 and 30 miles above sea level, ozone is a vital ingredient of ecological balance, deflecting 90 percent of the sun's harmful ultraviolet rays. Without the stratosphere's mostly natural shield of ozone, the ultraviolet rays reaching Earth would overpower most life forms.

Stratospheric ozone is continuously created by a natural photochemical reaction that converts oxygen to ozone and then back to oxygen. When ultraviolet radiation strikes ordinary oxygen molecules (O_2), it splits them into separate atoms. These so-called free atoms link up with other oxygen molecules to form ozone (O_3). The ozone molecules then absorb more ultraviolet rays and are split again, forming ordinary oxygen once again.

However, the natural balance of this cycle is thrown off by chlorine. Most of the chlorine released into the atmosphere comes from human-made sources, especially CFCs and related compounds like carbon tetrachloride, halons, and methyl chloroform. Loose chlorine molecules attack ozone molecules and break them up. Scientists estimate that a single chlorine molecule can destroy as many as 100,000 ozone molecules over its long lifetime of 75 to 100 years.

The discovery by the British scientists of a 40 percent loss of stratospheric ozone over Antarctica represented the lowest stratospheric ozone reading ever recorded. And it was greeted with skepticism that mirrored the doubts raised a decade earlier by the Rowland-Molina warnings about the destructive nature of CFCs.

Experts wondered why such a dramatic occurrence hadn't been picked up by ozone-monitoring devices on satellites. The answer was simple: The NASA Nimbus satellites had indeed been recording decreased levels of ozone, but because no one anticipated such a large and seemingly sudden loss of ozone, the computer programming had been set to disregard such drastic readings as anomalies or mistakes.

Since then, scientists have paid close attention to the ozone readings from satellites and observed some even more dramatic depletions ranging as high as 60 percent. In 1986, a U.S. team went to Antarctica to take its own readings and test theories about what was causing the ozone hole. The following year, a far larger expedition of 150 scientists returned to the icy continent. They measured a 50 percent ozone loss from mid-August to October, and over some portions of Antarctica the stratosphere was found to be totally devoid of ozone.

Annual ozone depletion over the South Pole raises the natural question. What about the North Pole? When scientists sampled the Arctic skies, they found an estimated 4 to 10 percent loss of stratospheric ozone during the springtime months. A 1988 scientific expedition reported finding enough ozone-depleting chemicals in the Arctic atmosphere to produce a 5 percent wintertime loss of ozone over much of the northern hemisphere.

What causes this extreme loss of ozone over the polar regions? It is generally thought to be the result of a chemical mechanism that is aggravated by the unique climate of these areas. In Antarctica, and to a lesser extent in the Arctic, swirling winds and frigid temperatures create atmospheric conditions known as "polar vortexes." With little or no sunlight reaching these regions during the coldest months of winter, air temperatures fall to very low levels and the clouds freeze. Scientists believe that the ozone hole is created after chlorine — which is carried to the two polar regions by global wind patterns — condenses on the surface of the frozen clouds. When sunlight returns with the polar springtime, it liberates chlorine from the clouds, initiating a series of accelerated chemical reactions within the vortex that rapidly destroy ozone.

As temperatures rise with springtime, this ozone hole closes. The replacement ozone has to come from somewhere, and one theory is that stratospheric ozone over other portions of the globe moves into the polar regions to replace the ozone destroyed by the chlorine. This, of course, reduces the amount of ozone available to shield more populated areas of our Earth from dangerous ultraviolet radiation.

WHAT ARE THE EFFECTS OF OZONE LOSS?

Just as scientists have measured ozone loss over Antarctica, they have recorded higher levels of ultraviolet radiation reaching that continent and beyond. The extremely high readings in Antarctica have deadly implications for its ecosystem. Laboratory experiments show that reproduction of algae, the base of the food chain, can be disrupted when exposed to sunlight unfiltered by ozone. Algae in Antarctic waters are necessary for the development of krill, the tiny surface-dwelling creature that is the main diet of a number of species, including many types of whales.

Recent studies have confirmed that the ozone hole is becoming larger each year, spreading outward to the inhabited land masses surrounding Antarctica. In addition, in December 1987, three out of five Australian ozone-monitoring stations reported a sharp drop in stratospheric ozone levels shortly after the polar vortex broke up. In 1989, researchers reported elevated ultraviolet readings in portions of Australia.

However, danger signs exist closer to our own homes. Lower ozone readings have been found above Bismarck, North Dakota; Caribou, Maine; Canada, Switzerland, and West Germany. During a recent 3½-month trek through Siberia, members of a Canadian-Soviet expedition received unusually severe sunburns. The suspected cause was higher levels of ultraviolet radiation reaching the trekers as a result of ozone depletion.

Not only does ultraviolet radiation cause sunburn, it also can promote skin cancer. There has been a steady rise in this disease in the United States for the past 10 years, especially among Caucasians. Incidences of squamous and basal cell carcinoma, the two most common — but rarely fatal — forms of skin cancer are increasing in the United States at the rate of 600,000 new cases each year. The most deadly form of skin cancer, melanoma, attacks more than 25,000 Americans annually and accounts for about 8,000 deaths. If we continue to destroy the ozone layer, the numbers could become far more staggering.

The Environmental Protection Agency recently warned that unless action is taken to halt ozone depletion, "the United States can expect 40 million additional skin cancer cases and 800,000 deaths of people alive today and those born during the next 88 years." The EPA's warning was based on the assumption that worldwide production of CFCs would grow at 2.5 percent a year. Some estimates show they're already growing faster than that.

Ultraviolet radiation is also a major cause of cataracts, a

clouding of the lens of the eye that causes blurred vision and eventual blindness. The EPA estimates that unchecked ozone depletion would bring this affliction to anywhere from 555,000 to 2.8 million Americans born before 2075. Like mild forms of skin cancer, cataracts can be treated with relatively simple surgery. Needed medical services would be available to residents of the developed world, albeit with the increasing cost to national resources. But a lack of medical treatment in less-developed countries would leave an escalating percentage of the world's burgeoning population at far greater risk of going blind or dying from skin cancer. The bulk of this neglected population would be the poor who live closer to the Equator and who now contribute least to ozone destruction.

There is yet another danger to humans from increased exposure to ultraviolet radiation. Too strong a dose can lower the body's ability to resist such attacking organisms as infectious diseases and tumors. Some medical experts worry that excess exposure will undermine the inoculation programs that have controlled diseases that once caused epidemics. Instead of protecting people from a disease, an inoculation could inflict the disease on those whose immune system has been damaged by excessive exposure to ultraviolet radiation.

Other species will share the sad results of ozone depletion. For the many plants that are sensitive to ultraviolet radiation, continued exposure at higher-than-normal levels can impede photosynthesis, resulting in lower crop yields. A study by the University of Maryland found that soybean yields can drop up to 25 percent when these vital food crops are subjected to a 25 percent ozone loss. As with global warming, there is a danger that ozone loss may be occurring too rapidly for some plant species to adapt. The faster the depletion, the less chance there is for a particular specie's survival.

At the foundation of the aquatic ecosystem are small organisms known as phytoplankton. They live on the surface of water and depend on sunlight for survival, making them extremely vulnerable to changes in levels of ultraviolet radiation. Too much exposure to ultraviolet rays can kill phytoplankton, setting off a destructive, possibly deadly, reaction in the marine food chain—first affecting larger microorganisms, then fish larvae that feed on them, then small fish, then larger fish and marine mammals, and even aquatic birds that depend on water creatures for their food. There is no real timetable for this environmental destruction. But marine biologists warn that in recent years there have been reduced populations of krill.

WHAT ARE CFCS?

The major contributors to ozone destruction are compounds containing chlorine and bromine. Most of the chlorine entering our atmosphere comes from the breakdown of CFCs, a laboratory product that has become widely used worldwide. In the manufacturing process, these chemicals seem perfect; they are nontoxic and won't ignite. As refrigerants, they help cool our homes, offices, theaters, and vehicles. They are in our refrigerators. They clean computer chips. They are used to produce foam products. Some items like insulation help us save energy. Others, such as foam food containers made with CFCs, are pure waste.

No matter how CFCs are used, they find their way into the atmosphere. Some of the chemical escapes during manufacturing processes. About 85 percent of the cars in the United States have air conditioners with CFC coolant. What doesn't leak during normal operation most often gets vented during servicing and when the car is sent to a junkyard. The tens of millions of refrigerators in our homes are time bombs. When they wear out and are disposed of, the CFC coolant will head toward the stratosphere except in the odd case where a recycler captures the chemical.

When you see discarded plastic foam in a landfill or a foam fast food container beside the road, you are witnessing a release of stored-up CFCs if those chemicals were used in the product's manufacture. If you go to Europe and buy a spray deodorant, you will then most likely be pumping more CFCs into the atmosphere. The use of CFCs as aerosol propellants was banned in the 1970s by Canada, Sweden, and the United States because of the Rowland-Molina findings. Their use remains legal and widespread elsewhere, making spray cans the world's largest source of CFC emissions.

Global consumption of CFCs hit 1 billion pounds in 1970 and dipped after the three nations banned their use in spray cans — a ban that in the United States was generated more from adverse reaction by consumers than environmental protection leadership by government. By 1984, CFC production world-wide had surpassed pre-1974 levels and was rising about 7 percent a year. In 1986, there were 2.5 billion pounds of CFCs consumed worldwide. Despite its restrictions on using CFCs in aerosol cans, the United States accounts for 29 percent of global consumption, and Americans use 6 times more CFCs than the global average.

WHAT HAS BEEN DONE TO CURB CFCS?

The discovery of the Antarctic hole forced political leaders in the industrialized world to recognize that something needed to be done. In 1987, 24 nations gathered in Montreal to sign a

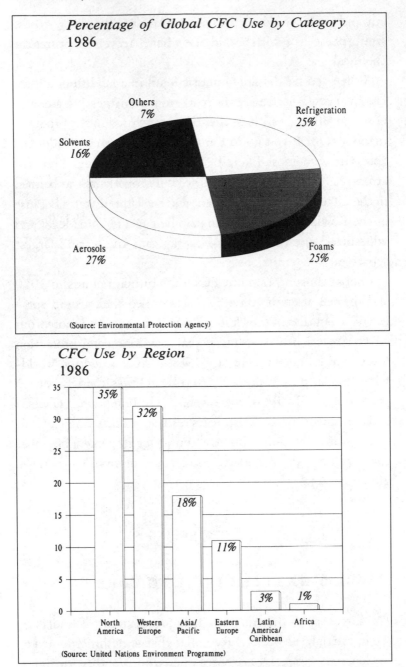

Percentage of Global CFC Use by Category
1986

Others
7%

Refrigeration
25%

Solvents
16%

Aerosols
27%

Foams
25%

(Source: Environmental Protection Agency)

CFC Use by Region
1986

North America 35%
Western Europe 32%
Asia/Pacific 18%
Eastern Europe 11%
Latin America/Caribbean 3%
Africa 1%

(Source: United Nations Environment Programme)

protocol to cooperatively reduce consumption of CFCs. Since then, more than 40 nations have ratified what is now commonly known as the "Montreal Protocol." If followed, the protocol could curb global production of chlorofluorocarbons by up to 50 percent by 1998. However, critics say that loopholes could limit reduction to only 30 percent.

The drive to conclude this major international effort was partly spearheaded by the Reagan administration, which otherwise had a poor environmental record. By September 1988, the Environmental Protection Agency was urging a rewriting of the protocol to produce a worldwide cutback in CFC production of 85 percent.

In the wake of the CFC treaty, there were further encouraging signs. DuPont, the world's largest producer of CFCs, announced a crash program to develop safe alternatives. General Motors says that by the early 1990s it will require its dealers to recycle CFCs when servicing automobile air conditioners. Nissan says it will stop using CFCs in its mobile air conditioners by 1993. And AT&T says it will end its extensive use of the chemicals by 1994.

These are steps in the right direction, but they do not go far enough. CFCs are a global time bomb, and nobody can say just when it will explode.

The very first CFCs produced and released are still active in the stratosphere and are continually destroying ozone. So is every molecule released since then, except those that are still working their way up to the stratosphere. Scientists say it takes a CFC molecule 6 years to rise through the atmosphere before it reaches the stratospheric ozone layer. This means that the ozone hole discovered by the British expedition in 1984 was the result of CFCs released before 1979. The destruction from CFCs released in the last 6 years is yet to be experienced, but they will continue damaging an already depleted ozone layer for as long as a century.

The most frightening aspect of venting CFCs is the uncertainty about the extent to which we are causing damage. In congressional testimony, scientists have said they have no way of knowing when we will have gone too far and reached the so-called crossover point: the theoretical moment when the total amount of CFCs released into the atmosphere is sufficient to ensure that no matter what we do next, we have already guaranteed enough ozone depletion to threaten life on Earth.

Even if we never added another CFC molecule to the atmosphere, knowledgeable scientists have warned it could already be too late to halt ozone destruction short of this crossover point. Then again, the final fatal CFC molecule could be released next week, next year, or after the turn of the century. We're playing a global game of roulette, and nobody knows when the wheel will stop spinning, let alone whether humankind will win the gamble.

PEOPLE MAKING A DIFFERENCE

•

LYNDA DRAPER

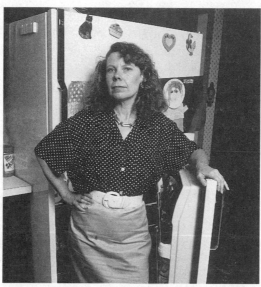

MILBERT ORLANDO BROWN

Lynda Draper's fight against chlorofluorocarbon (CFC) emissions began in the kitchen of her Ellicott City, Maryland, home in early 1989 after learning that General Electric (GE) was in the process of replacing compressors in 1 to 2 million of its refrigerators. After finding her model on the repair list, a call to GE's 800 phone number brought a repairman to Draper's kitchen.

"He asked me to open the window," Draper recounts. "I thought it was an odd request. I had no idea why he wanted me to do this, but I did it. Then I heard a whooshing sound, and I knew what was happening. CFCs were escaping. It was too late to stop him."

Draper told the repairman that she didn't think venting CFCs into the atmosphere was a very good idea. She relates, "He said there's nothing to be concerned about; it's only a small amount, four or five ounces. I was really upset."

Her calculations told her that the few ounces of CFCs vented from her refrigerator meant that somewhere between 125 to 312 tons were entering the atmosphere through GE's compressor-replacement program. At the high end, the released CFCs totaled nearly 10 percent of the amount of CFCs slated by the Environmental Protection Agency (EPA) for refrigeration production in the United States in 1989.

For Draper, the incident in her kitchen was doubly vexing. She grew up in GE country—Schenectady, New York. Her grandfather and father had been long-time employees of the appliance giant, and her husband had worked for GE for 10 years. "GE was a symbol of 'bringing good things to our lives,'" she admits.

Draper picked up the telephone and complained to a GE spokesman, who pointed out that the company was doing nothing illegal. He said, notes Draper, "They had a perfect right to vent the CFCs. He acknowledged that CFCs cause problems for the ozone layer. But he said they were adding only a small amount to the atmosphere and that the benefits to people from refrigerators far outweigh damage to the ozone. I told him that I thought GE could do something. I told him I would take the matter to the government and the public."

Draper's complaints to the EPA and state and local officials led to media attention and eventually to a meeting in Washington, D.C., involving Draper, GE officials, environmental groups, and Senator Albert Gore of Tennessee. Pressured to find an alternative to venting CFCs during refrigerator repairs, GE stated several months later that it would offset these CFC emissions by recapturing an equal amount elsewhere in its vast operations.

Before the incident in her kitchen, Draper's environmental efforts were local: battling a road extension because of the accompanying air and noise pollution and halting a bike path extension into wetlands. Now her horizon is broader. She has lobbied the Maryland General Assembly on environmental issues and has stalked the hallways of Congress urging more controls on CFCs.

"It's interesting how I've gone from being basically a PTA volunteer to getting involved in environmental issues," she notes." There are things that can be done. We're just not doing them. Stopping even a small thing makes you realize that one person can make a difference. I intend to keep fighting. If more people were fighting, we'd make more progress."

WHAT WE CAN DO

The Montreal Protocol to reduce global use of CFCs is a hopeful sign, but it needs to be followed up by a complete ban. Our obvious and ultimate aim must be to replace ozone-depleting chemicals with substitutes that do not harm the ozone layer. Some replacements have already come on to the market, but we can't expect a complete changeover from CFCs to happen overnight. Chemical companies are claiming that toxicity testing and "investment lags" will keep many substitutes from widespread distribution for at least 5 years.

However, there are short-term actions that can reduce CFC emissions substantially and swiftly. We must become aware of products such as auto air conditioners that contain CFCs and stop venting the chemicals into the atmosphere whenever these products are discarded or serviced. We must use alternate products whenever possible. By promoting CFC reductions through the power of our dollars, our voices, and our votes, we can make a significant dent in emissions.

INDIVIDUAL ACTIONS

In 1974, more than half of two common CFC varieties—CFC-11 and CFC-12—went into aerosol sprays. As we have already seen, consumer reaction in this country forced the U.S. spray can industry to abandon its use of CFCs. In much of the world, however, aerosol cans still contain and release CFCs.

A decade later, American consumers won another CFC victory, this time over the CFCs used to puff liquid plastic into foam for food packaging. With the help of people such as Senator Robert Stafford of Vermont, citizens targeted McDonalds, writing letters and picketing under the "golden arches" until the company agreed to stop using food containers and other packaging material manufactured with CFCs. Other fast-food chains followed suit, helping to give environmentalists leverage they needed to work out a deal with fast-food packaging manufacturers to completely phase out use of the most destructive CFCs within a year.

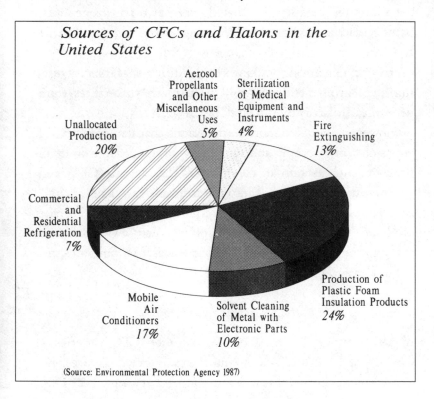

Sources of CFCs and Halons in the United States

Aerosol Propellants and Other Miscellaneous Uses
5%

Sterilization of Medical Equipment and Instruments
4%

Unallocated Production
20%

Fire Extinguishing
13%

Commercial and Residential Refrigeration
7%

Production of Plastic Foam Insulation Products
24%

Mobile Air Conditioners
17%

Solvent Cleaning of Metal with Electronic Parts
10%

(Source: Environmental Protection Agency 1987)

Refrigerants

Refrigeration and air conditioning equipment accounts for 30 percent of combined CFC-11 and CFC-12 consumption in the United States. The Environmental Protection Agency estimates that car air conditioners account for as much as 25 percent of U.S. CFC use. Once again, as with CO_2 emissions, cars are a primary target. So let's start here:

• The best thing we can do is buy a car without air conditioning. Unfortunately, that's easier said than done. More than 85 percent of the models arriving at showrooms are equipped with air conditioning. But a U.S.-built car can be factory-ordered without air conditioning. If fewer people bought auto air conditioners, fewer would be offered.

- Get your state legislature into the act. For instance, Vermont's voted to ban CFCs from auto air conditioners as of 1993.

- 65 percent of all mobile air conditioner coolant is lost before the system is ever repaired. That's because these units are prone to leakage. Don't wait until most of your coolant leaks out before you take your car in for service. To avoid leaks, run your car air conditioner a couple of times during the winter; it keeps hoses from drying and cracking. Have your car air conditioner checked regularly and replace hoses before leaks begin.

- Don't top off your air conditioning coolant with the do-it-yourself cans of CFC refrigerant available in auto parts stores. You'll not only ensure that CFCs reach the atmosphere, but you're risking harm to yourself and your air conditioner if you don't do the job properly. This is a task for an environmentally responsible professional.

- When car air conditioners are serviced, it is common practice to drain the coolant and let it evaporate. Recovery systems called "vampires" allow repair shops to pump refrigerant out of the compressor, purify it, and recycle it back into the automobile. Make sure your air conditioner is serviced or recharged at licensed service stations that use refrigerant reclaiming systems. If there is no such station in your area, pressure your local mechanic to purchase the equipment. If all service shops had to recycle CFCs, emissions from this source would be cut in half. For more information on recycling car air conditioner refrigerant, contact Simon Oulouhojian, president of the Mobile Air Conditioning Society at (215) 352-6080.

- If you junk your car, try to find a junk yard that will properly dispose of not only the CFCs in the air conditioner, but all the environmentally harmful fluids in the vehicle.

Together, home and commercial food refrigerators and freezers account for about 7 percent of total CFC and halon emissions. This number can be reduced substantially through consumer pressure and attentiveness.

- When your refrigerator or freezer needs servicing, try to find a repair person who will agree not to vent CFCs into the atmosphere. The same type of "vampires" used for car air conditioners can be used for refrigerators. If a repair shop lacks the portable equipment to recapture CFCs, keep looking until you find one.

Again, most CFC emissions from refrigerators and freezers occur when they are discarded. Opportunities to properly recover CFCs from refrigerators and car air conditioners need to be encouraged at the political as well as the consumer level.

- Push your state and local governments to require recovery of CFCs when refrigerators and automobiles are disposed of. On a local level, there are a number of possibilities to consider, including establishing centralized reclamation centers for refrigerants (perhaps at existing recycling centers) or requiring discarded automobile air conditioners and home refrigerators to be picked up by licensed salvagers or the local sanitation department. Another option to consider is a deposit/refund system to ensure the return of these units.
- Utilities often pick up old refrigerators. Consider working with your local utility and government agencies to design programs under which the utility removes old refrigerators

for customers, retrieves the CFCs, and safely disposes of highly toxic PCB-laden oil that is frequently found in older refrigerators.

Foam Blowing

CFC-blown foams are used in more than packaging. In fact, CFC-11 is widely used in the construction and refrigeration industries as insulation.

- Rigid home insulation represents a huge store of banked CFCs that eventually will make their way into our atmosphere. When buying insulation for your home, shop for products that are not made with CFCs. Several alternate sheathing materials are available, such as fiberboard, fiberglass, foil-laminated board, and gypsum. Cellulose fiber insulation—a recycled wood fiber product made from newsprint and flame retardants—is a good alternate product to sprayed, blown, or poured wall and ceiling insulation. When buying such insulation, make sure it is approved by the Cellulose Industry Standards Enforcement Program and it carries a CISEP label.
- Try not to disturb existing foam insulation. It will only release CFCs.

Solvents

CFC-113 and methyl chloroform, both of which deplete ozone, are used in paints and as solvents to clean and degrease metal parts, printed circuit boards, and semi-conductors. Emissions of these two substances represent approximately 25 percent of all ozone-depleting emissions. The cleaning process is most commonly performed in open systems, allowing evaporation of solvents into the environment. Emissions are virtually immediate; three-fourths result from vapor losses, the rest from waste disposal. As a result, emissions of CFC-113 and methyl chloroform may be some of the easiest and most economical to control. Some large computer companies are already beginning to recover and recycle CFC-113, which costs about twice as much as other CFCs.

- Pressure CFC emitters in your area to increase solvent recovery. Target polluters by looking at their Form R, a list of toxic chemical release information that must be submitted by companies under section 313 of the federal Right to Know Law. (See Chapter 5 for information on how to obtain and use right-to-know information.) Check specifically for emissions of CFC 113 (listed as Freon 113), carbon tetrachloride, and methyl chloroform (listed as 1, 1, 1-Trichloroethane). If you discover a polluter in your area, put the pressure on them through elected representatives and the press.

Halons

These ozone-destroying chemicals are some of the most effective substances for fighting fires. Many new buildings contain systems that will flood them with halon in the event of a fire. When first installed, these flooding systems are usually tested by releasing all the halons. The cumulative effect of such discharge testing contributes more emissions to our atmosphere than does actual firefighting. We need to promote alternate testing procedures. We need to have local laws that require the use of safe flood-testing agents instead of Halon 1301. When buying a hand-held fire extinguisher, look for one that doesn't contain halons. Read the label or ask the salesperson.

Packaging

It's difficult to determine exactly how much CFC is used in food packaging. Until substitutes are commercially available, polystyrene foam manufacturers are turning to HCFC-22 as an interim replacement for CFC-12. Because of its chemical makeup, HCFC-22 has only 5 percent of the ozone destruction power of the chemicals it replaces. The Food and Drug Administration (FDA) has approved HCFC as a blowing agent for hinged food containers used in fast-food restaurants and is considering its use for other products.

Since HCFC-22 is not regulated under the Montreal Protocol, there is the danger that its use could greatly expand, resulting in substantially increased loads of chlorine being added to the atmosphere. With a lifetime of 20 to 25 years, HCFC-22 can be expected to have a significant effect as a greenhouse gas if it is present in the atmosphere in high enough amounts. HCFCs represent a substantial improvement, but only as an interim measure. As consumers, we would be better off avoiding these products altogether, since they contribute to our solid waste woes as well.

- Avoid purchasing polystyrene foam products. This will encourage the plastic foam manufacturing industry to cease using at least the most destructive CFCs. And if manufacturers use HCFCs, as consumers we should encourage them to find completely harmless substitutes. Purchasing available paper products reduces the release of ozone depleters and the amount of plastics in our solid waste stream. Packaging made from molded recycled pulp and other paper products is readily available if manufacturers get the message from consumers. For example, egg cartons made from molded pulp are readily available and are superior to foam cartons for preventing breakage. Meats and sandwiches can be wrapped in paper just as effectively.

- Urge your supermarket to use alternative packaging. Ask your local restaurant to use paper rather than styrofoam for carry-out. Patronize fast-food outlets that wrap their burgers in paper. Tell the managers of foam-using establishments why you're taking your business elsewhere.

Aerosols

Avoid aerosol spray products where alternatives are available. Some spray cans—for example, dusting sprays, noise horns, and party streamers—may contain CFCs that have slipped through a regulatory loophole.

GETTING POLITICAL

The Montreal Protocol will not totally protect the ozone layer. It allows for a continued use of ozone-depleting CFCs and doesn't even cover other ozone-depleters like carbon tetrachloride and methyl chloroform. Even with widespread participation by all nations, the protocol's inadequate goal of halving worldwide CFC use by 1998 will not be met.

While there is much that we can do in our individual lives, halting ozone destruction can only be accomplished through global participation in an effective anti-CFC program. The United States, a voracious consumer of CFCs, should be a leader in this battle by following up its ban on CFC-spray cans with bans on all CFC fronts. Your voice is important.

The case may seem clear to you, but don't count on it being clear to Congress. The CFC producers and users—giant chemical and auto makers—are a tenacious and powerful lobby that traditionally puts profits ahead of the environment. Legislators need to hear from their constituents on this issue, not just well-heeled industry lobbyists. Call or write your representative and your senators. Let them know you're concerned about the fate of our Earth and want an early halt of the production and use of CFCs. Demand:

- A halt in U.S. production of CFCs, carbon tetrachloride, halons, and methyl chloroform by 1995 at the latest.
- A thorough EPA review of the safety of alternative chemicals.

• An immediate ban on CFC-user industries from venting ozone-destorying gases and a requirement that they recover and recycle them.

The EPA has estimated that CFC producers will reap $2 to $7 billion in windfall profits over the next 10 years as current regulations and the Montreal Protocol restrict supply and CFC prices rise.

• Push Congress to require that such windfall profits go not into corporate coffers, but to the U.S. Treasury to support environmental improvement.

Although chemical manufacturers are spending some $100 million annually to develop safe chemical substitutes, they have little interest in alternate product designs that would cut into their markets. The federal government must fund research on development of technologies that do not rely on ozone-depleting chemicals, such as new refrigeration and air conditioning and insulation processes.

To get active in a national campaign to ban CFC production and use, contact:

Friends of the Earth/FOE
218 D Street, S.E.
Washington, DC 20003
(202) 544-2600

National Toxics Campaign
37 Temple Place, 4th Floor
Boston, MA 02111
(617) 482-1477

Environmental Defense Fund
257 Park Avenue South
New York, NY 10010
(212) 505-2100

PEOPLE MAKING A DIFFERENCE

NORMA SULLIVAN-KARL STEHLE

JOHN JORDAN

Public opinion polls have shown consistently that a majority of Americans say they are willing to pay for a cleaner environment. School children in the New Jersey township of West Milford are living proof of that.

The statistics came to life one day in the social studies class Karl Stehle was teaching at West Milford High School. His students' discussion centered on a newspaper article reporting that the local school board had decided to continue using styrofoam trays in school cafeterias because each costs 5 cents less than a paper tray.

Tenth-grader Tanja Vogt voiced anger over this move. She thought students would pay an extra nickel at lunch if they had a choice between nonbiodegradable foam and biodegradable paper trays.

Stehle mentioned the classroom discussion to Norma Sullivan, a science and language arts teacher at neighboring Macopin Middle School. They decided to broach the foam-versus-paper-tray issue to the school board. Sullivan says the response was basically, "Let the students put their money where their mouths are."

In a week-long test of the two types of trays, students had a choice in the cafeterias: Use foam for free or pay an extra 5 cents for paper. The results were 86 percent of the middle school students and 72 percent of the high schoolers chose paper. Duly impressed, the school board ordered a switch to paper trays. The following school year, the board went one step further, switching to old-fashioned washable dishes for the cafeterias. Not only did this cut down on the amount of trash generated by the cafeterias, it was also cheaper than paying for throwaways.

Inspired by making a difference, Stehle, Sullivan, and their young environmental activists ventured beyond their own schools. Students wrote letters to principals of 700 other schools throughout New Jersey urging them to stop using plastics in their cafeterias. Sullivan says officials of many schools agreed to consider alternatives.

The West Milford high school activists urged local merchants to stop using and selling plastic products. They picketed a McDonald's franchise demanding a switch from foam to paper. Noting that local supermarkets were using plastic bags exclusively, Sullivan recounts, "The kids pushed their moms to demand paper bags, and now the stores are giving people a choice between plastic and paper." And the West Milford town government banned use of disposable plastic products in its offices and required the use of recyclable or reusable nonplastic products. "Kids are a formidable lobby," comments Sullivan. The campaign in West Milford has made her more hopeful than ever about the ability of people to change habits and halt environmental degradation. She adds, "I believe the only way we're going to clean up the environment is through grassroots efforts. If you wait for the government, it takes too long. The greatest thing I can do as a teacher is create awareness, light a spark."

CHAPTER FOUR

A Breath of Clean Air

FIGHTING AIR POLLUTION

America's biggest hazardous waste dump isn't on the Environmental Protection Agency's superfund list of the nation's worst toxic waste sites slated for cleanup. It's the air we breathe. And day by day that dump in the sky is getting larger and dirtier.

As we open the environmental decade of the 1990s with the 20th anniversary of the first Earth Day, it's easy to look back to 1970 with sadness and frustration about the condition of the air we breathe. Our air was supposed to be cleaner today, not more polluted.

When Congress rode the crest of the green wave created by Earth Day and passed the Clean Air Act in 1970, it took clear notice of the hazards of continued degradation of our skies. Said Congress: "The growth in the amount and complexity of air pollution brought about by urbanization, industrial development, and the increasing use of motor vehicles has resulted in mounting dangers to the public health and welfare."

The Clean Air Act and strengthening amendments adopted in 1977 directed the EPA to establish health-based ground level (or ambient) air standards for six of the most common and widespread air pollutants. These are sulfur dioxide, particulates, carbon monoxide, nitrogen dioxides, ozone, and lead. The EPA was directed to set performance standards to reduce pollution from such major stationary sources as power plants and from our ever-growing fleet of motor vehicles. Requirements were established to prevent significant deterioration of the air around such places as national parks and wilderness areas that still had particularly good air quality.

Actually, remarkable progress was made in cutting urban air pollution after the passage of the Clean Air Act. Motor vehicle emission standards mandated by Congress forced automakers to build cars that were 6 to 8 times cleaner than the cars of the late 1960s. Much credit goes to the development of the catalytic converter, which removes some pollutants from exhaust.

For vehicle-related pollutants other than smog, pollution levels declined by the mid-1980s to a third of what the dirtiest cities experienced in the early 1970s. A major factor was the decrease in lead levels after growing numbers of cars were made to burn lead-free gasoline. The number of days when air quality standards were violated steadily declined from 1970 to 1986, dropping by as much as 90 percent in the most polluted cities.

CRITERIA POLLUTANTS OF
THE CLEAN AIR ACT

Pollutant	Health Effects	Welfare Effects	Major Sources
Sulfur Dioxide (SO_2, a gas)	Aggravates symptoms of heart and lung disease, obstructs breathing (particularly in combination with other pollutants); increases incidence of acute respiratory diseases, including coughs and colds, asthma, bronchitis, and emphysema.	Toxic to plants; can destroy paint pigments, erode statues, corrode metals, harm textiles; impairs visibility; precursor to acid rain.	Electricity-generating stations, smelters, petroleum refineries, industrial boilers.
Particulate (solid particles or liquid droplets)	Can carry heavy metals and cancer-causing organic compounds into the deepest, most sensitive parts of the lung; with SO_2, can increase incidence and severity of respiratory diseases.	Obscure visibility; dirty materials and buildings; corrodes metals.	Industrial processes and combustion; about 7% from natural, largely uncontrollable, sources (wind-blown dust, forest fires, volcanoes).
Carbon Monoxide (CO, a gas)	Interferes with blood's ability to absorb oxygen, thus impairing perception and thinking, slowing reflexes and causing drowsiness, unconsciousness, and death. CO inhaled by pregnant women may threaten the unborn child's growth and mental development. Long-term exposure is suspected of aggravating arteriosclerosis and vascular disease.		Motor vehicles.
Nitrogen Dioxide (NO_2, a gas)	High concentrations can be fatal; at lower levels, can increase susceptibility to viral infections, such as influenza, irritate the lungs, and cause bronchitis and pneumonia.	Toxic to vegetation, reducing plant growth and seed fertility when present in high concentrations; causes brown discoloration of the atmosphere; is a precursor to acid rain and ozone.	Electric utility boilers and motor vehicles.
Ozone (a gas)	Irritates mucous membranes of respiratory system, causing coughing, choking, impaired lung function, reduced resistance to colds, and serious diseases such as pneumonia; can aggravate chronic heart disease, asthma, bronchitis, emphysema.	Corrodes materials such as rubber and paint; can injure and kill many crops; trees, shrubs.	Formed by chemical reactions in the atmosphere from two other airborne pollutants—NO_2 and HC.
Lead (a metal)	Affects blood-forming, reproductive, nervous, and kidney systems; can accumulate in bone and other tissues, posing a health hazard even after exposure has ended. Children are particularly susceptible, and behavioral abnormalities including hyperactivity and decreased learning ability have recently been demonstrated.		Motor vehicle exhaust; lead smelting and processing plants.

(Source: National Clean Air Coalition, *The Clean Air Act: A Briefing Book to Congress*, April, 1985.)

But after these years of steady progress in reducing dangerous levels of air pollution, the hot, drought-ridden summer of 1988 provided an ominous sign that our nation's air quality was beginning to deteriorate once again. City after city recorded their highest levels of ozone and carbon monoxide in a decade. Thirty-seven cities and rural areas where air quality had satisfied ozone health standards in 1987 found themselves violating those standards in 1988. The number of "violation days"—times when carbon monoxide (CO) or ozone standards are exceeded—nearly quadrupled between 1986 and 1988, increasing from 380 days to 1,250. By the summer of 1988, more than half of all Americans—137 million people in 121 different cities and towns—lived where smog or carbon monoxide levels exceeded safe levels.

We have long had statistics and measurements on the amount of pollutants causing smog problems. It was not until the late 1980s that the nation learned of the horrifying volume of toxic chemicals routinely dumped into the air. According to reports filed by over 18,000 companies, more than 2.7 billion pounds of toxic chemicals, many of them known or suspected carcinogens, were coughed into the American sky in 1987. There are indications that this massive spewing of poisons represents only a fraction of the emissions of toxics into the air we breathe. Thousands of factories that produce or use chemicals either are exempt from reporting their emissions or have ignored the reporting requirements mandated by Congress in the 1986 right-to-know law that forces industries to reveal data about emissions.

In addition to the assault from smog and toxic air pollution, mounting scientific evidence gathered throughout the late 1970s and 1980s spotlighted a growing problem that was not foreseen by the authors of the original Clean Air Act. This is acid rain. Acid rain is created in the atmosphere from emissions of sulfur dioxide and nitrogen oxides, most often by coal-burning power plants. Rain downwind of such facilities is sometimes as much as 120 times more acidic than normal rain. In some instances, acid rain has been as acidic as battery acid. This acidified precipitation falls over most of the eastern United States, the Southeast, parts of the West, eastern Canada, and throughout other regions of the world. Acid rain has been shown to cause not only destruction of aquatic ecosystems, reduced forest growth, and billions of dollars in damaged roads, bridges, and buildings, but also reduced agricultural production and thousands of premature deaths each year.

Clearly, America's air is still a major threat to our health, our environment, and our future. We can no longer rely on the 20-year-old Clean Air Act to protect us. Before we can see what action should be taken by individuals and the nation, let's first look at what causes different forms of air pollution and how they can be controlled. We'll begin with the most visible form, urban smog, and the nation's capital of urban smog, Los Angeles.

URBAN SMOG

As the sun rises on Los Angeles, heralding another warm, beautiful day, hundreds of thousands of cars, trucks, and buses inch along the freeways in a daily ritual that is repeated across the country. But the concentrated mixture of motor vehicles and warm sunlight in Southern California results in more than overheated cars.

Smog—the visible manifestation of ozone pollution—results primarily from a combination of vehicle exhaust and sunlight. Ozone pollution stems from the chemical reaction that occurs when nitrogen oxides (NOx) and volatile organic compounds (VOCs) are "cooked" by the hot sun. Motor vehicles are the major source of NOx and VOC emissions in the United States, contributing approximately 45 percent of NOx pollution and 40 percent of all VOC emissions. Coal-burning power plants are another major source of NOx pollution. Other big sources of VOCs include house paints and the gasoline vapors that escape when cars are being fueled or gasoline is being pumped into underground storage tanks.

Los Angeles, with its sunny climate and huge numbers of vehicles, is a perfect smog factory. But it is not alone. Ozone pollution is a serious health and environmental problem for nearly every large city, many smaller cities, and rural areas as well. In the summer of 1988, 101 cities, towns, and rural areas suffered from ozone pollution above the level considered safe for humans. From Acadia National Park on the coast of Maine to Lake Charles, Louisiana, from Columbia, South Carolina, to Kewaunee County in Wisconsin, and from Tulsa, Oklahoma, to Owensboro, Kentucky, excessive ozone readings were recorded in the summer of 1988 — the hottest part of the hottest year in recorded U.S. climate history.

Nearly every American living in a high ozone area has at one time or another experienced its immediate adverse effects — breathing difficulty, burning eyes, headaches, nausea. But it is long-term exposure to ozone that poses the most serious threat to health. Research by the American Lung Association indicates that continued exposure to ozone levels above the federal standard can accelerate aging of the lungs as well as increase a person's susceptibility to infections by hindering the human immune system. Children, the elderly, pregnant women, and people with respiratory illnesses are affected most adversely.

Even healthy people who regularly exercise outdoors can suffer minor lung damage from breathing air containing ozone that is at the federal standard of 0.12 parts per million. Joggers

BEYOND THE LIMIT

Metropolitan areas that failed the ozone test,
exceeding the federal ozone smog standard of .120 ppm
in the air from 1986 to 1988

Metropolitan Area	Highest ozone level (parts per million)	Average # of days above standard each year
Los Angeles, CA	.340	145.4
New York, NY	.217	18.0
Chicago, IL	.193	21.2
Houston, TX	.190	12.6
Milwaukee, MN	.183	9.1
Baltimore, MD	.181	13.3
San Diego, CA	.180	11.1
Muskegon, MI	.180	9.0
Philadelphia, PA	.180	8.9
Portsmouth-Dover-Roch., NH-ME	.179	7.8
Hartford, CT	.179	6.9
Louisville, KY-IN	.171	5.6
Fresno, CA	.170	11.6
El Paso, TX	.170	8.1
Parkersburg-Marietta, WV-OH	.169	7.2
Sheboygan, WI	.167	9.5
Worcester, MA	.167	7.3
Atlanta, GA	.166	10.2
Boston, MA	.165	10.0
Huntington-Ashland, WV-KY-OH	.165	6.2
Baton Rouge, LA	.164	4.1
Washington, DC-MD-VA	.163	8.3
Springfield, MA	.162	7.3
Providence, RI	.162	6.6
Bakersfield, CA	.160	37.8
Sacramento, CA	.160	8.9

Beaumont-Port Arthur, TX	.160	4.5
St. Louis, MO-IL	.159	7.5
Knox Co., ME	.158	8.1
Cincinnati, OH	.157	5.4
Portland, ME	.156	5.4
Hancock Co., ME	.153	12.0
Greensboro-Winston Salem-High Point, NC	.151	7.2
Visalia-Tulare-Porterville, CA	.150	8.5
Pittsburgh, PA	.149	6.6
Charlotte-Gastonia-Rock Hill, NC	.149	5.7
Charleston, WV	.148	2.7
Kewaunee Co., WI	.147	5.5
Memphis, TN-AR-MS	.146	2.7
Cleveland, OH	.145	5.8
Portland, OR	.145	1.8
Detroit, MI	.144	3.3
Jefferson Co., NY	.143	5.1
Atlantic City, NJ	.143	3.7
Birmingham, AL	.143	3.7
Grand Rapids, MI	.143	3.1
Salt Lake City-Ogden, UT	.143	3.1
Miami, FL	.143	2.4
Richmond-Petersburg, VA	.142	4.4
Raleigh-Durham, NC	.141	4.4
Reading, PA	.141	3.4
Modesto, CA	.140	6.0
Dallas, TX	.140	5.8
San Francisco, CA	.140	3.4
Edmonson Co., KY	.140	2.1
Phoenix, AZ	.140	1.4
Nashville, TN	.139	6.0
Greenville-Spartanburg, SC	.138	4.8
Poughkeepsie, NY	.138	1.7
Owensboro, KY	.137	4.1
Allentown-Bethlehem, PA-NJ	.137	3.1
Lewiston-Auburn, ME	.137	1.5
Dayton-Springfield, OH	.136	2.7
Manchester, NH	.136	2.4

Toledo, OH	.136	2.4
Harrisburg-Lebanon-Carlisle, PA	.136	2.2
Montgomery, AL	.135	1.8
Knoxville, TN	.135	1.8
Canton, OH	.135	1.7
Youngstown, OH-PA	.134	2.5
Columbus, OH	.134	1.4
Norfolk-Virginia Beach-Newport News, VA	.133	3.0
Johnstown, PA	.133	2.5
Lake Charles, LA	.132	2.0
Buffalo, NY	.131	3.4
Sussex Co., DE	.130	3.6
Stockton, CA	.130	2.3
Kansas City, MO-KS	.130	1.7
Santa Barbara, CA	.130	1.7
Scranton-Wilkes-Barre, PA	.129	3.0
Erie, PA	.129	2.4
Altoona, PA	.129	2.0
Livingston Co., KY	.129	1.8
Tampa-St. Petersburg-Clearwater, FL	.129	1.7
York, PA	.129	1.5
Lexington-Fayette, KY	.128	2.7
Anderson, SC	.127	3.1
Lincoln Co., ME	.127	2.4
Essex Co., NY	.127	1.8
Albany-Schenectady-Troy, NY	.126	4.0
Lafayette-West Lafayette, IN	.126	2.1
Columbia, SC	.125	1.6
Fayetteville, NC	.125	1.4
Greenbrier Co., WV	.125	1.4
Lancaster, PA	.125	1.3
Indianapolis, IN	.124	1.1
Tulsa, OK	.123	1.1
Huntsville, AL	.122	1.1
South Bend-Mishawaka, IN	.121	1.1
Jacksonville, FL	.120	1.1
Waldo Co., ME	.120	1.0

(Source: Environmental Protection Agency)

and tennis players may actually be creating future respiratory problems by pursuing their fitness activities in air heavily laced with ozone.

Exposure to ozone pollution is analogous to a sunburn. Repeated doses of ozone stiffen lung tissue, decrease lung-function capacity, and may cause premature aging of the lungs. Only 10 percent of the ozone we inhale is exhaled. The other 90 percent remains within us, irritating and inflaming lung tissues and causing coughing, shortness of breath, tightness in the chest, sore throats, and increased susceptibility to respiratory infections.

Children are more susceptible to lung damage from ozone because their more rapid breathing patterns draw air more deeply into their lungs. In a 1988 study, children at a summer camp during five days of ozone smog experienced lung problems that lasted for several days. The elderly are also particularly susceptible because their lungs have already lost some capacity, limiting their ability to tolerate further decreases in lung function.

In most heavy ozone areas, hospital admissions for asthma, bronchitis, and pneumonia increase with rising ozone levels. Seven percent of the population has some sort of lung ailment, but the EPA hasn't considered this a significant enough number to tighten the federal standards for ozone. The American Lung Association estimates that the nation spends as much as $40 billion each year in health-care costs and lost productivity caused by air pollution.

Besides harming humans, ozone smog increases the vulnerability of crops and trees to attack by insects and diseases. One study showed that smog actually "seasoned" some foliage, making it more appetizing to insects. The National Crop Assessment Program estimates that ozone damage to corn, peanuts, soybeans, and wheat costs the nation between $1.9 and $4.5 billion each year.

Ozone pollution is damaging our forests. It is responsible for premature death and stunted growth in the San Bernadino National Forest and the Sierra Nevada Mountains in California. And it is a prime suspect in the forest dieback that has occurred at high altitudes throughout the Appalachian Mountains. Despite the Clean Air Act's requirements that significant deterioration be prevented around national parks, ozone pollution has impaired the vistas at such parks as Acadia in Maine, Grand Canyon in Arizona, and Shenandoah in Virginia, to name just a few.

TOXIC AIR EMISSIONS

The image of the "midnight dumper" is dramatically etched in our environmental consciousness: A truck, its headlights off, moves slowly down a dirt road, heading for a secluded spot to illegally dump barrels of toxic waste that will pollute a groundwater supply and make a neighborhood uninhabitable.

But there's another villain in the vicious world of toxic pollution that does its dirty work by day, by night, often around the clock. Billions of pounds of toxics are being loaded into our environment every year by the thousands of facilities that manufacture and use dangerous chemicals. Worse still, it's perfectly legal to pump most of these poisons into our atmosphere.

Controls on the disposal of toxic waste into land dumps or water were established in the 1970s as Love Canal, Times Beach, and flaming waterways in Cleveland awoke the nation to the consequences of indiscriminate dumping. But the air—that essential life-sustaining element—has remained largely unprotected from toxics and is fouled by hundreds of chemicals, including dozens that cause birth defects, cancers, genetic mutations, and severe illnesses.

In 1987 alone, more than 2.7 billion pounds of toxic chemicals were routinely pumped into the air. In the same year, 92 industrial facilities each admitted to releasing more than 500,000 pounds of one or more cancer-causing chemicals. This data comes from the first series of chemical-release reports that industries filed with the EPA by order of Congress. As startling as these reports are, they give us an incomplete picture of the amount of toxics being dumped into the air in virtually every part of America. The EPA estimates that as many as 4 out of every 10 facilities obligated to reveal this disturbing information never even bothered to file reports. The 2.7 billion pounds we know about do not include toxics released into the air by industrial accidents.

A 1985 study by the EPA said that just 17 toxic air pollutants cause an estimated 2,000 more cancer cases a year than the United States should expect to have. This study didn't cover the numbers of cancers caused by other toxics in our air or the other adverse health effects caused by the 17 pollutants.

Routine, business-as-usual releasing of toxics doesn't grab headlines. The regular venting of 30 metric tons of methyl isocyanate from a plant over the period of a year won't make the news as does the sudden escape of an identical amount of the chemical as occurred, for instance, at the Union Carbide facility in Bhopal, India, in 1984. It's easy to fix the blame for the deaths of more than 2,500 people in the Bhopal chemical cloud or from similar, but less tragic unplanned releasing of toxic substances in this country. It's vastly more difficult to assign blame for the high rates of certain cancers around chemical plants, especially in places like the huge complex in West Virginia's Kanawa Valley and "cancer alley," the petrochemical

20 COMPANIES WITH THE HIGHEST
TOXIC AIR EMISSIONS

	Total reported TRI* air emissions in 1987
Amax Magnesium, Rowley, UT	68,112,700 pounds
Chlorine	68,110,000
Also: titanium tetrachloride	
Avtex Fibers Front Royal, Front Royal, VA	50,990,000 pounds
Carbon disulfide	49,390,000
Chlorine	1,600,000
Courtaulds North America, Le Moyne, AL	42,292,605 pounds
Carbon disulfide	42,290,000
Also: sulfuric acid and zinc compounds	
Tennessee Eastman Co., Kingsport, TN	39,484,508 pounds
Acetone	31,900,000
Methanol	2,270,000
Methyl isobutyl ketone	1,428,000
Ethylene glycol	1,111,000
Also: toluene, acetaldehyde, p-xylene propionaldehyde, ammonia and o-xylene	
Unocal Chemicals Division, Kenai, AK	30,203,400 pounds
Ammonia	30,181,000
Also: 1,1,1-trichloroethane and formaldehyde	
El Paso Products Co., Odessa, TX	26,970,200 pounds
Ethylene	18,360,000
Propylene	8,021,700
Also: xylene, vinyl acetate, 1,1,1-trichlorethane, benzene, 1,3-butadiene, toluene, ethylbenzene and styrene	
Eastman Kodak Co., Rochester, NY	22,606,909 pounds
Dichloromethane	8,920,000
Methanol	6,000,000
Acetone	3,640,000
Also: toluene, hydrochloric acid, xylene, ethylene glycol, 1,2-dichloropropane, cyclohexane and m-butyl alcohol	

Triad Chemical, Donaldsonville, LA   19,817,220 pounds
     Ammonia   19,281,800
     Also: methanol

CF Industries Inc., Donaldsonville, LA   16,241,000 pounds
     Ammonia   14,835,000
     Methanol   1,350,000

Union Camp Corp., Savannah, GA   15,795,000 pounds
     Methanol   14,084,000
     Acetone   1,000,000
     Also: hydrochloric acid, and toluene

BASF Corporation, Hamblen, TN   15,474,500 pounds
     Carbon Disulfide   15,300,000
     Also: methanol, biphenyl and ethylene glycol

3M Mag Media & Consumer Products Plants
McLeod, MN   15,293,755 pounds
     Methyl ethyl ketone   10,219,000
     Toluene   4,710,000
     Also: xylene, methanol, methyl isobutyl ketone,
     ethylbenzene, and diethyl phthalate

Agrico Chemical Co., St. James, LA   14,679,355 pounds
     Ammonia   14,031,995
     Also: methanol, sulfuric acid and chlorine

Agrico Chemical Co., Mississippi, AR   14,640,000 pounds
     Ammonia   14,200,000
     Also: methanol

Mississippi Chemical, Yazoo, MS   13,253,300 pounds
     Ammonia   13,249,500
     Also: chlorine

Aluminum Company Of America, Calhoun, TX   12,487,000 pounds
     Aluminum oxide   8,790,000
     Sodium hydroxide (solution)   2,500,000
     Also: sulfuric acid, hydrogen fluoride and methanol

Hoechst Celanese, Giles, VA   11,221,804 pounds
     Acetone   10,014,000
     Also: benzene, dichloromethane, methyl ethyl
     ketone, and ethylene

Brunswick Pulp & Paper Co., Glynn, GA	11,150,410 pounds
Methanol	9,190,000
Also: acetone, chloroform, chlorine, chlorine dioxide and sulfuric acid	
Westvaco, Alleghany, VA	10,930,500 pounds
Methanol	8,480,000
Hydrochloric acid	1,300,000
Also: chlorine, sulfuric acid, ammonia and sodium hydroxide (solution)	
Westinghouse Electric, Hampton, SC	10,447,680 pounds
Methanol	8,500,000
2-Methoxyethanol	1,300,000
Also: acetone, toluene, methyl ethyl ketone, xylene, formaldehyde, cresol and styrene	

*Toxic Release Inventory
(Source: Based on air emissions in 1987 reported to the Environmental Protection Agency under the Toxic Release Inventory Program as compiled by the Natural Resources Defense Council)

---

metropolis lining the banks of the Mississippi River northwest of New Orleans.

In 1987, the 38 major companies in "cancer alley" reported discharging nearly 400 million pounds of toxics into the surrounding environment. Down-river from the chemical plants, cancer rates in New Orleans are among our nation's highest. In 7 of the 10 parishes, or counties, along "cancer alley," cancer rates are higher than the national average, and in every parish, cancer rates are rising faster than the national average. Cancer rates among women in one parish, St. Charles, are rising 18 times faster than they are for American women as a group. In West Virginia, health department records covering the 1968 to 1977 period show an incidence of respiratory cancer 21 percent above the national average.

Many of the corporations that helped put 2.7 billion pounds of toxics into our nation's air in 1987 argue that there is no relationship between their routine emissions and the higher-than-routine rates of cancer and other illnesses around their facilities. The victims don't agree, and a growing number of physicians, public health officials, and medical researchers don't either.

The EPA has been derelict about controlling the toxic chemicals being pumped into our air. It has set health-protecting emissions standards for only seven of the hundreds of toxic substances entering our atmosphere. Only one of these seven, benzene, is among the 25 toxic chemicals most frequently produced and used by American industry.

We may think we are protecting our water and land from these poisons by enacting laws against direct dumping. But the toxics that are put into the air also settle on the land and water, often many miles away from the source. As with global warming, we cannot wait for absolute, irrefutable proof of cause and effect before controlling the fouling of our air by toxics. We know these substances cause cancer. We know people should be protected against them. We know that billions of pounds are entering our atmosphere each year. That's all we should need to know.

ACID RAIN

When thinking about acid rain, you need to look beyond the familiar picture of Adirondack lakes left crystal clear but lifeless by this controllable form of air pollution. Look beyond the well-known and growing devastation acid rain is causing Vermont's maple syrup industry. Look instead at human health, a less known but obviously crucial effect of this worsening problem.

And listen to Dr. Philip Landrigan, a professor of community medicine and pediatrics at Mt. Sinai School of Medicine in New York: "Current levels of acid air pollution are able to produce substantial adverse health effects in certain segments of the American population and particularly in children." Testifying in 1987 before a subcommittee of the Senate Environment Committee, Landrigan and other witnesses helped shift the focus of the acid rain debate away from woodlands and into our hospitals and clinics.

Landrigan estimated that acid rain is probably the third largest cause of lung disease in our nation after active smoking and passive smoking. The congressional Office of Technology Assessment estimated that some 50,000 premature deaths may occur each year in the United States and Canada by the same airborne chemicals that produce acid rain.

There are other acid rain-related health dangers, such as contamination of drinking water. High acidic levels in surface water and shallow groundwater are likely to leach toxic metals like cadmium, copper, and lead from soil and pipes into water that comes from faucets. Many wells in the Adirondacks contain levels of toxic metals that are as much as 4 times higher than national safety standards for drinking water. Long-term ingestion of such water can cause Alzheimer's and Parkinson's diseases, hypertension, kidney damage, and, especially in children, brain damage.

Rain and other water can be neutral, acidic, or alkaline, as measured on the so-called pH scale. A reading of 7 is neutral. Higher readings show water is akaline, while readings below 7 show acidity. Normal rainfalls are slightly acidic, measuring 5.6 on the pH scale. What is called "acid rain" measures 5.0 or lower. In especially troubled parts of the United States and Canada, rain is 30 to 40 times more acidic than normal rain and has pH averages of from 4 to 4.3. A lake that has had its pH reduced to 4.5 by repeated doses of acid rain can no longer

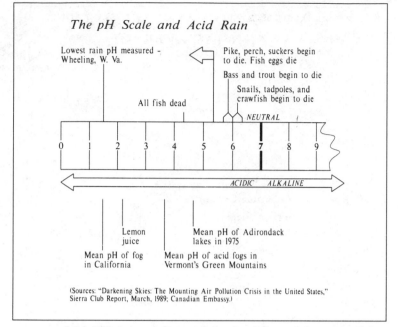

The pH Scale and Acid Rain

Lowest rain pH measured -
Wheeling, W. Va.

Pike, perch, suckers begin
to die. Fish eggs die

Bass and trout begin to die

Snails, tadpoles, and
crawfish begin to die

All fish dead

NEUTRAL

0 1 2 3 4 5 6 7 8 9

ACIDIC   ALKALINE

Lemon
juice

Mean pH of Adirondack
lakes in 1975

Mean pH of fog
in California

Mean pH of acid fogs in
Vermont's Green Mountains

(Sources: "Darkening Skies: The Mounting Air Pollution Crisis in the United States,"
Sierra Club Report, March, 1989; Canadian Embassy.)

support fish. With a reading of 2, the lake might as well be lemon juice.

The key chemicals in the acid rain equation are sulfur dioxide and nitrogen oxides—SO2 and NOx. More than half this country's emissions of SO2 come from burning coal and other fossil fuels to produce electricity. Power plants produce about one-third of the NOx emissions. Motor vehicles are responsible for nearly half the NOx emitted in the United States.

Once airborne, SO2 and NOx mix with other airborne chemicals and water to form secondary pollutants, such as sulfuric acid, nitric acid, sulfates, and nitrates. When this mixture falls to earth with rain, snow, sleet, or hail, it's acid precipitation.

Emissions of SO2 and NOx have risen sharply since World War II. SO2 is up 50 percent; NOx a whopping 400 percent. Emissions are higher in the 31 eastern-most states, where a

MOST ACID RAINFALL, 1987:
ANNUAL AVERAGE

State	Monitor Location	Average pH	# Times More Acid Than Pure Rain
Pennsylvania	Leading Ridge	4.08	33
Pennsylvania	Penn State	4.10	32
Ohio	Caldwell	4.15	28
Pennsylvania	Kane Experimental Forest	4.15	28
New York	Aurora Research Farm	4.19	26
New Jersey	Washington Crossing	4.20	25
New York	Bennett Bridge	4.20	25
Ohio	Oxford	4.21	24
Ohio	Wooster	4.22	24
West Virginia	Parsons	4.22	24
New York	Chautauqua	4.24	23
New York	Jasper	4.24	23
Pennsylvania	Milford	4.24	23
Tennessee	Walker Branch Watershed	4.26	22
Illinois	Bondville	4.27	21
New York	West Point	4.27	21
Maryland	White Rock	4.28	21
Maryland	Wye	4.28	21
Michigan	Kellogg Biological Station	4.28	21
New York	Biscuit Brook	4.28	21

(Source: "Darkening Skies: The Mounting Air Pollution Crisis in the United States," Sierra Club Report, March, 1989; Natural Resources Defense Council.)

preponderance of coal-burning power plants are located. Eighty percent of the SO2 comes from this region, as does 65 percent of the NOx. It is estimated that unless these pollutants are controlled, SO2 emissions will rise another 30 percent and NOx another 50 percent by 2010.

Most reports of acid rain damage, at least initially, came from the northeastern United States and eastern Canada, which are downwind of the midwest, which has the nation's largest concentration of coal-fired plants. The Office of Technology Assessment estimates that the eastern United States has some 17,000 lakes and 117,000 miles of streams in areas sensitive to acid rain. One study said that one-quarter of the nitrogen entering Chesapeake Bay originates in acid rain. Nitrogen has been blamed for excessive algae growth, loss of oxygen, and decline of the bay's marine life. But studies are turning up more and more instances of reduced pH levels in western lakes as well.

In 1987 in Jacksonville, Florida, acidic precipitation ate away the paint on 2,000 luxury BMWs that had just arrived from West Germany. That rainfall had economic ramifications for Jacksonville: BMW moved its point of entry out of the city. Of the 20 most acidic rain samples collected in this country in 1987, one was from Alabama, another from Tennessee, a third from Florida, and three from North Carolina. The National Acid Precipitation Assessment Program says that over the coming 30 years acid rain will cause major changes in the chemistry of the soils that support southern forests.

Like toxic air pollution, acid rain is controllable. Utilities and industries must clean up their dirty smokestacks. It's not inexpensive to outfit these coal-burners with equipment to prevent SO_2 and NO_x emissions. Outweighing this cost, however, is the toll acid rain damage takes on human health and the environment. Coal that produces less pollution is available, if the utilities would agree to use it. And auto exhausts can be cleaned up. Moreover, energy conservation means less air pollution as do cars that achieve better gas mileage than the vehicles now being sold. We have the means to rid our polluted air of not only acid rain but toxic chemicals and much of the smog and carbon monoxide fouling our populated areas. We simply must make the commitment to use them.

PEOPLE MAKING A DIFFERENCE

·

JIM HARRIS

© 1989 DAN YOUNG

The year that Jim Harris became principal of the elementary school in Rothschild, Wisconsin, the state Department of Natural Resources (DNR) installed equipment to measure sulfur dioxide (SO2) emissions reaching the school from the nearby Weyerhaeuser paper mill. "It was somewhat naive of me, but it was reassuring to think that the DNR would be protecting the kids if the levels were high," he says.

For seven years, he watched DNR workers come and go, taking SO2 readings. He also sometimes saw as many as 25 children with asthma and other respiratory ailments go outside for recess and return coughing, wheezing, and having to take medication to continue classes.

"It was clear that something was wrong," recalls Harris, who organized health forums where parents could voice their concern about the children's safety to the DNR. State officials said they could do nothing because the plant complied with SO2 emission limits set by the federal Environmental Protection Agency. Critics say the limits were too weak because they leave asthmatics exposed to dangerous levels of SO2. At this point, there seemed to be little more that Harris could do.

Rothschild, a 3,400-resident suburb of Wausau, is, Harris says, "a company town. Everyone either works at the mill or has a friend, neighbor, or relative who does. It's the town's biggest employer. We couldn't bank on mass support because we wouldn't get it. Had we tried to be real vocal, we would have been shouted down."

Less than a year later in mid-1988, luck came Harris's way in the form of Robert Yuhnke, an Environmental Defense Fund lawyer who was battling EPA over improving the SO2 emission limits. At a conference in California, a Wisconsin DNR employee alerted Yuhnke to the problems in Rothschild.

The lawyer visited the school and talked with parents at a meeting arranged by Harris. Yuhnke carried their videotaped complaints to an SO2 hearing in Washington, D.C., and convinced EPA to look into the situation. Officials found that the state's monitoring device was limited. It could detect SO2 only up to 1 part per million (ppm). A better device showed that children sometimes were being exposed to at least five ppm when the mill vented SO2 during recesses. Medical researchers say that exposure to as little as 0.4 ppm for five minutes can narrow an asthmatic's sensitive airways.

Yuhnke demanded action and even threatened to sue the EPA. The agency, unable to force change under its own regulations, sued Weyerhaeuser under a Wisconsin public nuisance statute prohibiting pollution that causes health hazards. In March 1989, the company settled the case, agreeing to spend $9 million on new SO2-control equipment. In the interim, Weyerhaeuser agreed not to emit SO2 when schoolchildren were outside for recess.

Harris views the new equipment, due to be operating in 1991, with "some skepticism. Having been taken to the cleaners for seven years, I'm not willing to trust this is all over. One thing I learned is, you can't trust the bureaucracy to take care of you. You have to watch them and keep them honest. For a lot of years, I sent children out for recess into badly polluted air, thinking that a state agency was going to protect their health."

WHAT WE CAN DO

Air pollution is responsible for most of our exposure to toxic substances. It's not just that our air is awash with pollutants; it's the volume of air we breathe that causes alarm. While on the average, individuals drink two liters of water per day, we each breathe approximately 15,000 to 20,000 liters of air.

We tend to give the most attention, deservedly, to the massive volumes of air pollution generated by industrial sources. In order to force industry to clean up its act, we must pressure Congress and the states to strengthen clean air laws. We must force the EPA and state environmental agencies to enforce those laws aggressively. And, in some cases, we must apply pressure directly on individual polluters through grassroots campaigns.

Air pollution is a problem with many fronts. But the most practical and logical place to start fighting air pollution is in our own homes.

INDIVIDUAL ACTIONS

In Your Home

Concentrations of hazardous air pollutants can be 10 to 40 times higher inside than outside. Approximately 20 to 100 hazardous chemical compounds are present in the typical American home, often reaching levels that would be illegal if found outdoors. Fortunately, you have a lot more control over your own house or apartment than over a polluter whose smokestack may be miles away. Indoor air pollution can be relatively easy to curb once you know the sources of pollution and how to deal with them.

Wood Stoves

There are approximately 10 million wood-burning stoves in use in the United States today. While these stoves are traditionally viewed as signs of environmental self-sufficiency, they can emit significant levels of dangerous air pollutants, especially carbon monoxide (CO). Some cities, like Denver, with dire CO problems have actually banned the use of wood stoves on high pollution days. If stoves can pollute outside air, imagine what they do to your home environment if improperly used and maintained.

- The CO—as well as sulfur dioxide and other pollutants— emitted by wood stoves can lead to serious respiratory problems if allowed to build up inside the home. Make sure that your stove is properly installed, vented, and maintained. Consult the instructions that came with your stove or call a professional.

- If you rely on a wood stove for heating, make sure it is properly adjusted. Consider purchasing a newer, more energy-efficient model with more sophisticated pollution control equipment. A less expensive option would be to retrofit your current stove with emission controls to capture and recombust pollutants.

Asbestos

If your home was built before 1970, chances are it contains asbestos. The asbestos won't cause health problems as long as it remains bonded to other materials. But if its tiny fibers become loosened and airborne, they can lodge in the lungs, where they will never dissolve or be expelled. Asbestos causes cancer of the lung, stomach, and chest lining and the fatal lung disease known as "mesothelioma." There is no safe level of exposure to asbestos.

- Carefully survey your home for exposed asbestos that is "friable"—loose or crumbly. You are likely to find asbestos in wall or ceiling insulation, in panels behind stoves or radiators, or wrapped around hot water tanks or pipes.

- Don't count on your ability to identify asbestos; it comes in many forms and has no apparent odor or color. If you find something that you suspect might be asbestos, have it tested by a lab. You can find asbestos testing labs listed in the yellow pages. The EPA can supply you with a list of accredited asbestos testing labs if you call (202) 554-1404.

- If the substance is asbestos, do not try to remove it yourself! Improperly done, removal of asbestos can present more of a hazard than leaving it undisturbed. Find a certified asbestos removal contractor to assess the situation and decide whether to remove it or stabilize it. Contact your state environmental agency to obtain the names of certified removal contractors in your area.

Passive Smoke

Most people are familiar with the health hazards posed by smoking. But the dangers of environmental tobacco smoke, also known as second-hand or passive smoke, are less well-known. Passive smoke comes directly from burning tobacco or indirectly from smoke exhaled by a smoker.

Studies indicate that exposure to passive tobacco smoke may increase the risk of lung cancer by an average of 30 percent in nonsmoking spouses of smokers. Very young children exposed to smoking at home are more likely to be hospitalized for bronchitis and pneumonia. Passive smoking also substantially increases the risks posed by other pollutants, including radon and asbestos.

- QUIT SMOKING! Ask visiting smokers to smoke outdoors.

Formaldehyde

Formaldehyde, a colorless, strong-smelling gas, is a by-product of combustion processes, including smoking. It can also be found in carpets, draperies, furniture, particle board, plywood, and wood paneling. In a process called "outgassing," formaldehyde escapes from these products into the air. While it's at its highest level when the material is brand new, outgassing can continue for many years.

Even low levels of formaldehyde can cause chronic respiratory problems, dizziness, lethargy, nausea, and rashes. Continued exposure may lead to central nervous system disorders or possibly cancer. In mobile homes, where extensive use of formaldehyde products is often combined with poor ventilation, formaldehyde is especially threatening. According to EPA estimates for mobile home residents, the risk of developing cancer over a 10-year period can be as high as 2 in 10,000.

Formaldehyde is often an ingredient in the adhesive used to bind pressed or veneered wood products. Countertops, paneling, and inexpensive furniture may contain high levels of loose formaldehyde. Medium-density fiberboard, which is used in cabinet doors, drawer fronts, and furniture tops, is the highest emitter of formaldehyde among pressed wood products.

- Avoid the purchase of formaldehyde products.
- Ask about formaldehyde content in pressed wood products, including building materials, cabinetry, and furniture before purchasing them. Another possible source, especially in older homes, is urea-formaldehyde foam insulation.
- Buy some house plants. Philodendrons, spiders, and some other house plant species can actually clean indoor air of low levels of some dangerous pollutants. In one 24-hour experiment, an elephant ear philodendron removed almost 87 percent of airborne formaldehyde in a closed chamber.
- Control your indoor climate. Formaldehyde levels, as well as those of other indoor air pollutants, tend to increase with heat and humidity.
- If you notice any symptoms of exposure to formaldehyde in

yourself or a family member, have your home tested. Many
city, county, and state health agencies conduct tests in the
home for levels of formaldehyde.

- For more information on formaldehyde and products, contact the EPA Toxic Substance Control Act assistance line at
(202) 554-1404.

Radon

Over the past decade, radon has emerged as one of our most
serious forms of indoor air pollution. Unlike most other forms,
it is not caused by human activity. Radon is the natural by-
product of decay of uranium and radium in the soil. It pene-
trates our houses through cracks, pipes, sump pits, and other
openings in a building's foundation.

The EPA estimates that 1 in 8 homes may have levels of radon
above the recommended level of exposure. The EPA also estimates that between 5,000 and 20,000 lung cancer deaths per
year can be attributed to radon.

- Check your home for radon. Testing kits cost between $25
and $50 and are available in hardware and drug stores.
"Alpha track" detectors are recommended for reliability;
they require exposure to your indoor environment for a
month or more.

- If your home tests positive for radon levels above the
recommended standards, hire a professional diagnostic
service. Names of companies with demonstrated ability to
measure radon in homes have been compiled by the EPA
and should be available from your state radiation protection office.

- If your house registers high levels, your diagnostic service
should recommend the next step. For more information on
how to select a contractor and how to evaluate proposals for
reducing radon, write for a copy of the EPA's *Radon Reduc-*

tion Methods: A Homeowner's Guide. Copies should be available from your state radiation protection office. If not, contact your regional EPA office. (See Appendix for address.)

- Some interim steps to reduce radon risks include: sealing cracks in the floor of your basement or foundation with a quality sealant; covering and sealing other foundation openings such as floor drains and sump pumps; covering exposed soil inside your home with concrete; and ventilating crawl spaces, basements, and attics.

Your Clothes

By trying to take good care of clothes through dry-cleaning or storing them in mothballs, we may actually be bringing health hazards into our homes. The distinctive scent of dry-cleaned clothes comes from a solvent called "perchloroethylene." This toxic chemical has caused cancer in laboratory animals, as have some of the chemicals used in mothballs. Properly dry-cleaned clothes shouldn't reek of chemicals. If they do, they haven't been dried long enough.

- If your dry-cleaned clothes smell of chemicals, take them back to the dry cleaner and ask to have them cleaned correctly. When you get them home, hang them outside or on a porch until any smell subsides. Better yet, cut down on your use of dry cleaners.
- Avoid chemical moth-repellants. Instead, when storing clothes, make sure they are clean and kept in tightly closed containers. If you do this, you shouldn't need moth repellants. Mothballs (or cake, flakes, and wreaths) are made of a range of chemicals, including napthalene and para-dichlorobenzene. Not only have they been found to cause cancer in animals, they insidiously permeate indoor air.
- Air fresheners and toilet bowl cleaners in the form of solid

blocks often contain dichlorobenzene. Avoid these products.

In Your Car

Another source of air pollution over which we have direct control is, of course, our car—a four-wheeled, mobile pollution machine.

- The most important ways that we can fight air pollution are by cutting down on driving and increasing the efficiency of our cars. Just as carbon dioxide emissions are reduced by increased efficiency in cars, so too are other pollutants. (Tips in this area are contained in Chapter 3's section on "What We Can Do.")

- Don't mess with your car's catalytic converter! According to the EPA, 5 percent of car owners tamper with this vital environmental device in an attempt to increase car performance. In states without vehicle inspection programs, 8 percent of car owners do so.

Home Energy Efficiency

The primary source of power in most homes is electricity. Most electricity is generated by coal-burning utility plants, which are major contributors to air pollution. By saving electricity in the home, we can all play a role in reducing pollution at the smokestack.

A 1987 study of one midwest utility region, which emits one-third of our nation's sulfur dioxide (SO_2) pollution, found that the region could reduce SO_2 emissions by 7 to 11 percent during the 1990s through energy conservation measures alone. The less energy we use, the less we have to produce—and the less pollution we emit. Few of the following tips will seem radical or new, but it doesn't hurt to list them for a refresher course. More importantly, they work! A more complete booklet of tips should be available from your local utility. Or for more information, contact the Conservation and Renewable Energy Inquiry and Referral Service, Box 8900, Silver Spring, MD, 20907, (800) 523-2929.

Almost half the residential energy use goes to heating and cooling our homes. For more information on maximizing efficiency in your furnace, see Chapter 2's section on "What We Can Do." Here are some tips on insulating and keeping cool:

- If you have a thermostat, keep it at 65 to 68 degrees during hours when you're active and between 50 to 60 degrees when you're in bed or away from home. You can buy a thermostat timer to do this for you. If you have radiators, service them regularly. They should be kept clean. They should not have a cover over them when they are working.

- Minimize your use of air conditioning. The thermostat should be set no lower than 78 degrees. Turn the system off when you'll be out of the house or room more than a couple of hours. Keep filters very clean. Keep outside units free of leaves and debris that may clog vents.

- Consider alternatives to air conditioning. Keep windows closed and shades drawn during the hottest hours. Attic and ceiling fans use a fraction of the energy of an air conditioner and frequently supply adequate comfort. Close off unoccupied rooms. Shut off heat or air conditioning vents or turn off room air conditioners in these spaces.

- Keep your home air tight. Each year we lose as much energy through window panes as flows through the Alaska pipeline. You can test your windows and doors for air tightness by moving a lighted candle around the frame. If the flame dances, you need weather stripping. If your windows leak, don't think that replacing them is your only option. The money would often be better spent on window repairs or perhaps a more efficient furnace. Caulking and weatherstripping windows is a straightforward process. The necessary materials are available at any hardware store.

- A door sweep on the bottom edge of exterior doors can help keep your home air tight. You can make a draft guard yourself by taking an old bedsheet or any old fabric, sewing it into a tube shape, filling it with sand, and sewing it shut. Place it along any open space between the floor and the bottom of the door.

- Insulate your attic to the levels recommended for your area. Be sure to weatherstrip around the attic hatch or door and caulk around all plumbing running through the attic floor. Insulating without sealing these other passages is a waste of money and effort.

- In the summer, lights, stoves, and such appliances as washers and dryers generate heat and increase the load on your air conditioner. Keep lights low or off whenever possible. Try to schedule cooking and use of other appliances for the cooler hours of the day.

- Plant a few trees strategically around your house to keep it cooler. (Chapter 2 tells you how.)

- Dress for the weather, inside and out. Dark colors absorb more heat, keeping us warmer. Light colors reflect heat, so we feel cooler. In the winter, a lightweight long-sleeved sweater will add 2 degress warmth; a heavy sweater 3.7 degrees; and two light-weight sweaters 5 degrees. The space between the two layers serves as insulation.

Bringing water into our homes is an extremely energy-intensive process. It requires energy to pump it from the ground, reservoir, or river. It needs to be cleaned, filtered, and then pumped again to its place of use. It is finally disposed of through an energy-intensive sewage treatment system. Fifteen percent of the electricity we consume at home is used to heat water.

- Conserve water as a general practice. A shower requires only about half as much water as a bath. Water-saver shower heads cut the flow by 40 to 60 percent. Don't let your faucets leak. One drip a second can waste up to 200 gallons a month. Invest in faucet aerators and toilet dams.
- Don't use hot water unless you have to. Run cold water to operate your trash disposal — it actually works better with cold water.

The rest of the electricity we use at home goes for cooking, lighting, and running appliances. Refrigerators alone use over 10 percent.

- Buy energy-efficient appliances. Your refrigerator is especially important. Unlike most household appliances that operate only periodically, the refrigerator runs 24 hours a day, 365 days a year. The American Council for an Energy Efficient Economy (ACEEE) publishes a guide to the most energy-efficient appliances. For a copy of the 1990 edition, write to ACEEE, Suite 535, 1001 Connecticut Avenue, N.W., Washington, DC, 20036, (202) 429-8873.
- Use the most energy-efficient light bulbs and the lowest wattage possible for your needs. The new screw-in fluorescent bulbs cost more initially, but they last far longer, use much less electricity than incandescent bulbs, and will save you money over their lifetime.
- Turn off lights in unoccupied rooms. Use electrical appliances sparingly.

GETTING POLITICAL

As individuals, we can cut down on our driving and drive as efficiently as possible, but our cars will only be as clean as Detroit is willing to make them. We can conserve electricity, but the energy we consume has got to come from somewhere, and that somewhere is very probably a polluting coal-fired plant. We can make a dent in the pollution problem by changing our individual lifestyles, but to really clean up our air, we are going to have to retool our entire industrial and transportation sectors. This type of change requires federal leadership.

Even as this book went to press, Congress was reviewing the Clean Air Act. As in earlier legislative review processes, the industries covered by the law were fighting proposals to strengthen it. In some cases, such as allowable levels of pollution from autos, they were even trying to weaken them. Faced with the power of these industry lobbies, it seems at times that compromise is inevitable. As citizens, we must send a resounding message to Congress that we cannot afford to compromise on clean air!

Write to your representative and senators; tell them of your concern and specifically ask them to:

- Set a new round of NOx, hydrocarbon, and carbon monoxide standards that force manufacturers to develop new and more effective control technologies for conventional cars. Technology for controlling emissions from automobiles has improved dramatically since 1981, driven by tougher regulatory requirements and engineering advances. We must continue to push for advances in science through regulation.

- Force municipal transportation planners to incorporate air quality objectives in their plans, promote less driving in congested areas, improve mass and rapid transit, and provide other alternatives to single-occupant transportation systems.

- Reduce risks of cancer and other severe illnesses from exposure to airborne toxic chemicals to below 1 in 1 million. Congress must require industry to develop "closed loop" systems that contain toxic substances from the air. Congress must require the best available pollution control technologies for mobile sources and smaller area sources of toxic air pollutants that, when combined, account for up to 50 percent of the toxic air pollution problem.

• Establish a chemical safety investigation board to look into the causes of chemical accidents and establish standards for industry to follow in order to prevent accidental releases.

• Reduce emissions of acid rain by cutting emissions of sulfur dioxide and nitrogen oxides by half and then hold emissions at those levels by promoting more efficient energy use and development of safe, nonpolluting alternative sources of energy.

• Maintain and strengthen legal requirements to protect air quality and visibility in national parks and wilderness areas.

The federal government can only do so much. Once Congress issues its mandate, states and municipalities are still charged with developing state implementation plans (SIPs) for meeting those standards. Then the plans must be aggressively implemented.

To date, states have been lax in implementing SIPs. That's why we are suffering from such high levels of carbon monoxide and ozone pollution today. There are clear reasons for this, not the least of which is that the federal government has lacked the political will to force states to comply. Clearly, we cannot just rely on the feds to push from above; as citizens we must also be pushing from below.

SIPs are usually designed to bring violating areas into compliance with federal standards. SIPs are usually drafted by local planning commissions appointed by elected officials. The plans are then approved by a state air quality control commission—a body with authority to adopt rules and regulations and approve a statewide plan.

When it comes to the hard choices for your area, the local board analyzes the potentially available solutions and drafts the plan. It's at this level that creativity and imagination come into play. If a good-faith effort to put together an effective plan doesn't happen here, it won't happen at all. Unfortunately, it's also at this level that industry launches its first attack. And these local air planning boards typically receive very little input from anyone except industries and local governments that will ultimately be affected by the plan. By the time local air planning boards hold public hearings, all the real decisions have already been made.

We cannot let this process remain an insider's game.

- Find out if your municipality is not complying with any federal clean air standards. The areas violating the ozone standards are listed earlier in this chapter. You can find out about other violations of other "criteria pollutants" by calling your regional EPA office (see Appendix).

- If your area is not complying, find out through an elected official or your health department about the local air planning board. When does it meet? Who is on it? Often these boards are stacked with industry types. Is there adequate citizen or environmental support?

- These meetings are open to the public. Attend them. Or hook up with a local environmental group that is doing so. Do your research and make sure that the board is taking a creative, aggressive approach to developing and implementing a plan.

- If you aren't satisfied with the board's progress, try to learn as much about the interest groups on the other side of the issue as possible. What is their financial or political clout? What ties do they have to board members? Use media to highlight any potential conflict-of-interest or bought votes.

A breath of clean air should be something we take for granted. But because it is not, we must guard against all types of air pollution in whatever way we can. Whether it's a simple lifestyle change, such as leaving your car home and riding your bicycle whenever you can, or a more involved effort, such as monitoring the work of local planning commissions and attending public hearings, every little bit makes a difference.

PEOPLE MAKING A DIFFERENCE

—————————— • ——————————

ELLEN FLETCHER

© 1989 RENEE BURGARD

Ellen Fletcher was no stranger to bike wars when she set about making Palo Alto, California, one of the nation's most bicycle-friendly cities—so friendly that at last count an estimated 14 percent of its residents who work in town commute on two wheels.

As a young girl, Fletcher had to battle a foster mother for permission just to ride a bicycle. Then, she fought college administrators who wouldn't let her bring her bike inside during bad weather. And as a bike-commuter in New York City in the 1950s, she dodged taxis and heard cops yelling at her to get off the busy streets.

By 1973, Fletcher was a self-described "typical California housewife and mother" of three. Her bike-riding days seemed over, until the oil embargo reactivated her transportation roots. "I refused to wait in gas lines," she states.

Setting out to establish bike rights in Palo Alto, Fletcher soon was chairing the Citizen's Technical Advisory Committee, which focused on bicycle issues and pioneered what eventually became the work of the local Bicycling Advisory Committee. The community had some bike lanes on its streets, but additional work needed to be done to lure more commuters out of their polluting vehicles.

One of the advisory committee's first proposals was for downtown facilities where commuters could safely park their bikes. Fletcher wrote a position paper on the issue and lobbied the planning commission to establish a bike parking policy. She later expanded her paper into a booklet that became the definitive reference work on bike parking facilities.

In 1977, she began the first of three four-year terms on the City Council, giving official clout to her voice and mission. Setting an example, she bikes all around Palo Alto. For trips to San Francisco and Sacramento, she uses a folding bike and public transportation. Her 1963 car, used extensively when her children were young, languishes at home.

The results of Fletcher's crusade include improvements like Palo Alto's "bicycle boulevard"—a 2-mile stretch running through the city with restricted access for motorized vehicles. New commercial and residential developments must provide enclosed, locking bicycle storage areas and customer-service facilities must have bike parking racks. New businesses and industries must provide showers so bike commuters can freshen up. (For example, the Xerox Research Center has a towel service; one of every five of its employees is a bicycle commuter.) Businesses with drive-in facilities must provide access for bicycles. Palo Alto's traffic lights were adjusted to give bikes more time to cross intersections. City workers get per-mile cash reimbursements for using bicycles. There is an Effective Cycling Course for seventh graders. And the Police Department conducts a remedial program for juvenile traffic offenders.

Fletcher's fight for bicycle rights goes beyond her love of bikes. "I've always been a strong environmentalist," she admits. "I don't like what I consider the misuse and overuse of the automobile. Being on the council brought me the realization that tremendous resources are spent on trying to deal with traffic problems. Accommodating the car is tremendously expensive, from the cost of roads to the space devoted to parking. It seems such an unnecessary waste. It doesn't lead to pleasant living."

CHAPTER FIVE

Defusing the Toxics Timebomb

·

CLEANING UP OUR AIR, WATER, AND FOOD

"**T**each your children what we have taught our children, that the Earth is our mother. Whatever befalls the Earth befalls the sons of the Earth. Man did not weave the web of life. He is merely a strand in it. Whatever he does to the web, he does to himself."

When Chief Seattle of the Suquamish tribe, in what is now the state of Washington, said this to President Franklin Pierce in 1854, he had seen enough of the white man's ways to be concerned about the future of the environment. Seattle's eloquent plea for the new Americans to respect the air, water, land, and wildlife describes some early symptoms of our present disease: the plains littered with the rotting carcasses of a thousand buffalo shot from a passing train; the "lack of a quiet place" in our cities; destruction of forests; "the view of ripe hills blotted out by talking wires;" the disappearance, even then, of the eagle; the "stench" in the air.

We can only guess at Chief Seattle's reaction to a toxic waste dump such as Love Canal, which focused our attention on 50 years of careless production, excessive use, and indiscriminate disposal of hazardous chemicals. Beginning in the 1920s, an array of toxic substances was deposited in an abandoned canal between the upper and lower Niagara rivers near Buffalo, New York. With the postwar building boom in full swing, developers in 1953 filled in the rest of the old channel and constructed homes and schools on the site.

Over the next two decades, the buried chemical soup bubbled and oozed its way to the surface. Love Canal residents began noticing putrid odors and strange substances in their neighborhood and even seeping into some basements. In 1976, high concentrations of extremely toxic, cancer-causing PCBs were found in storm sewers bordering the old canal. It took New York's Department of Health two years to order the evacuation of pregnant women and young children from 239 homes in Love Canal. By then, Love Canal's "Tales of Toxic Terror" were mounting: babies born with abnormal hearts and kidneys and two sets of teeth; four mentally handicapped babies on the same block; rates of epilepsy, liver disease, nervous disorders, rectal bleeding, and miscarriage far above normal. Finally, the 900 families living in Love Canal were evacuated, and the long, expensive process of cleaning up the mess was begun.

The disaster of Love Canal could be attributed, at least in its formative days, to ignorance about the dangers posed to human health and the environment by the growing numbers of chemicals that our burgeoning petroleum-based civilization was creating.

But the destruction of the small Missouri town of Times Beach? This catastrophe occurred as a result of pure callousness and carelessness at a time when the dangers of toxics were quite clear. In the mid-1970s, town officials hired a contractor to spray oil on 10 miles of unpaved roads to hold down the dust of summer. The truck the contractor used to oil Times Beach was also used regularly to haul waste sludge from a chemical factory. Over at least two summers, the roads of Times Beach were coated with oil contaminated by this toxic sludge residue. Among the contaminants were dioxins, one of the most toxic substances in the world. Times Beach was evacuated and is a ghost town today.

THE EXTENT OF THE TOXICS PROBLEM

Love Canal and Times Beach are the two most infamous toxic waste sites in our nation. But they are far from the only ones: The overall dimension of our toxic timebomb is staggering. The Environmental Protection Agency says there are as many as 29,000 waste sites that could qualify for its superfund cleanup program—which tackles only those toxic dumps that are considered the nation's worst. The Congressional Research Service of the Library of Congress estimates that our nation may be littered with as many as 300,000 hazardous waste dumps. Many are leaking poisons into the underground drinking water supplies that serve 120 million people, including 95 percent of rural Americans.

In its 1988 report *Environmental Progress and Challenges*, the EPA reported shocking statistics on the extent of toxic releases into the ground and water. Besides the 29,000 potential superfund sites, at least 180,000 pits, ponds, and lagoons contain chemical poisons; an estimated 500 hazardous waste disposal facilities and 16,000 municipal and private landfills contain toxics; and thousands of "injection wells" deep underground are filled with liquid wastes in an environmentally uncertain disposal process.

Waste dumps are merely one indication of the severity of our toxics problem. On a larger scale, we live in a society addicted to chemicals. In our nation, there are roughly 12,000 chemical manufacturing plants producing over 70,000 different chemicals, including 37,000 types of pesticides. Most of these compounds were on the market before federal controls were instituted and have never been adequately tested for safety. American industry each year generates more than 1 ton of chemical waste for every citizen—that's roughly 260 million tons a year. While chemical complexes and factories create a large amount of this dangerous refuse, the hazardous waste stream is fed by a wide variety of sources, including auto repair shops, the construction industry, dry cleaners, equipment repair shops, careless disposal of dangerous household products, laundromats, photo labs, and printers.

Our management of these various chemicals is marked by carelessness. Nationwide, there are around 5 million buried tanks storing petroleum products and chemicals. The EPA estimates that from 15 to 25 percent of these tanks may be leaking harmful substances into the ground. According to reports filed with the EPA, 19,000 industrial facilities released more than 7 billion tons of waste into the air, land, and water in 1987 alone. An additional 3 billion tons were sent to hazardous waste treatment facilities.

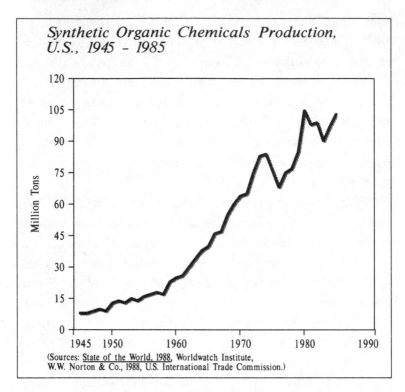

Synthetic Organic Chemicals Production, U.S., 1945 – 1985

(Sources: State of the World, 1988, Worldwatch Institute, W.W. Norton & Co., 1988, U.S. International Trade Commission.)

Most chemicals are released deliberately and slowly during routine production and manufacturing processes. A distinct minority of our chemical emissions is the result of catastrophic accidents with immediately devastating consequences, such as the disaster in Bhopal, India. In the middle of the night a valve broke at Union Carbide's Bhopal plant, releasing 30 tons of deadly methyl isocyanate gas. At least 2,500 people were killed and 17,000 permanently disabled by this avoidable accident. In the United States, the EPA has documented more than 6,900 accidental chemical releases between 1980 and 1985, resulting in 138 deaths, 4,717 injuries, and the evacuation of 200,000 people.

Compounding this problem is the tendency for chemical and petroleum plants to cluster together in "hot spots." The

250,000 people living in West Virginia's Kanawa Valley share the area with 13 major chemical plants, each spewing a deadly brew into the air. An 80-mile area along the Mississippi River from Baton Rouge to New Orleans has the nation's biggest concentration of petrochemical plants. This stretch has been dubbed "Cancer Alley."

There was a time when a community would fight to attract a computer factory—perceived as a "clean" industry packaged neatly in a low-slung, modern building. Since then, we've learned that not only does the manufacture of microchips help destroy the atmosphere by its heavy use of chlorofluorocarbons, but the process also produces huge amounts of toxic waste. Silicon Valley in Northern California, a center of microchip production, is experiencing rising rates of birth defects and cancer, as well as contaminated drinking water wells.

U.S. military installations and their stable payrolls are still very popular with local officials. But we've learned that, largely because of sloppy procedures with huge volumes of such chemicals as cleaning solvents, military installations are among our biggest toxic polluters. They have fouled the ground not only in this country, but around the globe. Part of Guam's water supply has been ruined by our military. Add this toxic waste problem to the chemicals mishandled by other U.S. agencies and we have the federal government as one of our biggest polluters. Nobody really has a handle on the dimensions of government pollution or how much money we the taxpayers will have to spend to clean up the mess. But shortly after Congress ordered the EPA to place federal facilities on its superfund cleanup list, the names of 115 of them were added to our "toxics hall of shame."

In our intricately connected "web of life," all these chemicals sooner or later turn up in the air, soil, groundwater, rivers, lakes, and oceans as well as in our food and ultimately our bodies. The polychlorinated biphenyl (PCB) levels in fish caught in the Great Lakes have gotten so high that people have been warned to limit their intake of these fish; pregnant women and children are advised against eating any at all.

Of the 1.2 billion pounds of pesticides used each year, only 10 percent is estimated to reach the targeted organisms. The other 1.1 billion pounds land elsewhere in our environment. Many of the fruits and vegetables that people eat every day often contain dangerous levels of pesticide residues. The salad you ate yesterday may have contained such unwanted ingredients as endosulfan on the lettuce, methamidophos on the tomatoes and peppers, and dimethoate on the broccoli. The potential hazards from long-term exposure to these chemicals include birth defects, cancer, kidney and liver damage, and nervous system disorders. Fresh meat may also be pumped so full of antibiotics and growth hormones that it can retard our body's natural ability to fight infection.

Unlike processed foods, there are no labels on fresh produce and meats to warn us about unwanted substances. The Food and Drug Administration tests only about 1 percent of the fresh fruits and vegetables sold in the United States each year. When produce is tested, pesticide residues have been found on half of all samples. A 1987 study of produce from California—the nation's biggest domestic source of fresh produce—found that 10 percent of its fruits and vegetables had pesticide residues exceeding legal limits.

A 1988 EPA report states that "hundreds of different chemicals. . . could reach groundwater and potentially contaminate drinking water wells. . . . The agency's major concern is with man-made toxic chemicals such as synthetic organic chemicals that are pervasive in plastics, solvents, pesticides, paints, dyes, varnishes and ink." In fact, the agency examined groundwater in 38 states and detected the presence of 74 pesticides, 18 of

FREQUENCIES OF DETECTABLE PESTICIDE RESIDUES IN FRUITS AND VEGETABLES AS MONITORED BY FDA AND CALIFORNIA FOOD PROGRAMS 1982-85

Commodity	Percent of Domestic and Imported Samples with Pesticide Residues
Strawberries	63
Peaches	55
Celery	53
Cherries	52
Cucumbers	51
Bell peppers	49
Tomatoes	45
Sweet potatoes	37
Cantaloupes	34
Grapes	34
Lettuce	32
Apples	29
Spinach	29
Carrots	28
Green beans	27
Grapefruit	22
Oranges	22
Pears	22
Potatoes	22
Cabbage	20
Broccoli	13
Onions	10
Cauliflower	5
Watermelon	4
Bananas	1
Corn	1

(Note: These data may not accurately reflect true contamination rates because many pesticides are undetectable by FDA methods, including widely used fungicides on fruits. Also, the FDA program lacks a sampling design to ensure representative sampling of all fruits and therefore certain fruits are sampled more rigorously than others.)

(Source: *Intolerable Risk: Pesticides in Our Children's Food,* A Report by the Natural Resources Defense Council, February, 1989; *Pesticide Alert: A Guide to Pesticides in Fruits and Vegetables,* L. Mott and K. Snyder, Sierra Club Books, 1988.)

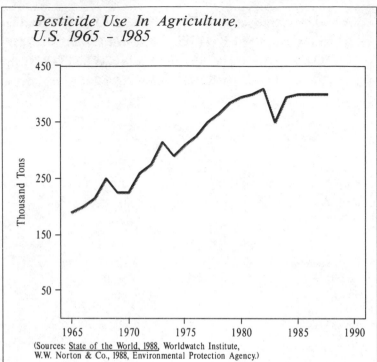

Pesticide Use In Agriculture, U.S. 1965 - 1985

Thousand Tons

(Sources: State of the World, 1988, Worldwatch Institute, W.W. Norton & Co., 1988, Environmental Protection Agency.)

them known carcinogens. Many of these, such as DDT are pervasive. Even after DDT's use was banned, the pesticide was still showing up in one-third of the wells tested.

Because 90 percent of rural households get their drinking water from the ground, contamination of groundwater has the potential of causing many serious health problems. The EPA has tried to reduce the leaching of pesticides into groundwater, but as long as the farming industry is dependent on chemicals, the contamination of rural drinking water will increase. But even with reduced use of chemical pesticides, our groundwater will still be threatened by the many other toxics leaching into the soil from leaking underground storage tanks and illegal dumping of toxic wastes.

Chief Seattle's words should haunt us: "Whatever befalls the earth befalls the sons of the earth." The National Human

Adipose Tissue Survey, a detailed chemical analysis of actual human fat samples, detected the presence of regulated hazardous chemicals in 100 percent of the tested samples. Benzene, a known carcinogen, was found in 96 percent of the human tissue tested; PCBs in 83 percent; DDT in 55 percent. Even mothers' milk, the symbol of purity and wholesomeness, has been found to be contaminated with dioxins, PCBs, and pesticides.

Chemical accidents have immediate, often dramatic consequences. But what are the effects of chronic exposure to toxics and the overall burden this places on our bodies? No one knows for sure, but the indications are frightening. Cancer rates are rising about 1 percent every year. Childhood cancers have increased almost 32 percent since 1950. A 1978 study by the National Academy of Science estimated that pesticide residues in food alone could cause over 1 million cases of cancer by 2050. Since 1978, there have been twice as many carcinogenic pesticides found on food.

Cancer isn't our only concern. Terms like "chemical sensitivity," "environmental illness," and "sick-building syndrome" have been added to our medical vocabulary. Learning disabilities are increasingly linked to very low levels of exposure to environmental contaminants. One study showed a direct correlation between the level of lead in a mother's blood and developmental delays in her children.

In 1989, the Natural Resources Defense Council said in its report, *Intolerable Risk: Pesticides in Our Children's Food*, that "our nation's children are being harmed by the very fruits and vegetables we tell them will make them grow up healthy and strong. These staples of children's diets routinely, and lawfully, contain dangerous amounts of pesticides, which pose an increased risk of cancer, neurobehavioral damage and other health problems."

The report went on to say that exposure to only eight of the most widely used pesticides during preschool years may result in as many as 6,200 children developing cancer sometime in their lives. Because of their small body sizes and the large amounts of fresh fruits and vegetables they consume, children receive 4 times greater exposure than adults to the eight most widely used cancer-causing pesticides. Worse still, children are much more susceptible to carcinogenic substances than adults. Separate studies have shown that half of a person's lifetime cancer risk from exposure to pesticides occurs during the first 6 years of life.

We do not need to lace our food with pesticides. Chemicals are not the only way to control insects and weeds. A small, but growing number of farmers are turning to Integrated Pest Management that uses natural methods, such as insect predators and different planting patterns, to produce their crops. But to escape from our pesticide dependency, we are going to have to reorient the Department of Agriculture from its almost exclusive bias toward chemical farming and its polluting and poisoning alliance with the agrichemical industry.

The tragic irony is that our increasing use of pesticides is not working. Insects and weeds develop resistance to chemicals. Over the last 30 years, our farmers have increased the use of agrichemicals elevenfold, but their crop losses to chemical-resistant insects have doubled.

Our profligate use and disposal of toxics threatens more than the health of humans. The EPA says that "potential impacts of groundwater contamination on the environment include adverse effects on surface waters and damage to fish, vegetation and wildlife. For example, 15 percent of our endangered species rely upon groundwater for maintaining their habitat."

THE LEGISLATIVE RESPONSE

Our lives are filled with products whose manufacture, use, or disposal results in toxic threats. Behind our plastic jugs is a trail of organic chlorine compounds and organic solvents; behind common medicines we find organic solvents and residues and heavy metals like mercury and zinc; paint manufacture requires the use and disposal of heavy metals, pigments, and organic residues and solvents; leather production leaves behind heavy metals and organic solvents; and textile waste includes dyes, heavy metals, organic chlorine compounds and solvents. Other vast quantities of hazardous waste are created by the complexes that produce our metals, motor fuels, and pesticides. And, of course, the end products themselves must be disposed of when their useful lives are through.

We have responded to these threats with a patchwork of laws and regulations drafted and amended over the last 40 years. Some laws, such as the Clean Air Act, the Clean Water Act, the Federal Food, Drug, and Cosmetics Act, the Safe Drinking Water Act, and portions of the Federal Insecticide, Fungicide, and Rodenticide Act, have tried to protect the end points of pollution. By setting standards for our air, water, and food, it was hoped that the industrial behavior behind the damage would change.

All these laws approach the problem by defining allowable levels of pollution. The Clean Water Act, for example, allows industrial facilities and municipal sewage treatment plants to obtain permits to discharge polluted waste into streams, lakes, and oceans. It was based on the premise that if the concentrations of dangerous substances were kept relatively low, the waste problem would be taken care of by dilution in the receiving waterways. The Clean Air Act is structured in much the same manner. Unfortunately, this approach has not accounted adequately for the long-term cumulative effects of all these discharges.

We've seen the development of "toxic hot spots" in our waterways—areas where the natural water was polluted to unsafe levels, even though each discharge pipe supposedly was meeting the requirements of its permit. It became clear that toxic substances in our air and water were building up, not disappearing. Laws aimed at protecting food and drinking water ran into similar problems. The EPA has spent years trying to set standards for "allowable" contamination of produce and tap water. Because of the complexity of this task, very few contaminants have enforceable standards, and these standards change constantly as scientific evidence accumulates. Moreover, none of these standards takes into account the cumulative effect of all the contaminants we are ingesting. Because these laws have not stopped the flow of toxics into our environment, increasingly complex and expensive technologies are required simply to measure levels of dangerous chemicals in our air, water, and food, let alone repair the damage.

THE FEDERAL INSECTICIDE, FUNGICIDE, AND RODENTICIDE ACT (FIFRA) AND THE TOXIC SUBSTANCES CONTROL ACT (TSCA)

In addition to the general goals of assuring clean air, water, and food, this country has been concerned with controlling the flood of specific new chemicals and pesticides into the market. Laws such as the Federal Insecticide, Fungicide, and Rodenticide Act (FIFRA) and the Toxic Substances Control Act (TSCA) were passed over the strenuous objections of the chemical industry. FIFRA requires that a new pesticide must be approved by the EPA before it can be marketed. But TSCA allows new chemicals other than pesticides to be marketed without EPA approval. The agency must simply be notified and supplied with any available health studies. If the EPA later concludes—based largely on studies supplied by the manufacturer—that the health or environmental risks of a new chemical outweigh its economic benefits, the substance can be regulated or banned. So far, only one toxic chemical—polychlorinated biphenyls—has been singled out under TSCA for such postmarketing regulation by the EPA.

Under both FIFRA and TSCA, existing chemicals, including pesticides, may continue to be marketed, but they are supposed to undergo extensive testing by the producing company. The EPA can order them removed from use if they are found to pose "unreasonable risks" to health, safety, or the environment. Since testing is costly, time-consuming and often reveals bad news, companies have been dragging their feet. Partly because of a lack of funding, the EPA has not moved aggressively in this area, and the majority of chemicals on the market still have not been shown to be safe.

For example, we have no information on the possible toxic effects of 79 percent of the existing chemicals. About 90 percent of the cancer risk from pesticides is posed by those approved before 1978, when standards were far weaker than today. Amendments made to FIFRA in 1988 require the EPA to either approve or ban all existing pesticides within 10 years.

The 1989 Natural Resources Defense Council's (NRDC) report on pesticide risks for children set off a wave of controversy over pesticides, particularly daminozide, which is marketed under the name Alar. This chemical is used primarily for cosmetic purposes by apple growers. It makes apples redder and shinier, increases their shelf life, and makes them easier to harvest. Alar is also a potent carcinogen. The NRDC and consumer advocate Ralph Nader had been trying for years to get the EPA to ban Alar. Uniroyal Chemical, the manufacturer, was forced to withdraw Alar in 1989 when a storm of public protest erupted after the NRDC report was aired on CBS's "Sixty Minutes."

FIFRA uses a risk-benefit analysis process to determine the "acceptable" residue level for a particular pesticide. This is the level that will result in roughly one excess death for every 1 million people. However, these analyses do not consider the cumulative effects from the dozens of pesticides that can be used together. Nor do they consider the risks posed to sensitive populations such as children. The "Delaney clause" of the Federal Food, Drug, and Cosmetic Act sets a much higher standard for food additives than FIFRA's risk-benefit approach to pesticides. Under Delaney, no food additive, including artificial flavors, dyes, and preservatives, can be used if it causes cancer in animals. It was this authority that was used for the much-publicized ban on Red Dye No. 2.

The clash between these two approaches—no acceptable cancer risk for additives versus the cost-benefit analysis for pesticide residues—has resulted in an effort by industry and the EPA to reinterpret the Delaney clause to allow consideration for the economic effects of banning a particular food additive. For example, there is ongoing debate about the cherries in canned fruit salad. The most effective dyes, the ones that make cherries stay bright red after months of sitting in sugar syrup, all carry some level of health risk. Under the traditional interpretation of Delaney, these dyes should be banned. But fruit salad manufacturers have prevented this from happening by arguing that without those bright red cherries, sales of their product would plummet.

Another major point of contention about chemicals concerns the definition of "unreasonable risk." How many additional cases of cancer constitute a "reasonable" price to pay for a new substance that will make apples shinier, cherries redder, or laundry brighter? However this question is answered, problems remain. Enforcement of food-protection laws has been minimal, at best. Food imported from countries without stringent pesticide controls can virtually evade regulation. The Food and Drug Administration tests only 1 percent of the produce shipped into the United States. Even when inspectors find problems, importers rarely are fined, and the contaminated produce usually is not taken off the market.

RESOURCE CONSERVATION AND RECOVERY ACT
(RCRA)

One of the most ambitious attempts to solve the toxic waste crisis is embodied in the Resource Conservation and Recovery Act (RCRA, pronounced "rick-ra"), a detailed plan for tracking and managing waste "from cradle to grave." This law, passed in 1976, controls the generation, transportation, treatment, storage and disposal of hazardous waste. Its mandate is to prevent the creation of new Love Canals. Although RCRA could be used to address the problem of excessive waste generation, its implementation has focused instead on waste treatment and disposal.

Facilities that treat, store, or dispose of hazardous waste must have EPA permits and follow prescribed procedures in handling the waste. Operators of licensed hazardous waste landfills must prevent leakage and continually monitor the quality of groundwater around their facilities. They must report any contamination to the EPA. They must handle certain waste in specific ways, such as solidifying liquid waste before putting it in a landfill. When a licensed landfill reaches its capacity and is closed, the operators must cover it with a leakproof cap and monitor the nearby groundwater for 30 years. Within a few years of passing the hazardous waste disposal law,

Congress realized that additional steps were needed because hazardous waste facilities were still being operated in ways that endangered human health and the environment. From this came strengthening amendments in 1984 that banned land disposal of untreated hazardous waste and required hazardous waste landfills to have double liners and systems to collect any waste before it could migrate out of the landfill.

The 1984 amendments also forced the EPA to speed up the permitting process. As of November 1985, the nation's 1,500 disposal facilities that lacked permits to operate were supposed to certify to the EPA that they had met the groundwater monitoring and financial requirements of RCRA. The facilities were also supposed to apply for permits. Instead of complying with RCRA, two-thirds of the facilities decided to close. This created yet another problem. While these facilities could no longer legally accept hazardous waste, they nevertheless contained millions of tons of waste that had been dumped over the years. The threat of their leaking toxics remained.

Today, there are roughly 5,000 facilities covered by RCRA, but the EPA estimates that only 44 to 57 percent are actually in compliance with the regulations. A study by the congressional General Accounting Office found that EPA inspectors missed almost as many RCRA violations as they found. More than half the waste treatment and disposal facilities covered by RCRA — the dumps that were intended to safely handle industrial waste and prevent future Love Canals — are themselves in need of cleaning up.

As part of its responsibility under RCRA to regulate the storage of hazardous substances, the EPA has recently realized the importance of another widespread source of drinking water contamination. Buried underground in all parts of the nation are from 5 to 6 million storage tanks, some 97 percent of them used for petroleum products. There are upwards of 5 billion gallons of gasoline stored below ground at service stations and distribution centers. The EPA estimates that some 400,000 of these underground tanks are leaking. We can expect that number to grow as tanks age and deteriorate. Many of the older tanks are made of steel, which rusts and leaks. One-third of our underground tanks are more than 20 years old, with a heavy percentage of them dating back to the service station construction boom of the 1950s and 1960s.

A leak in a storage tank may be insignificant to a service station owner, but it can be a major threat to groundwater purity. A station pumping 30,000 gallons of gasoline a month may hardly notice a leak rate of one-third of a gallon an hour. But when calculated by the month, this means 210 gallons of gasoline are released into the soil below the tank!

If water contains as little as 1 part of gasoline for 1 million parts of water, the water is considered undrinkable by public health authorities. That means just 1 gallon of gasoline can render 1 million gallons of water unpotable. Gasoline contains up to 1,200 different chemical compounds. While much of gasoline floats on the surface of water, some of its most dangerous components dissolve in water. These include benzene, lead, toluene, and xylene. Benzene is a known carcinogen, considered dangerous at 15 parts per billion parts of water. That means it takes only 1 teaspoon of benzene to dangerously contaminate 80,000 gallons of water. Even very low levels of lead in water can produce neurological and motor disorders, with children being the most vulnerable.

In 1986, Congress initiated a nationwide campaign against leaking underground storage tanks. A trust fund of $500 million was earmarked to help states set up and operate programs to find leaking tanks and replace them with newer varieties that are supposed to be more environmentally safe. As with the money for toxic dump cleanups, the trust fund amounts to nothing more than a down payment on this expensive task. Removing and replacing the tanks at the average service station can cost upwards of $50,000.

However, this does not include excavation of contaminated soil, which occurs only about 10 percent of the time. If the gasoline-laden soil is not removed, the poisons it contains will continue to percolate deeper into the earth. An unknown volume of these poisons are heading toward our underground water supplies. An EPA study of 12,500 leaking tanks showed that 3,500 had released chemicals into groundwater. Cleaning up contaminated water is extremely costly—even assuming that such a process could successfully purify a very large aquifer.

How has RCRA worked over the years? Not very well, according to William Kovacs, who was chief counsel to the House subcommittee that helped write the original legislation. "EPA's implementation of the law can only be described as tardy, fragmented, at times non-existent and consistently inconsistent," Kovacs wrote in his contribution to *The Solid Waste Handbook.*

THE COMPREHENSIVE ENVIRONMENTAL RESPONSE COMPENSATION AND LIABILITY ACT (CERCLA OR SUPERFUND)

Commonly known as the superfund law, the Comprehensive Environmental Response Compensation and Liability Act (CERCLA) was passed in 1980 as an after-the-fact plan to clean up the result of years of grossly negligent mismanagement of toxic waste. Though superfund was originally envisioned as a short-term program, toxic dumps are being discovered and added to the superfund list much faster than old sites are being cleaned up.

Congress allocated the EPA $1.6 billion to begin cleaning up our worst toxic dumps. The superfund law and the money arrived just about the time the Reagan administration brought its anti-environmental, deregulation campaign to Washington. Before it ever had a chance to begin operating, the new superfund program was engulfed in scandal. Among a variety of questionable actions to circumvent EPA procedures, Rita Lavelle, Reagan's first superfund chief, channeled cleanup efforts to areas where partisan officials thought Republican candidates for office would be helped. Lavelle ended up in jail after she was caught lying to Congress about the cleanup program.

Congressional authors of the superfund law, such as Representative James Florio of New Jersey, believed the scandals set back the progress of the cleanup program by several years at least. The damage can be seen in the record of the first 5 years of superfund: Only six toxic waste dumps received what the EPA termed final cleanups, and one of these, the Butler Mine Tunnel in Eastern Pennsylvania, sprung a leak only months after it was declared stabilized and removed from the superfund list. Of the original $1.6 billion, less than 20 percent was spent on cleanups. Money was poured into paying contractors for repeated studies at some sites, while other sites were not addressed at all.

Since these early scandal-ridden and hunt-and-peck days, more than 1,000 sites around our nation have been visited by EPA inspectors and deemed a serious enough health threat to require action under the superfund program. More than 150 of those cleanups are in progress. And, in 1986, after a long and bitter congressional battle over the scope and future of the superfund, $8.5 billion was authorized for such cleanups through 1991.

Ridding our landscape of the profligate disposal of poisons is a complex and expensive process. A major cleanup can cost more than $100 million. The $10.1 billion earmarked in the 1980s for cleaning up toxic dumps is merely a down payment on the job. Estimates of the ultimate cost are little more than guesswork, but the lowest figure rarely drops under $100 billion, and some analysts have put it as high as $500 billion.

If the first decade of the superfund is any guide, taxpayers will be picking up much of this tab. The superfund law gives the EPA the authority to try to get the individuals and corporations responsible for creating toxic dumps to either conduct the cleanup themselves or reimburse the federal government for money the EPA spends to do the job. But through mid-1988, $4 out of every $5 spent on superfund cleanups came from the public's pocket.

One of the most heated backroom environmental battles during the Reagan administration involved bureaucrats from the Pentagon and Department of Energy, furiously fighting efforts to have the EPA, our experts in toxics, supervise the cleanup of federal toxic dumps. One of the key points in the fight was that the polluting federal agencies didn't want to be held to the same cleanup standards EPA imposes on private-sector polluters. Although the superfund amendments of 1986 gave the EPA greater authority over cleanup at federal sites, the problem of ensuring the proper and complete cleanup of waste still exists. An uneasy truce has been negotiated whereby the EPA is to work cooperatively with other government agencies in planning and carrying out these cleanups.

THE EMERGENCY PLANNING AND COMMUNITY RIGHT-TO-KNOW ACT (EPCRA)

The newcomer to the world of environmental laws is the Emergency Planning and Community Right-to-Know Act (also called EPCRA, SARA Title III, or simply right-to-know), which was passed in the fall of 1986 as part of the superfund amendments and has still not been fully implemented. At first glance, right-to-know seems to be a mere information-gathering device. However, it may well prove to be the most powerful tool of all in the effort to change this country's methods of handling and disposing of toxics.

Right-to-know emerged in the wake of the Bhopal disaster. As Americans heard and read about this tragedy, many began wondering about what chemicals were being produced in the plants in their communities. What exactly is routinely coming out of the exhaust vents? What would be unleashed into their communities in the event of a Bhopal-like accident? If an accident occurred, what emergency measures were in place to protect the public?

Members of Congress began considering these questions; when answers did exist, they weren't made readily available to people and their local governments. Before the right-to-know law of 1986, the producers of hazardous waste and the emitters of toxic air pollutants were not required to let the public know about the dangers existing in everyone's backyard. Neither were local officials and industries required to draft any type of emergency plans to respond to a severe accident.

The right-to-know law is intended to create a safer environment for everyone who lives or works in the vicinity of factories, refineries, warehouses, water treatment plants, and other sites that store, use, and manufacture hazardous chemicals. This landmark law requires hundreds of thousands of facilities to finally disclose the names and amounts of toxic materials they release into our environment. In addition, local officials are required to draft plans to respond to an emergency chemical accident such as the one that occurred in Bhopal.

Through this information and planning process, the right-to-know law seeks to reduce the threat of catastrophic accidents and the consequences of chronic pollution. The theory behind it is that if a community knows exactly what a local facility is releasing into the air and water, it will more readily take action to curb this pollution. Moreover, if a facility is forced to bare its previously private toxic secrets to its neighbors, it may take the initiative in reducing its toxic releases. This seemed to work in the case of the chemical giant Monsanto. In 1988, after reporting on releases by its 40 U.S. plants, Monsanto announced it would reduce its emissions of toxics into the air by 90 percent in 4 years.

But right-to-know, which was strongly opposed by the chemical industry, is still in its infancy. Compliance with its reporting requirements varies from state to state, ranging from 80 percent in some places to a mere 10 percent in others. The EPA has been slow to use its enforcement powers to improve compliance. Many communities still have not met the deadline for establishing emergency plans. And officials have been slow to make the right-to-know information submitted by companies easily accessible from any home computer.

The value of the right-to-know process is that it brings the grassroots into the battle to control toxic emissions. A community no longer has to wait for Washington or its state government to initiate action. The law makes available to everyone information about which chemical producers and users are polluting communities and just how much of this pollution is reaching our air and water. Armed with this vital knowledge, people back home are beginning to demand that their local, neighborhood polluters clean up their acts.

TOXICS USE REDUCTION

The number of abandoned dumps like Love Canal was startling to the nation, but this was a problem caused by past misdeeds and one that can be solved with cleanups—and lots of superfund money. The incomplete compliance with RCRA is a national concern, but it is a problem that can be solved with better management and enforcement. Even if both laws were fully enforced and implemented, we would still have problems, because we are continuing to create toxic waste.

Our nation's approach to toxics has been a dual one: "out of sight, out of mind" and "the solution to pollution is dilution." Right-to-know exposes the extent of our toxics dependency to public view. The use and inadequate disposal of huge amounts of toxics being brought to public attention make it obvious that we are quickly exceeding—and perhaps already have exceeded—the environment's capacity to dilute these poisons. We are using too many chemicals and producing too much hazardous waste to remain content with the idea that our waterways and our air can dilute them, rendering them harmless. The obvious solution is that we must produce and use fewer toxic chemicals. We must practice the same source reduction that is so effective when addressing such environmental problems as air pollution and solid waste disposal.

There are many alternatives available that can reduce use of toxic chemicals. For instance, the 3M Company—Minnesota Mining & Manufacturing—has cut its generation of waste in half by using fewer toxics and recycling as many hazardous substances as possible. Not only is source reduction good for the environment, but it frequently makes good business sense. A company that doesn't produce waste doesn't have to pay for its handling, treatment, and disposal, and it doesn't have to worry about its future liability. 3M says that since beginning this program in the mid-1970s, it has saved more than $300 million. And it has saved its neighbors considerable exposure to chemicals.

SELECTED SUCCESSFUL INDUSTRIAL WASTE REDUCTION EFFORTS

Company/Location	Products	Strategy and Effects
Astra Södertälje, Sweden	Pharmaceuticals	Improved in-plant recycling and substitution of water for solvents cut toxic wastes by half.
Borden Chem. California, United States	Resins; adhesives	Altered rinsing and other operating procedures cut organic chemicals in wastewater by 93 percent; sludge disposal costs reduced by $49,000 per year.
Cleo Wrap Tennessee, United States	Gift wrapping paper	Substitution of water-based for solvent-based ink virtually eliminated hazardous waste, saving $35,000 per year.
Duphar Amsterdam, The Netherlands	Pesticides	New manufacturing process cut toxic waste per unit of one chemical produced from 20 kilograms to 1.
Du Pont Barranquilla, Columbia	Pesticides	New equipment to recover chemical used in making a fungicide reclaims materials valued at $50,000 annually; waste discharges were cut 95 percent.

Du Pont Valencia, Venezuela	Paints; finishes	New solvent recovery unit eliminated disposal of solvent wastes, saving $200,000 per year.
3M Minnesota, United States	Varied	Companywide, 12-year pollution prevention effort has halved waste generation, yielding total savings of $300 million.
Pioneer Metal Finishing New Jersey, United States	Electroplated metal	New treatment system design cut water use by 96 percent and sludge production by 20 percent; annual net savings of $52,500; investment paid back in 3 years.

(Source: *State of the World, 1988,* Worldwatch Institute, W.W. Norton & Co.)

Chief Seattle reflected a centuries-old culture that believed then, and still does today, that humans merely share the Earth. We must live in sustainable harmony with all else; we can only protect the land, not own it. Chief Seattle never saw a hazardous waste dump, a drinking-water well poisoned by chemical pesticides, or a huge petrochemical factory pumping toxics into the air. But his words, spoken long before we began fouling our environment with chemicals, gave us fair warning about our current problems: "Contaminate your bed, and you will one night suffocate in your own waste."

PEOPLE MAKING A DIFFERENCE

———————— • ————————

PAT BRYANT

© 1988 SAM KITTNER/GREENPEACE

Pat Bryant and other black activists founded the Gulf Coast Tenants Leadership Development Project in 1982 in response to Reagan administration cuts in public housing and other poverty programs to help pay for its massive military buildup. Running a "Housing—Not Bombs" campaign among the poor of southern Alabama, Louisiana, and Mississippi, Bryant's project trained local leaders to mobilize their neighbors to demand social justice and better living conditions.

In 1985, public housing tenants organized by the project demonstrated in St. Charles Parish, Louisiana, for better living conditions. They got results: mass arrests, the ouster of a housing authority director, and $2 million for housing repairs. After this victory, Bryant focused his attention on another problem facing the poor tenants who live in "Cancer Alley," the lower Mississippi's industrial wasteland where one-quarter of America's chemicals are produced.

"The housing campaign was a great big success, but these people were miserable because they found their lives sandwiched between the Union Carbide and Monsanto complexes," Bryant says. "Their children were constantly having eye and respiratory problems."

Bryant realized that helping the poor involved more than racial justice, jobs, and housing. The equation included clean air and water. Bryant says he left St. Charles with a revised mission: "We've got to deal with the environment."

He and other project officials began learning about chemicals and how to get environmental data from the government. By early 1988, the black activists attended the Southern Environmental Assembly in Atlanta, a largely white conclave.

"You had differences of class," notes Bryant. "A lot of the environmentalists were middle class. We all speak English, but what we say doesn't always mean the same thing." Bryant says that meetings with Greenpeace activists helped him develop trust.

Within a year, there was a coalition linking Bryant's project with the mostly white members of the Sierra Club, Louisiana Environmental Action Network, and the Oil, Chemical, and Atomic Workers Union. "We must put aside foolish customs that divide us and work together, at least for the sake of our children," Bryant said as the coalition began the Great Louisiana Toxics March. For 10 days, protesters demonstrated through "Cancer Alley," from just north of Baton Rouge southeast to New Orleans, demanding reductions in toxic emissions they say are responsible for some of the nation's highest rates of cancer.

After that, Bryant became acting director of the Louisiana Toxics Project, which was formed to carry on the momentum of the march. Bryant added environmental aspects to a training program that develops local leaders, and his group ran workshops on race relations for black activists and white environmentalists. In 1989, the Louisiana legislature passed the state's first air quality law.

"The environment is the No. 1 problem in this country," Bryant says. "As an African-American, my hope and aspiration to be free are greatly dimmed by the prospect of environmental destruction. If we're going to make great strides on this problem, we're going to have to build African-American/ European-American coalitions. We have also got to act on the problem of racism. If we can do that in the context of the environment, it will be empowering for everyone."

PEOPLE MAKING A DIFFERENCE

·

GORDON WATKINS

I. JEFF CHRISTENSON

I f the United States ever recognizes chemical-free farming by naming a Secretary of Organic Agriculture, a logical choice for the post would be Gordon Watkins, who is already doing this job in northwestern Arkansas.

Watkins is a founder and leader of the Ozarks Organic Growers Association and two related organizations that are essentially a "private department of agriculture," providing natural farmers with the type of aid and comfort only chemical farmers currently receive from the U.S. Department of Agriculture (USDA).

It is ironic that Watkins is enmeshed in the organic farming movement considering he spent his boyhood on 2,000 acres in the Mississippi Delta where cotton and soybeans were raised with liberal quantities of chemical fertilizers and pesticides. Watkins left the farm for Memphis, where he counseled delinquent and drug-abusing teens until he burned out in 1973 and headed for Parthenon, Arkansas. There, he and his wife, Susan, began subsistence farming on an 80-acre homestead. By 1980, after much trial-and-error experience, they were producing organically grown fruits and vegetables in commercial quantities.

Watkins and a dozen other organic farmers began meeting to discuss a common problem: how to market their crops. This information exchange and support system evolved into the organic association, a nonprofit cooperative that began selling crops to wholesalers in 1986. "We had $12,000 in sales and were real excited," Watkins says. Sales tripled in 1987, went to $150,000 in 1988, and were expected to double in 1989, with members shooting for $1 million by 1992. Customers stretch from New York to Denver, from Chicago to Dallas. In 1989, the co-op had 150 certified farms as members, double the number in 1988. It's not easy to gain membership: A farm must be chemical-free for at least three years and stay that way.

Organic farmers have more problems than simply getting crops to markets. Banks are reluctant to loan money to natural farmers, and USDA-assistance programs are aimed at chemical farms. To fill the financial void, the organic association used a $36,000 grant from the Levi Strauss Foundation to create an autonomous arm that would guarantee repayment to banks which lend association members money for farm improvements and production.

The USDA's cooperative extension service all but ignores organic farmers in favor of chemical agriculture. So the association created its Ozark Small Farm Viability Project to mimic the service. Organic farmers take time away from their own crops to provide in-the-field advice to others about growing techniques, pest control, soils, and irrigation. Watkins has pressured the USDA, Congress, and the universities of Arkansas and Missouri to add organic farming to their agendas.

"It's tough," Watkins says. "We're struggling. We don't have the crop subsidy programs. We don't have the research programs. We don't have subsidized irrigation. Essentially, we finance ourselves. We're creating our own infrastructure. We feel we're unique because we're dealing with all the problem areas facing farmers. What we're producing is only touching the tip of the consumer-demand iceberg. We think the demand for organics will increase tremendously."

WHAT WE CAN DO

INDIVIDUAL ACTIONS

The problem of nationwide toxic overload can seem overwhelming. Many solutions must occur at state and national levels that require changes in laws and policies. New chemicals must be more tightly controlled and registered. Waste management laws such as RCRA must be strictly enforced. Above all, chemical producers and users must be forced to find less toxic alternatives.

For every product in your home, in the supermarket, or in a hardware store, think all the way back to where it came from and all the way forward to where it will end up. Pick up a can of bug spray. Think back: Every pesticide manufacturing plant in the United States is emitting dangerous materials into the air, land, and water. Think forward: Your nearly empty can will end up with millions of others in leaking landfills or polluting incinerators. And don't forget that the actual use of this poison is endangering your health as it settles on your skin and in you lungs.

Whenever you use a product made out of artificial, factory-made chemicals, you are becoming part of the chain of pollution as well as exposing yourself to risks. Remember that the health effects of exposure have not been determined. Even many chemicals that have been shown to cause health and environmental problems have not been withdrawn from the marketplace.

There are many concrete actions that individuals can take in their everyday lives to break this chain of toxics. The obvious first step is to "detox" your own home by using less polluting alternatives. This will reduce some immediate risks to you and your family. In addition, as more and more consumers come to

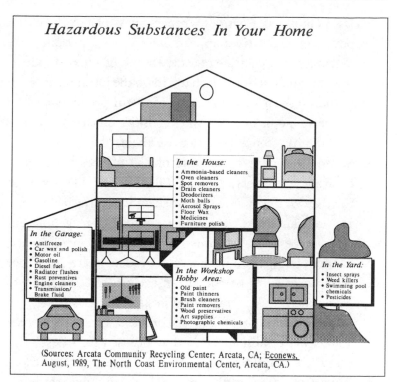

Hazardous Substances In Your Home

In the House:
• Ammonia-based cleaners
• Oven cleaners
• Spot removers
• Drain cleaners
• Deodorizers
• Moth balls
• Aerosol Sprays
• Floor Wax
• Medicines
• Furniture polish

In the Garage:
• Antifreeze
• Car wax and polish
• Motor oil
• Gasoline
• Diesel fuel
• Radiator flushes
• Rust preventives
• Engine cleaners
• Transmission/Brake fluid

In the Workshop Hobby Area:
• Old paint
• Paint thinners
• Brush cleaners
• Paint removers
• Wood preservatives
• Art supplies
• Photographic chemicals

In the Yard:
• Insect sprays
• Weed killers
• Swimming pool chemicals
• Pesticides

(Sources: Arcata Community Recycling Center; Arcata, CA; Econews, August, 1989, The North Coast Environmental Center, Arcata, CA.)

understand the dangerous cycle surrounding the manufacture, use, and disposal of toxic chemicals, they will reduce their dependence on "toxic products" both in and around the home and the office. As the demand for these products shrinks, the pollution that comes with their production and disposal will be reduced as well.

Detoxing Your Home and Office
The types of home-use products to look out for include air fresheners, automotive products, cleaning agents, glues, mothballs, paints, personal care products, pesticides, photographic materials, other home hobby products, solvents, and swimming pool chemicals.

Here are some general steps you can take to begin to detox your home:

- Use nontoxic alternatives whenever possible. A list of less polluting alternatives appears later in this section.

- When it is not possible to avoid the use of a toxic product, buy the smallest amount that will do the job and use it up. If you find you have an excess of useful products such as cleaners, motor oil, or paint, consider donating them to community groups that can use them.

- When it is time to dispose of any of these household hazardous products, DO IT PROPERLY! Do not pour them down the drain or throw them in the trash. Municipal waste facilities, whether general sorting-recycling centers, incinerators, landfills, or sewage treatment plants, are not equipped to deal with hazardous materials. Your toxic waste will just end up in the air, soil, or water to haunt the next generation. Whether it comes from your home or that huge chemical complex across town, hazardous waste must be treated at licensed facilities.

- Many communities now hold "Household Hazardous Waste Collection" days so people can bring toxic trash to a dropoff point for proper collection and processing. In the best programs waste is carefully sorted to separate products that can be reused, recycled, or neutralized before the remainder are disposed of at a licensed hazardous waste treatment facility. If there is no such collection in your neighborhood, you should consider organizing one, either as a one-time demonstration event or as a regular part of the community's waste management program. At first, you may want to interest a few other people willing to volunteer their time, money, or supplies. There are many detailed guides that will give you tips on getting the necessary permits, finding a hazardous waste collection company, advertising your event, and attracting sponsors. Start by contacting: The League of Women Voters, 1730

M Street, N.W., Washington, DC 20036, (202) 429-1965 or Golden Empire Health Planning Center, c/o The Local Government Commission, 909 12th Street, Suite 205, Sacramento, CA, 95814, (916) 448-8246.

Less Polluting Alternatives to Everyday Products
(The following helpful hints are drawn from the Greenpeace Publication, "Stepping Lightly on the Earth: Everyone's Guide to Toxics in the Home," Washington, DC.)

General Cleansers:
Use the simplest, mildest formula that will get the job done. First try warm water mixed with soap (or vinegar if the surface will show spots); add baking or washing soda, borax, or vinegar if needed.

Air Fresheners
Commercial fresheners work by masking smells, coating nasal passages, and deadening nerves to diminish the sense of smell. Instead:
- Find sources of odors and eliminate them; keep house and closets clean and well-ventilated; grow lots of houseplants.
- To absorb odors, place 2 to 4 tablespoons of baking soda or vinegar in small bowls in the refrigerator and around the house, and pour ½ cup of baking soda in the bottom of trash cans.
- For natural fragrance, boil sweet herbs and spices.

All-Purpose Cleaner
- Mix 2 teaspoons of borax and 1 teaspoon of soap in 1 quart of water for a cleaner you can store in a spray bottle.

Ammonia
- Use ammonia only when other cleaners won't do the trick. Ammonia cuts heavy grease and grime, but can be dangerous. Fumes irritate eyes and lungs and can be harmful to people with respiratory problems. Always provide good ventilation. Never mix ammonia with bleach or commercial cleansers; deadly fumes may form.

Disinfectant
- For a hospital-quality disinfectant, use ¼ cup of borax dissolved in ½ gallon of hot water. Keeping surfaces clean and dry reduces the need for disinfectants.

Scouring Powder
- If available, buy powder without chlorine, colors, detergents, or talc; or scrub with a sponge or fine-bristled brush, soap, and one of the following: baking soda, borax, or table salt.

Laundry:

Bleach
- Substitute ½ cup of borax per washload to whiten whites and brighten colors. If needed, occasionally use powdered, nonchlorine bleach.

Detergent
- Add ⅓ cup of washing soda to water before placing clothes in machine and substitute soap flakes or powder for detergent. Detergents are made from artificial chemicals and are not biodegradable. When making the initial switch

from a detergent to a soap laundry cleaner, wash items once with washing soda only. This will eliminate detergent residues that might otherwise react with soap to cause yellowing of fabrics. Add ½ cup of borax for additional cleaning power. If you have "hard" water, use a phosphate-free detergent.

Dry Cleaning

• Buy items you can wash or clean on your own. Most dry cleaning solvents, such as perchlorethylene, are toxic. If you must dry clean, air clothing out thoroughly before bringing indoors. Many garments whose labels specify "dry clean only" can be safely handwashed using mild soap or vinegar.

Fabric Softener

• Add 1 cup of vinegar or ¼ cup of baking soda during final rinse. To reduce static cling in tumble-dried synthetics, dampen hands when folding or line-dry instead.

Pre-soak

• Soak heavily soiled items in warm water with ½ cup of washing soda for 30 minutes. Rub soiled areas with liquid soap.

Spray Starch

• Dissolve 2 tablespoons of cornstarch in 1 pint of cold water in a spray bottle. Shake before each use. For delicate fabrics, dissolve 1 package of unflavored gelatine; or add 2 tablespoons of granulated sugar to 2 cups of hot water. Dip corner of fabric into solution to test; if fabric becomes sticky when dry, add more water.

Personal Care:

Bath and Hand Soap
- Use soaps without artificial scents or colors.

Deodorant and Antiperspirant
- To minimize body odors, apply baking soda, baking soda mixed with corn starch, or coconut oil.

Insect Repellent
- Apply very small amounts of citronella oil.

Medications

Medicines are much like any other toxic product in terms of their production and disposal problems.
- Follow your doctor's advice for all medications. But for diseases and toxic pollutants alike, "an ounce of prevention is worth a pound of cure." The formula is familiar and it works—clean, whole foods, fresh air, exercise, laughter, and rest.

Diapers
- Use cotton diapers rather than disposables. Diaper services usually cost no more than disposables.

Office Products:

Adhesive Tape
- Use nontoxic glues, paper clips, staples, or string whenever possible.

Carbonless Copies
- Use traditional carbon paper.

Glue
- Use stick-type glue or basic white glue. Avoid glues and cements that emit the smell of solvents (for example, hobby glue, rubber cement).

Markers
- Use china markers (wax pencils), colored pencils, or crayons, instead of solvent-based markers.

Typewriter Correction Fluid
- Use correction tape that covers errors or lifts them off without the use of solvents. When you must use fluid, use the water-based type made for photocopies.

Car and Garage:
Avoid skin contact with used oil and other automotive liquids; they contain metals and other highly toxic compounds and require special disposal, as do car batteries. Be sure to follow special procedures when disposing of products used in car maintenance.

Used Oil

- Each year Americans dump more motor oil into sewers and the ground than was released in the oil spill in Prince William Sound in Alaska! Take your used oil to a service station that will recycle it. If you live in a rural area, store it in a large receptacle, and arrange for periodic pickup from a used-oil recycler.

Solvents

- Store contaminated diesel fuel, kerosene, and other solvents in closed jars until particles settle out; then strain and reuse. When thoroughly used, these solvents may be mixed with waste oil for recycling. Do not use gasoline as a solvent since its toxic chemicals are absorbed through the skin, and it is difficult to dispose of safely when contaminated.

Transmission Fluid

- May be mixed with waste oil and delivered to a service station for recycling.

Batteries

- Scrap dealers will *pay you* for car and boat batteries! Appliance, camera, and hearing aid batteries are also valuable, but require a more thorough search to find a buyer. Another tactic is to request a "send-it-back" policy under which the retailer accepts the used battery when you buy a new one. This process places the responsibility on the retailer to find a collector for a large volume of recyclable batteries. It makes sense from both a collection and a recyclable materials marketing standpoint.

Controlling Indoor Pests:

- Avoid chemical pesticides. They are dangerous to you and to the environment.
- Don't overreact; one or two insects are not an invasion; some, such as spiders, help keep others under control.
- Locate and block pests' points of entry.
- Keep floors, garbage pails, and the kitchen clean to eliminate pests' food supplies.
- Remove clutter to eliminate nesting areas.

Cockroaches

- Caulk all cracks along baseboards, cupboards, pipes, shelves, and sinks. Use "roach motel" or other nontoxic traps to monitor population. Some commercial products and services now use an effective mixture of borax and diatomaceous earth.

Fleas and Ticks

- Routinely rub your pet's coat with brewer's yeast and add it to the pet's food. Avoid flea collars containing pesticides. To rid a house of fleas, vacuum frequently and use flea traps. Suspend lights a few inches above shallow dishes filled with soapy water. Heat-seeking fleas will jump toward the light, fall into the dish, and drown.

Moths

- Avoid conventional mothballs and flakes, which are made of toxic chemicals.
- Keep vulnerable clothes clean, dry, and well-aired. Store clothes in a cedar-lined closet or trunk.
- Seal clothes tightly in boxes or bags with moth-repellent

sachets; small cotton bags filled with cedar shavings, dried lavender, or equal parts dried rosemary and mint.

Lawn and Garden:

Insect Repellents

Many garden pests can be repelled from indoor and outdoor foliage by sprays. Here are two recipes:

- Blend two or three very hot peppers, ½ onion, and 1 garlic clove in water. Boil. Steep for 2 days and drain through a cloth. Can be frozen for future use. Thaw and put in a spray bottle. Avoid contact with eyes, mucous membranes, and skin.
- Mix 2 tablespoons of liquid soap with 1 quart of water. Use only pure soap. Additives and detergents may damage plants.

There are a wide variety of nontoxic and less toxic insecticides available commercially. The safer insecticides include:

- Diatomaceous earth—the powdered skeletons of tiny marine creatures. Avoid inhaling this substance.
- Pyrethrins—the extracts of certain chrysanthemums. Check the label carefully to make sure it does not contain other toxic ingredients.
- Bacillus thuringiensis—just one of a number of bacteria that attack insects.

Use Mother Nature's predator insects to combat the bad guys in your garden. Insect-killing insects include ladybugs and praying mantises. You can buy large supplies of these insects and turn them loose in your yard.

Snakes and spiders may not be your favorite creatures, but they're your friends when it comes to combatting the pests in your garden.

Keeping Chemicals Out of Your Food

With less than 1 percent of U.S. produce being tested for pesticide levels and a lack of consensus on what "safe" levels are, concerned consumers must start taking matters into their own hands. As with all consumer action, this has the double benefit of protecting individual health and creating broad-based pressure for institutional change.

Because of the national outcry about the use of Alar that followed the 1989 Natural Resources Defense Council report, many apple growers were eager to publicize their voluntary avoidance of Alar. In September 1989, five U.S. and Canadian supermarket chains—ABCO, Bread & Circus, Petrini's, Provigo, and Raley's—announced that by 1995 they would stop selling fruits and vegetables treated with cancer-causing pesticides. Clearly, consumer demands are beginning to be heard.

Your goal will be to purchase food that has been treated with as few dangerous artificial chemicals as possible. The obvious first place to look is your local grocery store or supermarket. Unfortunately, few of them now disclose the origin or chemical history of the produce they sell. If consumers are to make informed choices, this must change. The Consumer Pesticide Project, 425 Mississippi Street, San Francisco, CA, 94107, (415) 826-6314 has published an organizing kit with detailed tips for people to use in negotiating with supermarket managers for pesticide information and reduction.

- Look for signs indicating "certified organic" produce. This means that no artificial chemicals have been used on it. You are more likely to find it in farmers' markets, food co-ops, or natural food stores. Beware! The word "organic" used by itself is not controlled and can be misused by farmers who apply dangerous pesticides.
- When no pesticide information is posted, you may be

better off buying domestically grown produce. Many food-exporting countries have even weaker pesticide controls than the United States. Some still use pesticides that have been banned in the United States.

- Buy fresh produce. It may contain pesticide residues, but even more chemicals are used on crops that are destined to be canned or frozen. Residues can sometimes be washed off fresh produce, but it's nearly impossible to reduce residues in canned food.

- Thoroughly wash and rinse all fresh produce before eating it. The best way is to use a weak solution of dishwashing soap and water. Remove the peel or outside layers whenever possible. Outer leaves of lettuce and cabbage can contain up to 31 times as much pesticide residue as the inner leaves. Unfortunately, some pesticides like Alar are systemic. That is, they are absorbed throughout the plant. There is no way to wash, scrub, or peel it off your food. For more information on preparing food to reduce your exposure to pesticide residues, obtain *For Our Kids' Sake: How to Protect Your Child Against Pesticides in Food* from Mothers and Others for Pesticide Limits, P.O. Box 96641, Washington, DC, 20090.

- If you eat meat, be aware that most animals are raised on factory farms where they are fed large doses of growth hormones and antibiotics. Limit your consumption.

- If you have your own garden, you can grow your own produce without using pesticides and artificial fertilizers. Make your own fertilizer by composting your organic garbage. Learn about Integrated Pest Management and organic gardening techniques as a way of preventing pest problems. A good start is *The Encyclopedia of Natural Insect and Disease Control* by R.B. Yepson, Jr., published in 1984 by Rodale Press. You can also get information from the Bio

Integral Resource Center, P.O. Box 8267, Berkeley, CA, 94707.

Protecting Our Drinking Water

Sooner or later most toxic emissions end up in water. Airborne toxics can travel hundreds or even thousands of miles, but eventually they are deposited in soil or water. For example, dangerous levels of PCBs in the Great Lakes have been attributed to air emissions from distant smokestacks. Toxics in the air or soil eventually work their way into groundwater or into rivers and lakes.

What can you do to find out whether your water is safe?

- First, find out the source of your water. Does it come from a private well or a centralized community supply? The answer to this question will determine whether there is any supervision over the quality of your water. Unlike community sources that serve more than 15 households, private wells are not covered by the federal Safe Drinking Water Act. For more information, contact the Environmental Action Foundation for a copy of its *Re:Sources* on drinking water.

- If your water is from a private well, it should be tested periodically for bacteria, metals, and volatile carbon-based chemicals such as chloroform, gasoline, and solvents. There are no simple tests for all pesticides. If you know a particular pesticide was or is being used nearby, you can ask the testing laboratory to look for its presence in the water.

- If you get your water from a community supply, ask the provider for copies of their monitoring reports, which are required under the Safe Drinking Water Act. Providers are required to monitor for only 22 contaminants, even though hundreds of others have been found in drinking water. Ask your provider to test for additional substances.

- Keep in mind that your water provider will be testing the water at their well or at the water-treatment plant, not at your tap. Have your water tested if it smells or tastes suspicious; if you live in an older building that might have lead pipes; if there has been any unidentified illness among several members of your household; or if you are concerned about a nearby contamination source such as a gasoline station, industrial facility, or landfill. For more information, obtain *Testing for Toxics: A Guide to Investigating Drinking Water Quality* from U.S. Public Interest Research Group, 215 Pennsylvania Ave., S.E., Washington, DC, 20003 or *Safety on Tap* from the League of Women Voters Education Fund, 1730 M St., N.W., Washington, DC, 20036.

- If you do turn up a problem in your water, switch to bottled water until you find and eliminate the source of contamination. But beware! Many bottled water companies are simply selling packaged tap water. Choose a brand that identifies the source of the water.

- A dangerous source of exposure to toxics is skin contact with contaminated water. If a test has confirmed the presence of chemicals in your water, avoid bathing in it or using it for washing dishes. Finding an alternate water supply can be difficult and expensive. In some cases, you may be able to recover expenses from the parties responsible for the contamination of your water.

- Get to know your watershed. This is the land area that overlies an aquifer or feeds a particular stream or river. Investigate land-use patterns for industrial activity.

- People have been able to organize locally to provide protection to their water that state and federal governments have been unable or unwilling to provide. Under the Safe Drinking Water Act, an aquifer can get special protection if it supplies more than 50 percent of an area's drinking water. However, you must gather data to show this. Many localities designate "wellhead protection areas" and then prohibit such activities as underground tanks, landfills, and some industrial facilities from being located in those areas.

GETTING POLITICAL

Using Your Right-to-Know

The right-to-know law is one of the most powerful tools you have for dealing with toxics in your community. If citizens use this law and demand its full implementation, it will provide access to information about exactly what threats local industries pose to public health and the environment. The law will help your community reduce the threat of toxic accidents and chronic pollution; force companies to use fewer hazardous chemicals and reduce emissions; inspire governments at all levels to strengthen and enforce controls on hazardous chemicals; and give victims of toxics crucial information with which to hold polluters accountable.

The right-to-know law covers most medium-to-large size companies that use, store, or produce hazardous chemicals. They must disclose annually how much of each chemical they have on site and how much they have emitted into the air, water, and land or have taken to treatment facilities. They also must come up with an emergency plan to deal with fires or other accidents.

Companies are not required to provide right-to-know information directly to people who seek it. Instead, they must report their information to the State Emergency Response

Commission and the Local Emergency Planning Committee (LEPC) every year by July 1. You and your neighbors can get the information from these committees, which are composed of people such as firefighters, industry representatives, journalists, and concerned citizens.

- Plan a community event or press conference each July when local emissions reports become available. (See chapter 9 for details on how to plan such events.) Make maps or charts showing where local polluters are located and how much toxic waste they produce. Praise companies that show significant reductions from the previous year. Challenge all companies to do a better job reducing their toxics inventory and waste.

- Find out who is on your LEPC and ask them to report their progress, findings, and plans to the community.

- Develop a good relationship with LEPC members, and encourage them to provide easy public access to their information. If they resist this, put pressure on the LEPC through the news media or complain to the State Emergency Response Commission. Keep in mind that the LEPC is a volunteer committee. Help it do its job. Take adversarial action only when it appears that the LEPC is siding with industry, not the community.

- Encourage the LEPC to request *all* the information available to it. While some information will automatically be delivered to the LEPC, other information will be given to them only if they specifically request it. Under the law, an LEPC can request whatever information it feels is needed to produce a good emergency plan. This includes internal company studies and reports.

- Use the information you obtain from your LEPC to put political and community pressure on companies and regulating agencies to actually reduce risks.

- Join, support, or start a local activist group to use the right-to-know law to foster change in your community. Environmental Action has a number of useful publications on right-to-know and can help put you in touch with local groups.
- Inform others about what you are learning about the chemical threats in your community.
- Ask your state and local representatives to support more funding to strengthen right-to-know activities and the work of your LEPC.

Taking Legal Action

If you or your neighbors have been harmed by toxic pollution and you are fairly certain of its source, talk to a lawyer who specializes in "toxic torts." It can be a long, hard road, but people have successfully sued toxic polluters. A large dollar award can help you cope with your injuries and can send a strong message to industries. Information on legal action is contained in *Making Polluters Pay* by Andrew Owens Moore, which is available from the Environmental Action Foundation.

Most of the environmental laws allow citizens to sue companies for failing to comply with the law or to sue the EPA for failing to enforce the law. This is a difficult, expensive, and tricky process. It requires technical expertise to demonstrate noncompliance with the law. The courts will usually give the EPA the benefit of the doubt. But if you think you may have a good case, contact a state or national environmental group with a legal staff to discuss the specifics of your claims and possible next steps.

Political Goals We Should Work Toward

Anyone concerned about exposure to toxic substances realizes sooner or later that it is only through the combined efforts of citizens that policies will be significantly altered to get long-lasting results. Most of the existing environmental laws need to be strengthened. All of them need to be better enforced. For example, we need to get all levels of government to work toward the following goals:

- All municipal solid-waste management plans should include provisions for collecting household hazardous waste.
- The Food and Drug Administration should increase the quantity of food checked for pesticide residues and take prompt action to remove contaminated food.
- The EPA should be required to consider the effects on children when it sets health-based standards and should quickly remove pesticides and other chemicals from the market when they are shown to be toxic. Based on experiences with drugs like DES and Thalidomide, new chemicals should be considered guilty until proven innocent.
- Chemical lawn-care companies should be required to place prominent notices around treated areas. Government agencies should set an example against unnecessary use of chemicals and not employ these services. Government should be demonstrating nontoxic methods of grounds maintenance.
- RCRA should be strengthened and enforced to ensure that contaminated hazardous waste treatment and disposal facilities are cleaned up quickly and thoroughly.
- Commercial facilities should not be allowed to pour their liquid toxic wastes into our common sewer systems. They should pay for the complete pretreatment of any hazardous discharges.
- New laws should be enacted to protect our irreplaceable groundwater resources.

All these changes would help clean up our toxic mess. But if there is one clear, pressing need, it is for all our environmental laws and regulations at every level to require the overall reduction of toxic chemical use at the source.

- Facilities must redesign their production processes to use and produce fewer toxic materials and products.
- All companies reporting under the right-to-know law— and many companies that don't—should be required to conduct waste audits to determine the major sources of their waste. They should come up with specific recommendations for reducing their toxics use and waste generation by at least 80 percent.
- Government subsidies to agriculture must be altered to discourage excessive chemical pesticide use and encourage organic farming and Integrated Pest Management techniques.
- States and municipalities should demonstrate tgat they are pursuing toxics use-reduction strategies before authorizing any new incinerators, landfills, or other waste treatment facilities.

PEOPLE MAKING A DIFFERENCE

•

KAREN BLAKE

DAVID C. PIERCE

Karen Blake walked out of her house in a Buffalo, New York, suburb, took a deep breath of spring air, ran back inside, and collapsed: "I was so sick I felt I was going to die. And if I was going to die, I wanted to go kicking and screaming. I'm still kicking and screaming."

Nobody had to tell her the cause of her distress. She knew: It was the annual return of trucks carrying liquid pesticides and fertilizers to satisfy America's desire for the perfect lawn. In 1985, Blake saw chemical lawn-care trucks at 55 out of 60 houses in her neighborhood. Within two months, vague symptoms, apparent in previous years, developed into a full-blown chemical sensitivity that left her unable to tolerate odors from cigarettes, perfumes, and other common items.

"There's no escape from this witches' brew of toxic chemicals," says Blake, noting that lawn sprays often contain 2,4-D, an ingredient of Agent Orange. "We're not safe in our own homes. You can't just close the windows. The fumes seep in. We use this stuff like water. Nobody talks about it as poison."

Blake began her kicking-and-screaming campaign by cofounding HELP—Help Eliminate Lawn Pesticides—to warn others about the toxicity of lawn chemicals. By April 1986, HELP had stirred up enough interest that 250 people jammed a county-run information forum to hear accounts of humans and animals made ill by liquid pesticides and fertilizers. At another hearing two weeks later, lawn-care companies claimed their sprays were diluted and had low toxicity. HELP cited a New York State pesticide-applicator manual warning that poisoning can occur from "repeated, small nonlethal doses over a long period of time."

Blake and HELP continued to carry their warnings to the media and citizen groups in Buffalo and other parts of New York State. In mid-1987, the state legislature passed a law requiring lawn companies to give customers written contracts, provide copies of warning labels from the chemicals they use, and post warning signs on lawns for 24 hours after sprayings. Legal challenges by the industry delayed its implementation for two years.

Blake's pioneering work also brought chemical lawn-sprayers to the attention of state Attorney General Robert Abrams, who sued Chem-Lawn, the nation's biggest lawn sprayer, for allegedly making false and misleading safety claims. Abrams asked the courts to prohibit ChemLawn from telling customers that federal registration of a chemical is equivalent to an endorsement of its safety.

Blake welcomed the 1987 New York law for what it is, "just a right-to-know law, not a right to protection." She is especially concerned that a homeowner receiving a copy of a chemical's label will be misled by the fact that it is federally registered, as all such chemicals must be. "People believe the government wouldn't let it be used if it were harmful," Blake asserts. "The Environmental Protection Agency should tell people what registration means, that it doesn't guarantee the safety of a pesticide."

Blake vows to keep fighting until chemical lawn sprays are banned. She can't understand "people who get upset about a toxic waste dump, but don't realize what they're doing to their own property. It doesn't make much sense to give our kids organically grown apples for breakfast and then put them out to play on lawns treated with chemical poison "

PEOPLE MAKING A DIFFERENCE

---•---

RICHARD MOORE

DELGADO PHOTOS

For years, people in Albuquerque's Sawmill neighborhood complained with no results as their mainly Chicano community was continually dusted by "snow"—sawdust from an adjacent particle board factory. Nor could they interest city officials in the cracks they said were being created in their adobe homes by the pounding of the "hog"—the factory's huge wood crusher that thumped around the clock 364 days a year. So what if the well water in the low-income neighborhood tasted odd? It was as if Sawmill's pleas were being drowned out by the noise of the "hog."

The situation began changing with the arrival of the sympathetic ears of the SouthWest Organizing Project (SWOP), a community-based, nonprofit group formed in 1980 to help Chicanos, Native Americans, and blacks acquire social, racial, and economic justice through leadership development, community organization, and empowerment. SWOP programs include nonpartisan voter registration, issue education, and community and economic development. In 1985, SWOP added the environment to its agenda and selected Sawmill as its first target.

SWOP organizers, led by co-founder and executive director Richard Moore, canvassed Sawmill door to door to gain a community consensus about the neighborhood's most pressing problems. To no one's surprise, the particle board factory topped the list.

SWOP organized residents into the Sawmill Advisory Council, which turned years of solo complaints into a loud chorus. At an "accountability session," more than 200 residents confronted elected officials and administrators about air and water problems. SWOP and council leaders got the state legislature to call for resident participation in state and city negotiations with the plant owners. Petitions demanding action circulated in Sawmill. Residents alerted TV stations, elected officials, and city environmental agencies when the "snow" was especially heavy.

Testing by the New Mexico Environmental Improvement Division revealed that the ever-present sawdust, breathed and ingested by the neighborhood, was laced with formaldehyde. In addition, the well water was contaminated with toxins, including formaldehyde, nitrates, and toluene.

In late 1986, some 18 years after the factory opened, the city environmental officials decided that the 300-worker facility was violating air-pollution and noise-control laws. State officials demanded compliance with hazardous waste management regulations. Under what was the first agreement in New Mexico negotiated among government, a community organization, and a business, the factory began a $2 million multifaceted cleanup program to contain the sawdust, quiet the "hog," line toxic waste pits, and purify the aquifer serving Sawmill.

Moore says the experience of Sawmill demonstrates the need for people to confront environmental problems collectively, not individually. "There had been numerous complaints for years," he reports, "but until this community organized, nothing was done."

From its initial success in Sawmill, SWOP has tackled other environmental issues in Albuquerque and has advised community activists as far away as Denver and northern Mexico.

"We don't consider ourselves environmentalists," Moore says. "We prefer to be known as community activists working on environmental issues. We view environmental issues as issues of racial and social justice. We don't see it as coincidental that this kind of industry is located in our communities."

CHAPTER SIX

No Time To Waste

PROMOTING SOURCE REDUCTION AND RECYCLING

New Yorkers are building an architectural wonder on Staten Island. When completed in the late 1990s, this conical-shaped structure will be taller and heavier than the largest of Egypt's pyramids. The ancient Egyptians built their pyramids out of huge stone blocks. On Staten Island, the construction material is the garbage of 9 million New Yorkers. With an area of 3,000 acres, the Fresh Kills Landfill is the world's largest garbage dump. It receives an average of 18,000 tons of garbage each day and is the last remaining active landfill within New York City limits.

Our disposable society is catching up with us. Fresh Kills is but one example of a phenomenon that is striking fear in the hearts of local officials across the nation, especially in the northeast and portions of the midwest. Landfills throughout the country are filling up or being forced to close because they are polluting water supplies. Gone are the days of "out of sight, out of mind."

The solid waste disposal crisis facing our nation is only a symptom of a deeper illness that afflicts our society: the wasteful ways we use our resources. Take a look inside your garbage can. If you are a typical consumer, you'll find a disposable plastic razor or two, a newspaper, lots of junk mail, an orange juice carton, a plastic milk jug, soda bottles, trays from microwave dinners, plastic bags, metal cans, glass jars, last night's leftovers. If you have an infant, your trash can is likely to be stuffed with disposable diapers.

A visitor to your home from a resource-poor country would be astonished at the results of our throwaway lifestyle. We too should be astonished. We are a nation with dwindling oil supplies, yet we use petroleum to make plastic fast-food packages that get tossed out after 5 minutes of use. We have severe air pollution problems, yet we create still more pollution by manufacturing no-return bottles we use only once. An average American generates more than 3 pounds of trash every day. This adds up to 160 million tons of "municipal solid waste" every year. The U.S. Environmental Protection Agency says this would fill a convoy of 10-ton garbage trucks 145,000 miles long—or long enough to reach more than halfway to the moon. Eighty percent of our garbage gets buried in a dwindling number of landfills. Ten percent is incinerated. Only 10 percent is recycled.

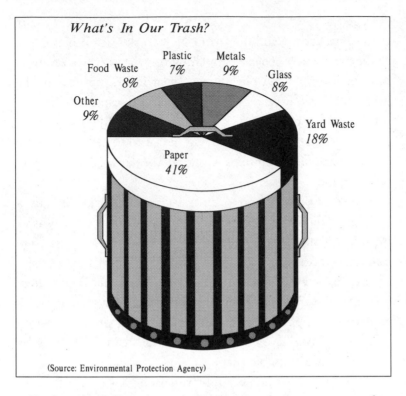

What's In Our Trash?

Food Waste 8%
Plastic 7%
Metals 9%
Glass 8%
Other 9%
Yard Waste 18%
Paper 41%

(Source: Environmental Protection Agency)

Environmentalists have long promoted the concept of a waste-management hierarchy that lists alternate methods of handling trash in order of preference. The most efficient approach is source reduction—reducing the amount of waste we generate. This method saves energy and natural resources as well as addressing a broad range of environmental problems over the entire life cycle of products from manufacturing to disposal. On the second rung of the waste-management hierarchy are recycling and composting, where valuable materials are recovered for reuse. By reducing the amount of trash we produce and by recycling as much as we can, waste volume can be cut by more than half. Recycling also reduces the environmental problems associated with extraction and processing of materials into manufactured products.

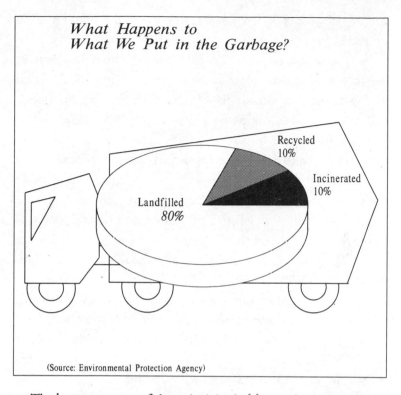

What Happens to What We Put in the Garbage?

Recycled 10%

Incinerated 10%

Landfilled *80%*

(Source: Environmental Protection Agency)

The bottom rungs of the priorities ladder are incinerators and landfills. These options should be explored only after we maximize source reduction and recycling. Today, however, our priorities most often are reversed, with source reduction and recycling playing second fiddle to burying and burning trash.

LANDFILLS

The EPA estimates that one-half of our landfills will be closed by 1995. Diminishing landfill space has sent disposal costs skyrocketing in some areas. Philadelphia, the fourth most populated city, no longer has an active landfill. It ships its trash to Maryland, Virginia, and even to Ohio. Philadelphia's bill for garbage disposal rose from $20 million in 1984 to $44 million in 1985.

New Jersey has one of the nation's worst disposal problems. It has to ship its waste as far as New Mexico. Even in the rural midwest, the cost of trash disposal soared fivefold in the second half of the 1980s. The rising price of trash disposal is clearly reflected in our tax bills.

States forced to export their waste are finding it increasingly difficult to locate communities willing to accept it. Remember the 6,000-mile odyssey of a garbage barge from the Long Island community of Islip? Its 3,186 tons of waste were rejected by six states and three foreign countries before the barge ended up in New York harbor to await a solution. The dark comedy of errors finally ended when the trash was incinerated, and the ash—some of it toxic—was buried in the Islip landfill.

Few communities want to bear the burden of somebody else's garbage. And nobody wants a landfill or incinerator in their area. The waste-management industry and some local governments have little patience with NIMBY—Not in My Backyard—concerns. But NIMBY makes a lot of sense when you look at just a few problems faced by people living near a landfill: explosions of methane gas, lower property values, noxious odors, toxic gas emissions, and vermin. Moreover, illegal dumping of hazardous wastes and other improper disposal practices at these landfills have forced hundreds of communities across the nation to stop drinking the water from their wells. Municipal solid waste landfills account for 20 percent of the sites on EPA's superfund list of the nation's worst toxic hotspots. When water percolates through a landfill, dangerous leachate can form and migrate into nearby groundwater supplies. In a 1984 survey, Minnesota found that leachate from one-third of its landfills had contaminated the drinking water of 10 municipalities.

While landfills poison[...]v generation of incinerators presents [...] its own. Many public officials, looking [...] o solve their trash-disposal problems, are j [...] incinerator bandwagon. An incinerator may provi [...] ix, but it also adds to toxic-waste problems and generates air pollution.

The systematic burning of trash is not a new idea. Incinerators have been combusting garbage since the start of the industrial revolution. At one time, there were hundreds of these trash burners in the United States. However, this early generation of incinerators lacked pollution-control equipment. Better air-quality standards forced many of these incinerators to shut down in the 1960s and early 1970s. Interest in trash burning was renewed during the mid-1970s as incinerator vendors offered "garbage-to-gold" promises with a new generation of equipment that supposedly would simultaneously solve trash woes and create energy for municipal use. But once again, inefficient technology and pollution problems kept the burner brigade on the sidelines.

As our solid waste problem worsened in the 1980s, the incinerator industry updated its sales pitch, claiming that new "cleaner burning" technology from Europe would ease our woes. This time, their campaign worked. There are more than 110 municipal incinerators in operation today, and more than 200 others are under construction or being planned.

The most common approach to burning our trash today is the so-called mass-burn facility. Burn plants range in capacity from a few hundred tons to 4,000 tons of trash a day. Most mass-burn plants are designed to generate electricity. In this so-called waste-to-energy process, the burning trash heats water in a boiler, which produces steam that drives a turbine to generate electricity.

Garbage is not an efficient fuel. Burning trash never generates as much energy as is conserved by recycling those same materials. Nevertheless, it's not hard to see why such incinerators seem to be an attractive option for local officials faced with soaring trash disposal costs. The incineration industry and its army of consultants has done a hard sell on America. They promise short-term results that require no changes in individual lifestyles or municipal waste collection patterns.

But using incinerators is simply replacing one type of pollution with other, potentially more dangerous environmental problems. Despite their claims of "new, cleaner" technologies, all incinerators produce large numbers of substances known to be harmful to human health and the environment. These poisons are found in the incinerator's emissions to the air or in the ash that remains after the garbage is burned. The worst offenders are toxic heavy metals, acid gases, and dangerous organic chemicals.

Incinerator stacks emit heavy metals like arsenic, beryllium, cadmium, chromium, lead, mercury, and selenium, which are highly toxic to humans. They can cause nervous system disorders and cancers. When trash containing chlorine compounds—materials such as bleached paper and some plastics—is burned, the combustion process forms highly toxic organic pollutants known as "dioxins" and "furans." Incinerators also pump substantial quantities of hydrochloric acid and sulfur dioxide into the atmosphere: Both are substantial contributors to the acid rain problem. Even if all trash burners were equipped with state-of-the-art pollution controls and were run at peak efficiency, they would still represent a significant new source of air pollution for most communities. To make matters worse, the history of incineration is littered with faulty controls and errors by human operators.

Ash is another troublesome environmental problem created by incinerators. Burning trash does not make it disappear; it simply reduces its volume by 70 to 90 percent. For every 10 tons of garbage burned, at least 1 ton of ash is produced. The conversion of garbage to ash simply concentrates the many toxic substances found in household trash, such as cleaners, insecticides, lawn chemicals, and paints.

Today's incinerators are producing between 4 and 5 million tons of ash every year. Incinerator ash, with its concentrated toxicity, is even more difficult to get rid of than unburned trash. For example, landfills throughout the East have rejected the ash from Philadelphia's two incinerators. So the city worked out a deal to pay $9 million to a Norwegian shipping company to haul its ash to Panama, where it would be used as a road-building material. At the last minute, Panama turned thumbs down because of environmental concerns. In Philadelphia, officials continue to hunt for a place to get rid of huge mounds of incinerator ash that grow by some 500 tons a day.

Philadelphia's dilemma is a grim sample of what will occur with increasing frequency if more incinerators are built. The wayward garbage barges of today will simply turn into the unwanted ash barges of tomorrow.

Even if we ignore the environmental problems, there are serious questions about the economics of incineration. A mass-burn facility designed to handle 2,000 tons of garbage a day costs from $250 to $300 million to construct. Cost overruns, mechanical failures, unscheduled shutdowns, miscalculations about the amount of salable electricity, and the rising cost of ash disposal have turned many incinerators into financial nightmares. Plans for more than $3 billion worth of mass-burn facilities were scrapped in 1987 and 1988 by municipal officials who had second thoughts.

The price tag of incineration is measured by more than the cost of construction and operation and the expensive environmental damage it creates. Part of the financial equation is that mass burning perpetuates our wasteful ways and diverts society from the real answers to its trash crisis: source reduction and recycling.

Often an incinerator company will pay for a trash-burning facility with its own money and then charge trash-burning fees to a municipality. In these cases, the profit-seeking company requires the community to supply a minimum amount of trash or compensate the company financially. These "put-or-pay" contracts are disincentives to source reduction and recycling. Once built, a $300 million, 2,000-ton-a-day garbage eater is a most inflexible beast.

Communities must do comprehensive planning that puts source reduction and recycling ahead of burning. If an incinerator must be built, it should be no larger than necessary to handle the portion of the waste stream that environmentally sound methods can't handle. Sadly, the incineration industry often captures the ear of public officials long before advocates of source reduction and recycling can get their attention. This happened in Seattle until incinerator opponents were given a fair shake in the planning process. After a case for source reduction and recycling was made, city officials placed an eight-year hold in 1988 on their plans for an incinerator. Seattle now has one of the nation's most aggressive source reduction, recycling, and composting plans; its goal is to avoid the incinerator completely by cutting its waste stream by 60 percent.

SOURCE REDUCTION

Throughout the country, communities, environmentalists, and even some forward-looking public officials are beginning to follow suit, taking the NIMBY response one step further and asking the question, "Why in anybody's backyard?" Why, indeed, when there are more environmentally sound ways than incinerators and landfills that will both reduce and manage our waste stream. As a nation, we are beginning to wake up to the fact that our garbage is actually a mixture of many materials and resources that can be conserved before they become part of our disposable society or recovered from brimming garbage cans for reuse.

We haven't always been a throwaway society. But in the post-World War II era, producers, packagers, and the advertising media have worked diligently and systematically to get us to buy more and then throw it away. In the mid-1950s, one marketing expert wrote in the *Journal of Retailing* that "our enormously productive economy demands that we make consumption a way of life, that we convert the buying and use of goods into rituals, that we seek our spiritual satisfactions in consumption. . . . We need things consumed, burned up, worn out, replaced and discarded at an ever-growing rate."

Source reduction is about reversing this lifestyle and building an economy that is environmentally sound, rather than one based on the throw-and-burn ethic. Narrowly defined, source reduction is designing, manufacturing, and using products with the goal of lessening their quantity and toxicity in the waste stream. If waste isn't created, it presents no disposal headache. In the long run, source reduction provides the most environmentally sound and cost-effective way of combating our growing solid waste problem.

To succeed, source reduction requires major changes in how

we produce and consume. It can be as simple as composting your own food scraps or as complex as retooling an entire factory so that it generates less waste. Source reduction turns producers and consumers into waste managers. It forces manufacturers to weigh environmental costs and benefits at every stage in a product's life, from creation to disposal. And it forces consumers to consider the environmental impact of their buying habits.

Source reduction translates into reusing items that are reusable, not just throwing them away; making products with fewer raw materials and with less toxic ones; producing goods that are more durable or easier to repair; and making products that are easier to recycle.

The place to start reducing waste is with packaging, which accounts for half the volume of our trash and one-third of its weight. The average American discards some 600 pounds of packaging each year. More than half the paper and glass and about one-third of the plastics produced in the United States are used in items with lifespans of less than 1 year. The Department of Agriculture reports that we spent more on food packaging in 1986 than all our farmers received in net income. Some packaging serves to protect a product, but more often what is found on store shelves is there merely to catch the buyer's eye.

Because of their role in the packaging explosion, plastics are a primary target for source reduction. And, because of their versatility, plastics have fueled the development of many nonrecyclable high-tech packages, such as microwaveable food trays, multilayer containers, and squeeze bottles. Techniques for recycling plastics are still in early stages of development, so plastics remain more difficult and expensive to recycle than glass or metal containers.

Source reduction seeks to decrease the sheer volume of packaging in the waste stream and to encourage manufacturers to design their packages for reuse, recycling, or at least environmentally sound disposal. For consumers, that means being a selective shopper; choosing items that are not overpackaged and that come in recyclable packages. For manufacturers, it means eliminating unnecessary layers of packaging; developing smaller packages for the same amount of product; avoiding the most environmentally damaging plastics like polyvinyl chloride (PVC); designing for recyclability; and removing toxic dyes and pigments from packaging.

As a consumer, don't be fooled by claims that a throwaway item will degrade harmlessly, particularly when such claims are applied to plastics. Companies that make so-called biodegradable plastics say they will actually reduce waste and litter, that the manufacture of such plastics helps the family farmer because they are produced with up to 12 percent corn starch. But environmentalists, recyclers, and many solid waste officials are convinced that degradable plastics will do more harm than good. There is very little evidence that they will break down completely in 2 to 5 years, as their advocates claim. The truth is, we know very little about the final byproducts of degraded plastics. While these plastics may work under optimal conditions, landfills are designed to minimize the degradation of all waste in order to prevent leaching and the formation of methane, a greenhouse gas. Excavations of old landfills have yielded decades-old materials, such as newspapers and food waste, still in their original form. Degradable plastics will fare no better.

Degradable plastics are also at cross purposes with plastics recycling. When mixed with other plastics refuse, degradable plastics contaminate batches of recycled resin. Plastics recyclers don't like degradables because they must separate them from other plastics refuse, which adds a costly and cumbersome processing step. Because plastics are made from nonrenewable resources such as petroleum and natural gas, we should be recycling them, not modifying them so they degrade into our environment.

Most importantly, by making plastics seem more environmentally acceptable, degradable plastics can perpetuate our reliance on plastics and disposable products in general. Why reduce or recycle when you can just toss something away and it will magically disappear? This perception may well lull consumers into a false sense of complacency and relieve the pressure on the plastics industry to develop more workable solutions such as source reduction and recycling.

RECYCLING

While source reduction is a concept made necessary by our modern consume-and-toss culture, recycling has been around since the first human realized that after using an animal's meat for food, its hide could be used for clothing. Before the end of World War II, recycling was second nature to most households. Old clothing became hand-me-downs or part of bed quilts. People refilled jars and bottles, straightened and reused old nails. In wartime, recycling was a patriotic duty. Everyone saved their nylons, scrap metal, tires, waste paper, and other materials vital to the war effort.

Although recycling went out of vogue immediately following World War II, interest picked up again in the late 1960s as problems with landfills and the first generation of incinerators fueled a growing environmental consciousness. When Earth Day galvanized the grassroots environmental movement in 1970, thousands of voluntary community-based recycling programs started up as a way to conserve natural resources and energy.

But this wave of successful recycling was hurt by the

mid-1970s recession, which forced many community recycling centers to close. By 1980, the emerging solid waste crisis brought a new constituency to recycling: city officials in charge of garbage disposal. In the 1980s recycling was increasingly embraced as a solution to the solid waste crisis. Two decades after the first Earth Day, recycling has gained a credible, if tenuous, foothold in large-scale solid-waste management plans. Today, one-fifth of our states have laws that mandate recycling, either by requiring waste generators to participate in recycling programs or by requiring local governments to provide recycling services. Ten states have "bottle laws," requiring payment of deposits on beverage containers in an effort to get them returned and recycled. And many other states and communities have active recycling programs.

The recycling of our waste stream has become a nationally recognized goal. EPA has set a goal of recycling 25 percent of our waste by 1992. Eighteen states have recycling goals ranging from 15 to 45 percent. Many communities have already surpassed the EPA's 25 percent benchmark.

All this points to the popularity of recycling as a solid-waste management tool. Like source reduction, recycling saves energy and natural resources. It also reduces the huge amounts of air, land, and water pollution associated with raw materials' extraction, processing, and transportation. By reducing the demand for virgin materials, recycling is pollution prevention of the highest order. According to the Institute for Local Self-Reliance, recycling a ton of steel prevents the production of 200 pounds of air pollutants, 100 pounds of water pollutants, almost 3 tons of mining waste, and the use of about 25 tons of water. One ton of resmelted aluminum eliminates the need for 4 tons of bauxite and almost a ton of petroleum coke and pitch. Burning a ton of paper may generate 1,500 pounds of carbon dioxide, the most prevalent greenhouse gas. Recycling that ton of paper saves about 17 trees, which live to absorb 250 pounds of carbon dioxide annually.

Recycling can combat global warming by reducing the use of energy, most of which is produced by the burning of fossil fuels. In manufacturing, energy is saved whenever recycled materials replace virgin materials. Less energy then goes to extracting, transporting, and processing raw materials. According to the Institute for Local Self-Reliance, more than half the energy the United States consumes is used to mine and process raw materials. Recycling aluminum cuts energy use by at least 90 percent, compared with producing new aluminum; for recycled paper and steel, the energy savings can be as much as 74 percent. Recycling glass can save up to one-third the energy needed to manufacture new glass.

While we've made progress on the recycling front, there is vast room for improvement. We recycle only 25 percent of our aluminum, 23 percent of paper, 9 percent of glass, and merely 1 percent of plastics. For some materials such as plastics, a major barrier to increased recycling is the lack of adequate collection systems.

Well-organized collection systems are essential for successful recycling. Many communities have curbside pickup programs that make recycling as easy as taking out the trash. While some solid waste officials argue that the cost of curbside pickup is more than the scrap value of the materials collected, this rationale ignores what a community saves by not sending the recycled material to a landfill or incinerator. Such savings, called "avoided cost," can be significant. While disposal costs vary regionally, it costs on average $40 to $60 to haul and dump a ton of trash to a landfill and from $70 to $120 to burn the same ton. Generally, it costs $20 to $30 a ton to run a weekly curbside collection and recycling program. As disposal costs continue to rise, recycling becomes a best buy for our tax dollars and a good deal for our environment.

Another type of collection system is the "bottle law." States requiring refundable deposits on beverage containers have achieved recovery rates in the 90 percent range for bottles and cans and in the 70 percent range for plastic soda bottles. In fact, if it weren't for these laws, we would have very little recycling of plastics. States with bottle laws account for more than 90 percent of the plastic bottles being recycled.

There are many other types of plastics—such as milk jugs and detergent containers—that could also be recycled. But they aren't, because the plastics industry has yet to build a recycling infrastructure to handle these items.

Another element essential for successful recycling is the availability of markets to absorb all the material collected. Without adequate markets, collected recyclables are nothing but ordinary trash that further congest landfills. The need for market development attracted national attention in 1989 as a glut of newspapers from increasing numbers of recycling programs caused the price of used newsprint to plummet. Many programs stopped collecting newsprint and waited for the market to improve.

Such situations will continue to occur until there are enough companies willing to buy recycled materials. In order to ensure a stable source of markets, states and communities are increasingly banding together to pursue regional marketing strategies. Other ways to stimulate demand for recycled materials include giving tax credits to businesses that invest in equipment that uses recycled material or requiring that governments purchase recycled goods. Governments and industry can also work together to research new uses for secondary materials.

Leaking landfills, incinerator ash without a home, wayward

trash barges, rising garbage disposal costs, and a decreasing number of safe places to put the results of our throwaway society have focused unprecedented attention and awareness on the solid waste crisis—enough to make it one of the major political issues of the 1990s. We are reexamining the way we take out the trash. After years of bury-and-burn, industry and government are beginning to move toward confronting the crisis. A basic question is whether they are going in the right direction?

At this crucial juncture, concerned citizens have a *unique* chance to influence this direction. Will we continue to squander our resources, to bury and burn valuable materials? Or will we find a new way of thinking about waste, looking at it as a resource, and learning how to use our resources to maintain the sustainability of our planet? If we can make the shift toward the latter, we will also go a long way toward solving many other environmental problems confronting our Earth. The energy used to process and transport raw materials adds to global warming if fossil fuels are involved. The extraction, processing, and transporting of raw materials adds to air and water pollution. Using new paper when recycled paper can do the job means the destruction of trees that might be the last habitat of a vanishing species.

PEOPLE MAKING A DIFFERENCE

DAVID BIRKBECK

JOHN J. KOULBANIS

Very often, trash recycling operations have a common thread: concerned citizen environmentalists forced to pressure reluctant governments to do something more sensible than spending scarce tax dollars on a controversial incinerator or expensive acreage for a new landfill. But when one-third of a local government is a sharp, creative, hands-on Connecticut Yankee like David Birkbeck, recycling can start at the top.

In 1983, Birkbeck was one of three part-time selectmen in North Stonington (population 4,300). His duties included overseeing the town's 40-year-old landfill, which was expected to be filled to capacity by 1990. Birkbeck, whose full-time job was town highway foreman, knew next to nothing about the mechanics of recycling, but common sense told him that if less trash were put into the landfill, it would last longer. "We couldn't wait until zero hour. If we began recycling now, we might gain a year or two before the dump filled up."

At this point, most towns would have hired outside experts to get them into the recycling business. North Stonington had no money for this, but it had a public official with do-it-yourself ingenuity. If there was an official start to North Stonington's recycling program, it came when Birkbeck waded into the landfill and rummaged through the trash, picking out cardboard and paper and bottles.

He campaigned on the street and in the local media to convince townspeople to voluntarily separate recyclables before they reached the dump. He cajoled trash-haulers. He visited businesses that buy recycled materials to study their operations and needs. He learned his lessons well, setting up a stable network of buyers who could depend on quality sorting from the landfill workers Birkbeck was able to hire out of money generated by his shoestring operation. When Birkbeck needed a machine to bail up used cardboard, he built his own. He acquired a used truck rig to haul recyclables to buyers. And some of the fabled boulders of New England were used as a foundation for a recycling ramp.

As North Stonington fell in behind his efforts, Birkbeck pushed for one of Connecticut's first local laws requiring people to separate their trash into recyclable and non-recyclable categories. At the town meeting that approved the law, the only "nay" from an eligible voter came from a trash collector.

"Recycling is now part of our way of life," Birkbeck says. "People who said it was a pain in the butt now say it's not so hard to do. We tried to make people aware it was a new way of living. It's a lot of work and you can get a lot of abuse. But if you get people to thinking, they come around. How can you argue with something that makes sense?"

Or, dollars and cents? One of Birkbeck's best arguments went to the heart and soul of his fellow Yankees: recycling is good business. An exhausted landfill means paying tens of thousands of dollars a year to haul the town's trash elsewhere.

How good has recycling been for North Stonington? Three years into the project, consulting engineer Lee Rowley said the amount of waste entering the landfill had been cut 65 percent. The town was saving $50,000 a year and could use the dump another 40 years or more if population and trash volume didn't increase substantially. "I know of no other program that has been as successful as this one," Rowley concluded.

WHAT WE CAN DO

INDIVIDUAL ACTIONS

The most effective way you can learn how much source reduction and recycling efforts can reduce the volume and toxicity of the waste stream is to start practicing them in your own home. Think of yourself and your household as a "waste producer."

Do a Waste Audit
To find out what your potential can be in reducing waste generation, monitor what you throw out over the course of a week.

- Separate the "good garbage" from the "bad." Separate recyclable glass containers, aluminum cans and foil, tin cans, newspaper and other paper, plastic soda and milk bottles, and put them aside.
- Inventory your "bad garbage." Is it mostly flexible plastics, such as foam, or nonrecyclable meat trays and clear plastic wrap? How many disposable diapers are you using? How much of your trash contains disposable products, such as pens, plastic packaging, and razors?
- Think about ways you can eliminate items from your "bad" garbage list by reducing consumption of those items, substituting reusables for disposables, and avoiding non-recyclable packaging.
- Your goal should be to make your home a "waste-free zone" as much as possible.

Become an Environmental Shopper
The next step in the process is to cut down on the number of wasteful products you buy. Here are some tips to get you started:

- Avoid buying products wrapped in elaborate, unnecessary

packaging. Buy products in bulk whenever possible to minimize packaging and save yourself money. At least get into the habit of bringing your own reusable tote bag to the grocery store. Ask clerks not to double- or triple-bag your purchases unless necessary; try to consolidate purchases in one bag rather than several. When buying only one or two items, don't take a bag at all.

- Buy liquid products such as juices and fabric softener in concentrates. Why pay more for the packaging, when you can add your own water?

- Invest in reusable containers for leftovers and sandwiches rather than wrapping them in disposable plastic wraps.

- Avoid buying products in multimaterial packages; many cannot be recycled. Examples include microwaveable packages; juices in soft-sided containers shaped and packed like bricks; and squeezable plastic bottles. Remember: The more materials a package is made of, the harder it is to recycle.

- Don't buy prepackaged fruits or vegetables that come in polystyrene trays covered by plastic wrap. Exercise your right to choose the produce you want.

- Buy beverages in refillable bottles, if available. Refillables can be reused up to 20 times; the process saves even more energy than recycling.

- Avoid buying disposables, whenever possible. Cut down on napkins, paper towels, plastic and paper plates, plastic utensils, and polystyrene cups. Use cloth towels and napkins instead. When buying "picnic-ware," sturdy products are available that can be washed and reused; microwave "disposable" trays and plates are ideal for this purpose.

- Consider switching from disposable diapers to cloth. Diaper services are usually less expensive than disposables and now provide cloth diapers with velcro tabs that make changing easier.

- Avoid the new generation of "disposable" products such as cameras and flashlights, which manufacturers are pushing as basic electronic equipment gets cheaper. Buy high-quality goods with extended warranties when possible; they're a better investment, and you will be reducing your contribution to the waste stream. Daily-use items such as lighters, pens, and razors can be replaced with better-quality, refillable models.

- Buy products with recycled content. Plenty of consumer products are now available that are routinely made of recycled materials. The list includes aluminium cans, greeting cards and writing paper, and plastic laundry detergent jugs. Products made from recycled materials generally carry the familiar three-arrow symbol or a statement to that effect.

- Try to buy products that you can recycle in your own community. If your dropoff center or curbside pickup program doesn't accept plastic containers, minimize your use of them. Choose glass and aluminum instead.

- Minimize your use of products with toxic ingredients. If you do have to buy them, make sure they are disposed of properly. Don't throw them out with the trash! See Chapter 5 for examples of less-polluting alternatives and tips on how to dispose of household toxics.

Recycle

Recycling programs are spreading like wild fire. If your community doesn't require recycling at the curbside, it should. And it probably will explore recycling as part of a comprehensive solid waste management plan in the coming years. In the meantime, you can take your glass, metal cans, newspapers, used aluminium, and other materials to a community dropoff center. If there is no dropoff center in your area, information later in this chapter will tell you how to start a pilot recycling program.

Here are some basic tips for setting up efficient and productive recycling practices at home:

- Designate a storage area for your recyclables. A space of about 3 feet square should provide enough room to store cans, glass, and newspaper for about a month. Have separate boxes or bags for each type of recyclable.
- Tie newspapers into bundles or put them into paper—not plastic—bags. Other types of paper such as junk mail, computer paper and cards should be stored separately from newspapers. They are made from a higher grade of paper. Some communities recycle junk mail. Others won't because sticky labels and plastic windows are not recyclable.
- Rinse and crush your aluminium cans before storing them. They'll take up less space.
- Rinse out jars and bottles and separate by color. Green and amber bottles contain dyes and usually must be recycled separately from clear glass. If you have a bottle law in your area, return all deposit bottles to your supermarket or collection site.

Compost

Yard waste, such as leaves and grass clippings, comprises as much as 20 percent of our solid waste stream. Food waste makes up as much as 8 percent. By taking advantage of the natural disintegration of organic materials, we could divert yard clippings and food scraps from the waste stream, vastly reducing waste volume and creating a highly useful—even salable—product. The end result of the composting process is free high-quality mulch and fertilizer for your garden. Your garden store or agricultural extension office can provide details about easy and successful composting methods. Here are a few tips for backyard composting:

- Enclose your compost pile with wire or wood fencing. Keep it under 5 feet high and slightly moist, but not soaked.
- Turn it with a pitchfork every few weeks. Shred bulkier items.
- If you want to get to another degree of sophistication, try layering the pile with green leaves (which supply nitrogen) and brown leaves or straw (which supply carbon).
- If you don't have a backyard in which to compost your food waste, don't give up. Pressure your community to set up a municipal composting program. It's a terrible waste for these materials to go to the dump.

COMMUNITY ACTIONS

Although many of the most important decisions in the solid waste arena are local decisions, they are all too often manipulated by powerful external forces, usually industry. This does not have to be the case. Local officials must be continually reminded that they are ultimately accountable to their constituents, not the public relations squad for the latest burning technology. Store owners—and product producers—need to make their decisions on the basis of consumer concerns, not the latest fashion in retailing. We need to organize in our communities to send out this message loud and clear.

Solid Waste Planning

The best way you and your neighbors can avoid being hoodwinked by a new landfill or an expensive incinerator is to get involved in the solid waste management planning process from the start. Too often, officials don't hear opposition to proposed

191

plans from enough people until it's too late—after the bonds are issued, contracts signed, sites decided, and equipment purchased.

- Take the time to attend public hearings and town council meetings when programs are proposed or new facilities are under consideration for siting in your community.

- If your town does not adhere to a process that guarantees your involvement, petition for the right to be heard. Use or create a Citizens Advisory Council to set up a formal review process of proposed plans.

- If your town is considering a landfill or incinerator, demand an in-depth cost analysis of the proposed facility before agreeing to move forward. Review the siting process carefully, and don't be afraid to hold it up if you are not satisfied with the plan's commitment to an overall recycling and source reduction goal. Make sure local officials fulfill their waste reduction obligations under existing policy before jumping to a quick-fix solution.

- If you do find yourself opposing a landfill or incineration facility, get in touch with other groups who are involved in similar fights. Share resources and learn from each other's victories and mistakes. A good contact to help hook you up with fellow activists is Work on Waste, Paul and Ellen Connett, 82 Judson Street, Canton, NY, 13617, (315) 379-9200.

- Even if you are not fighting an incinerator, you should be pushing for a positive alternative to our solid waste woes. If a recycling program exists in your community, support it. If not, organize your neighborhood to establish pilot recycling programs to prove to officials that they work. Many communities have successful recycling programs up and going; there is plenty of information to help you establish one. For information on model programs, contact the

Institute for Local Self-Reliance, 2425 18th Street, N.W., Washington, DC, 20009, (202) 232-4108.

Consumer Campaigns

Manufacturers don't assume that you favor environmentally safe products and packaging. Judging from the marketplace, they assume you want convenience. LET THEM KNOW OTHERWISE. They will produce environmentally sound products only if they know consumer demand for them is high and stable. While your voice as an individual consumer is important, the most effective way to reach these companies is through a consumer campaign.

- Target products that seem particularly wasteful, from either a nonrecyclable or an excess packaging standpoint. "Environmentally sound" purchasing guides are increasingly available to help you determine which manufacturers and products to support. A good starting point is the Pennsylvania Resources Council's "Environmental Shopping Guide," available by calling (215) 565-9131.

- Start a letter-writing campaign to tell manufacturers why you are avoiding their environmentally unsound products. Many packages and labels have toll-free consumer information numbers. Organize phone-a-thons to firms such as General Foods, Kraft, and Procter & Gamble. Point out a specific example of their packaging that is wasteful and should be reduced. Ask them to use more recyclable—and recycled—packaging, to sell concentrated liquid products, and to switch to packaging whose manufacture and disposal has a less negative impact on the environment.

- Work with your local supermarket. Pressure your retailer to install a bulk foods section. Request that they use recycled paper bags instead of plastic. Ask that they stock products in recyclable containers. Explain that you don't like prepackaged produce and it's bad for the environment. If the establishment seems receptive, try to get it to assist in your campaign. Stores could allow people to put up "environmental shopping" posters on walls. Stores could notify the community of their commitment through their advertising. They could print the location of recycling centers on their recycled paper grocery bags. They can provide dropoff recycling bins on their parking lots. All these and other steps have been taken by receptive stores. If the manager of the store you approach is not receptive, consider tabling or leafleting outside the store. You may be surprised at how quickly you'll get the manager to the bargaining table.

- Let your local newspapers and radio stations know about your campaign. It's a great human interest story with a strong environmental message. Explore the possibility of running public service announcements on the radio.

AT THE OFFICE

Recycling and waste reduction is a game of volumes. The more people involved, the quicker things can be turned around. To bolster this strength-in-numbers strategy, get recycling going at your office, workplace, or school. This can channel an enormous volume of garbage toward the recyclables market.

- Recycle aluminum, glass, newspapers, printer and copier ink cartridges, and valuable office paper. You will be amazed at the volume of paper collected just by putting a recycling box next to each printer and copy machine.
- Encourage use of ceramic mugs and metal spoons rather than disposable foam coffee cups and stir sticks.
- Reduce your paper use. Get into the habit of photocopying

documents on both sides of the paper. Circulate memos rather than producing copies for everybody.

- Talk to the person who buys paper for your office. Explain that creating a demand for a recycled product is a crucial link in the recycling equation. Urge them to purchase recycled paper for business cards, letterheads, and the photocopier.

- Encourage your purchasing department to buy durable office equipment and get it repaired rather than replaced. Take advantage of service contracts. If you must dispose of office equipment or furniture, donate it to charity or someone who will repair, recondition, or recycle it.

GETTING POLITICAL

Decisions at the state and national levels are sometimes made in a vacuum and too often with little real life data on solid waste management options. The time is ripe for citizen involvement in formulating a national solid waste policy. It is important for your community to realize that its information and experience are valuable to policymakers as they formulate short-and long-term goals.

While many solid waste decisions are best made at the local level, there are certain arenas in which state and federal leadership is paramount. For example, state and federal officials have a crucial role to play in building demand for recycled materials through market development. As the nation's largest consumer, the federal government can help build demand and set an example for the private sector by channeling its purchasing power into products made of recycled materials. Procurement guidelines to help purchasing departments obtain recycled products are already in place on a national level and in some states. We need to:

- Urge state and federal legislators to strengthen procurement guidelines and mandate purchase of certain recycled materials. Also urge them to consider other options such as offering tax advantages to businesses using recycled materials and publishing regional waste materials exchange catalogs that link disposers with recyclers. For example, a toy company might be able to use a bottle manufacturer's plastic scraps.

- Push legislators to see that recycling programs get their fair share of state and federal funding. For example, if EPA has set a 25 percent recycling goal for 1992, then 25 percent of the agency's solid waste budget should be going to reaching that goal.

- Urge Congress to strengthen existing requirements for municipal landfills—including double antileak liners, groundwater monitoring, leachate collections systems, and leak detection equipment—and to require the use of state-of-the-art technology to combat harmful emissions from all incinerators. To the degree that we do continue to use these two solid waste options, we must lessen their impact on the environment.

National groups are often in a position to refer activists to resources—from scientific data to legal recourse—that lead to better waste management. For more information on proper environmental control of solid waste incinerators and landfills, contact the Environmental Defense Fund, 1616 P Street, N.W., Washington, DC, 20036, (202) 387-3500. For more information on state and federal action on source reduction and recycling, contact Environmental Action Foundation's Solid Waste Alternatives Project at (202) 745-4879.

The federal government must take the lead in educating the public about the economic and environmental benefits of source reduction, recycling, composting, and reuse. As individuals, we need to get the word out to schools, civic and outdoors groups, as well as businesses. If you have come up with a successful strategy, let your state and federal decision makers know about it. Show your legislators and state officials that recycling can work, that business and industry will reform practices to incorporate source reduction.

PEOPLE MAKING A DIFFERENCE

•

PAUL & ELLEN CONNETT

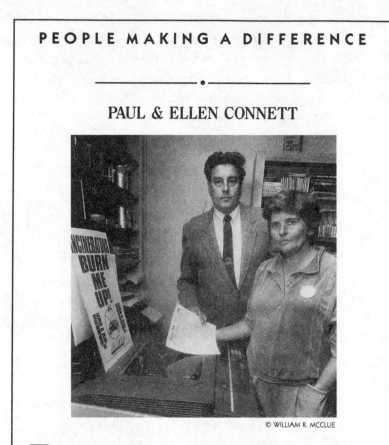

© WILLIAM R. MCCLUE

There's nothing like an incinerator to make Paul and Ellen Connett burn. And it doesn't have to be the huge facility that St. Lawrence County officials want to build near their home in Canton, New York. Any incinerator will spark their fury.

"I don't like rip-offs, and I think incineration is a rip-off, a tremendous mistake," Paul says. "The bottom line is, you can't run a throw-away society on a finite planet. What incineration tries to do is burn the evidence rather than face the problem."

Aroused in 1985 after the county announced plans to build a $36 million incinerator, the Connetts are perhaps the nation's premier grassroots source of information about the dangers of mass burning. They have the latest word about how dioxin fallout from a Swiss incinerator poisons cows' milk; or how a French study shows that the

198

nearer people live to an incinerator, the more prescription drugs they need; or how peas that end up in baby food are grown downwind of an incinerator in Rome, New York.

The Connetts are simultaneously war correspondents and combatants in the multifront battle raging in all parts of the nation as upwards of 200 governmental jurisdictions eye incinerators as the answer to overflowing landfills. Paul, a chemistry professor at St. Lawrence University, has presented his no-burn case more than 400 times in 36 states, urging people to recycle, compost, and not create waste in the first place. In an era of computer desktop publishing, Ellen uses a typewriter to produce "Waste Not," a weekly newsletter that gives the growing citizen network the latest scientific data and news about the victories and defeats of the anti-incinerator forces. "People were hungering for information, but there was little out there," reports Ellen.

One of the Connetts' accomplishments has been to help debunk the sales pitch of incinerator consultants and manufacturers that modern mass-burners are safe and that they are being used successfully in Europe. The Connetts went to Europe to investigate; they brought back a different picture and have alerted allies across the country. As a scientist, Paul is able to read technical reports that are adverse to mass burning and disseminate information vital to battling proposed incinerators.

The Connetts say that one major obstacle in their fight is closed minds. For example, the waste authority in their county, which is New York's biggest milk producer, won't consider alternatives to incineration. Neither will the state, which is planning to pay $200 million to subsidize 38 incinerators, but is offering only $5 million to foster recycling, according to the Connetts. Paul says the incinerator industry has captivated decision makers with "sleazy, smooth sales techniques." Ellen says that "the whole process is very corrupt. The consultants can't make money on low-tech alternatives." Paul says industry types have compared him with TV evangelists. His response: "God recycles, the devil burns."

However angry, the Connetts are optimistic. They celebrate whenever another community rejects an incinerator, and they see a cleaner environment resulting from the struggle. "The garbage crisis," Ellen says, "is bringing middle America into the environmental movement. It's exciting."

CHAPTER SEVEN

On The Nuclear Threat

HALTING RADIOACTIVE WASTE AND PROLIFERATION

Nuclear energy is a modern version of medieval alchemy with a terrible twist. When an alchemist's experiment to turn lead into gold went awry, it didn't expose hundreds of thousands of people to possibly lethal doses of radiation, and it didn't render huge areas uninhabitable for long periods of time. We have succeeded in converting uranium to electricity, but our modern day alchemy has very high costs and devastating risks.

In an instant in 1986, the Soviet city of Chernobyl went to the top of the growing list of failed nuclear experiments. They're still counting the toll from the worst tragedy in our relatively short Nuclear Era: 30 workers dead from radiation exposure in the first few months; more than 200 other workers and firefighters hospitalized for severe radiation sickness; hundreds of thousands of people forced from their homes and now waiting to see whether the explosion of the Chernobyl reactor sentenced them to death by cancer.

In the days following the blast, prevailing winds carried a radioactive plume across at least 20 European nations, exposing millions of people to varying degrees of radiation. The fallout pattern was so widespread and complex that scientists cannot determine the full effects of the accident.

The sequence of events in a nuclear accident is enlightening. Seldom do these tragedies occur solely because of mechanical problems. In many cases, human error is a factor, as graphically illustrated by Chernobyl.

On April 26, 1986, the operators of the Chernobyl 4 nuclear reactor were testing their emergency shutdown procedures. The operators ignored their own procedures and disconnected various safety systems, including the emergency core-cooling system. In the final step toward disaster, they started pulling from the reactor's core the rods that are used to control the nuclear fission reaction.

Soviet offiicals say that in just 4.5 seconds, power levels in the reactor rose to 120 times its rated capacity. The explosion hurled hot nuclear fuel and graphite high into the night sky. For the first time in history, the radioactive contents of a nuclear reactor were released directly into our atmosphere. Although U.S. civilian reactors are designed so an accident similar to Chernobyl won't occur, they can still release highly radioactive gas directly into the atmosphere and create an accident where the entire core of the reactor melts down.

In 1964, the old Atomic Energy Commission (AEC), the agency that preceded the Nuclear Regulatory Commission (NRC), painted this hypothetical worst-case accident scenario: 45,000 people would be killed, 100,000 people injured, $17 billion worth of damages inflicted (in 1964 dollars), and radioactive contamination covering an area the size of Pennsylvania. However, the AEC never revealed its calculations to the public. These horrifying projections had to be pried from federal files through a Freedom of Information action in 1973.

Our relatively brief experience with nuclear power is filled with accidents and frequent emergency shutdowns. The average nuclear power plant is forced to shut down about 6 times a year due to system irregularities. In 1985 alone, U.S. plants recorded almost 3,000 mishaps and an astonishing 765 emergency shutdowns. At least 18 of these shutdowns were the result of serious accidents that could have led to extensive core damage.

NUCLEAR POWER PLANTS IN THE UNITED STATES

Plant	Location
Arkansas 1	Russellville, AR
Arkansas 2	Russellville, AR
Beaver Valley 1	Shippingport, PA
Beaver Valley 2	Shippingport, PA
Bellefonte 1	Scottsboro, AL
Bellefonte 2	Scottsboro, AL
Big Rock Point	Charlevoix, MI
Braidwood 1	Braidwood, IL
Braidwood 2	Braidwood, IL

Browns Ferry 1	Decatur, AL
Browns Ferry 2	Decatur, AL
Browns Ferry 3	Decatur, AL
Brunswick 1	Southport, NC
Brunswick 2	Southport, NC
Byron 1	Byron, IL
Byron 2	Byron, IL
Callaway 1	Fulton, MO
Calvert Cliffs 1	Lusby, MD
Calvert Cliffs 2	Lusby, MD
Catawba 1	Clover, SC
Catawba 2	Clover, SC
Clinton 1	Clinton, IL
Comanche Peak 1	Glen Rose, TX
Comanche Peak 2	Glen Rose, TX
Cook 1	Bridgman, MI
Cook 2	Bridgman, MI
Cooper	Brownsville, NB
Crystal River 3	Red Level, FL
Davis-Besse	Oak Harbor, OH
Diablo Canyon 1	Avila Beach, CA
Diablo Canyon 2	Avila Beach, CA
Dresden 2	Morris, IL
Dresden 3	Morris, IL
Duane Arnold	Palo, IA
Farley 1	Dothan, AL
Farley 2	Dothan, AL
Fermi 2	Newport, MI
Fitzpatrick	Scriba, NY
Fort Calhoun 1	Fort Calhoun, IN
Fort St. Vrain	Platteville, CO
Ginna	Ontario, NY
Grand Gulf 1	Port Gibson, MS
Grand Gulf 2	Poqt Gibson, MS
Haddam Neck	Haddam Neck, CT
Hatch 1	Baxley, GA
Hatch 2	Baxley, GA
Hope Creek	Salem, NJ

Indian Point 2	Indian Point, NY
Indian Point 3	Indian Point, NY
Kewaunee	Carlton, WI
La Crosse	Genoa, WI
LaSalle 1	Seneca, IL
LaSalle 2	Seneca, IL
Limerick 1	Pottstown, PA
Limerick 2	Pottstown, PA
Maine Yankee	Wiscasset, ME
McGuire 1	Cornelius, NC
McGuire 2	Cornelius, NC
Millstone 1	Waterford, CT
Millstone 2	Waterford, CT
Millstone 3	Waterford, CT
Monticello	Monticello, MN
Nine Mile Point 1	Scriba, NY
Nine Mile Point 2	Scriba, NY
North Anna 1	Mineral, VA
North Anna 2	Mineral, VA
Oconee 1	Seneca, NY
Oconee 2	Seneca, NY
Oconee 3	Seneca, NY
Oyster Creek	Forked River, NJ
Palisades	South Haven, MI
Palo Verde 1	Wintersburg, AZ
Palo Verde 2	Wintersburg, AZ
Palo Verde 3	Wintersburg, AZ
Peach Bottom 2	Peach Bottom, PA
Peach Bottom 3	Peach Bottom, PA
Perry 1	North Perry, OH
Perry 2	North Perry, OH
Pilgrim 1	Plymouth, MA
Point Beach 1	Two Creeks, WI
Point Beach 2	Two Creeks, WI
Prairie Island 1	Red Wing, MN
Prairie Island 2	Red Wing, MN
Quad Cities 1	Cardova, IL
Quad Cities 2	Cardova, IL

Rancho Seco	Clay Station, CA
River Bend 1	St. Francisville, LA
Robinson 2	Hartsville, SC
Salem 1	Salem, NJ
Salem 2	Salem, NJ
San Onofre 1	San Clemente, CA
San Onofre 2	San Clemente, CA
San Onofre 3	San Clemente, CA
Seabrook 1	Seabrook, NH
Sequoyah 1	Daisy, TN
Sequoyah 2	Daisy, TN
Shearon Harris	Newhill, NC
Shoreham	Brookhaven, NY
South Texas 1	Palacios, TX
South Texas 2	Palacios, TX
St. Lucie 1	Hutchinson Island, FL
St. Lucie 2	Hutchinson Island, FL
Summer 1	Parr, SC
Surry 1	Gravel Neck, VA
Surry 2	Gravel Neck, VA
Susquehanna 1	Berwick, PA
Susquehanna 2	Berwick, PA
Three Mile Island 1	Londonderry Twp., PA
Trojan	Prescott, OR
Turkey Point 3	Florida City, FL
Turkey Point 4	Florida City, FL
Vermont Yankee	Vernon, VT
Vogtle 1	Waynesboro, GA
Vogtle 2	Waynesboro, GA
Washington Nuclear 2	Richland, WA
Waterford 3	Taft, LA
Watts Bar 1	Spring City, TN
Watts Bar 2	Spring City, TN
Wolf Creek 1	Burlington, KS
Yankee-Rowe 1	Rowe, MA
Zion 1	Zion, IL
Zion 2	Zion, IL

Nuclear power proponents attribute the Chernobyl accident to human error and faulty Soviet technology. They argue that the strict regulatory controls and the high-technology standards of U.S. facilities make an accident of Chernobyl's scale unlikely here. But prior to that accident, Chernobyl had one of the best service records in the world.

Reviewing the Soviet disaster, the Worldwatch Institute concluded that "one of nuclear power's fundamental problems is that even the most trivial incident could one day lead to catastrophe, a fact made possible by the enormous complexity of nuclear power systems. Significant nuclear incidents have already been initiated by hungry field mice, a worker's loose shirt tail, and an improperly used candle." In the high-stakes gamble of nuclear power, the United States has simply been luckier than the Soviet Union.

A strong watchdog is needed to help protect us from the potential devastation caused by an improperly operated nuclear power plant. Unfortunately, our watchdog, the NRC, has been negligent at its best and scandal-ridden at its worst. The NRC often seems more concerned with the survival of the nuclear industry than with public safety. Utilities across the country have cut corners, failed to report problems, and tampered with test records to obtain operating licenses. In many cases, the NRC has either failed to uncover violations or, worse yet, chosen to look the other way.

The Three Mile Island plant (TMI) operated by Metropolitan Edison in Pennsylvania is a chilling example. Six months before the 1979 accident there, both Metropolitan Edison and the NRC knew the Number 2 reactor was leaking water necessary for safe operation. Instead of shutting down the reactor and looking for the leak, the NRC allowed Metropolitan Edison simply to replace the lost water. In addition, the utility falsified leak-report records and destroyed test results.

After the partial meltdown in 1979, caused in some measure when increased leaking of cooling water uncovered the reactor core, a TMI employee reported the coverup to other NRC inspectors. The watchdog didn't bark. Rather than report these findings to the Justice Department, the NRC sat on them. When prosecutors discovered this evidence on their own, NRC officials defended the utility.

The Fermi 2 reactor in Michigan provides another example. In the Summer of 1985, Detroit Edison was in the final testing stages before applying for its full-power operating license. An operator violated NRC-mandated procedures by moving some control rods out of sequence. Within minutes the reactor was at full power—far beyond the generating level for this stage of testing. The operator regained control of the reactor, but Detroit Edison—despite a legal requirement to report any safety-related incident to the NRC—kept quiet, especially at the licensing hearing that led to NRC approval of full-power operation for Fermi 2. When Detroit Edison finally revealed the incident, the watchdog merely whimpered. The NRC ordered the utility to temporarily cut the reactor to 5 percent of full power.

These are not isolated examples. They illustrate how federal regulators that are bred to be watchdogs end up as the lapdogs of a regulated industry. In many respects, NRC's lack of strict supervision has made nuclear power a self-policing industry at best.

After the Three Mile Island accident, many nuclear power critics hoped the NRC would tighten its controls and show greater concern for public safety. However, this does not seem to be happening, not even after Chernobyl. On March 31, 1987, the NRC shut down the Philadelphia Electric Company's Peach Bottom 3 nuclear reactor because senior operators were sleeping and playing video games in the control room. It

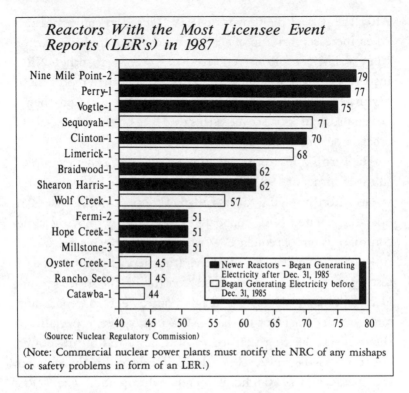

Reactors With the Most Licensee Event Reports (LER's) in 1987

Nine Mile Point-2	79
Perry-1	77
Vogtle-1	75
Sequoyah-1	71
Clinton-1	70
Limerick-1	68
Braidwood-1	62
Shearon Harris-1	62
Wolf Creek-1	57
Fermi-2	51
Hope Creek-1	51
Millstone-3	51
Oyster Creek-1	45
Rancho Seco	45
Catawba-1	44

■ Newer Reactors – Began Generating Electricity after Dec. 31, 1985
□ Began Generating Electricity before Dec. 31, 1985

(Source: Nuclear Regulatory Commission)

(Note: Commercial nuclear power plants must notify the NRC of any mishaps or safety problems in form of an LER.)

took 5 months—from the time the NRC learned about the misconduct until it took action—for the watchdog to even growl. This was an incredible delay, considering that at the time both Peach Bottom 2 and 3 topped the NRC's list of the nation's most poorly managed nuclear plants.

Nuclear facilities are only as safe as the people operating them. Every major accident at a nuclear power plant has been traced to human error. How carefully does the NRC work to ensure that operators maintain their skills?

In 1986, the NRC found that a surprisingly high number of nuclear plant operators were failing the requalification examinations used to test their ability to operate a plant safely. The Advisory Committee on Reactor Safeguards—created by Congress to advise the NRC on such safety matters and composed of

15 nuclear scientists and engineers—responded by recommending the elimination of the requalification exams on the grounds that many operators were becoming "demoralized" because they were flunking these tests!

The NRC's response was to develop a new system of testing. However, budgetary problems may limit the actual number of operators tested. Moreover, without full and adequate testing, the NRC remains in the dark about the potential for operator errors.

Occasionally, the ranks of the five-member NRC will include a commissioner who is a junkyard dog. In the 1980s, James Asselstine was one of this rare breed. During his tenure, he persistently criticized the agency and the nuclear industry. His insider conclusion about the NRC? "I'm afraid the commission is not likely to take any strong action," he noted. "The nation will have to suffer its own Chernobyl before the NRC seriously changes its attitude. We seem to need our own dead bodies first to prove there's a need for change."

DISPOSING OF NUCLEAR WASTE

Environmental and safety problems with a nuclear power plant don't center only on its operation. Forty years after our first commercial nuclear reactor began generating electricity, we still lack the means to safely and permanently dispose of the dangerous radioactive materials it and every other plant have created. The 122 licensed commercial nuclear power plants around the nation are holding more than 15,000 metric tons of high-level waste in temporary storage pools at plant sites. By the turn of the century, waste is expected to reach 40,000 tons. Experts say the spent fuel rods from reactors contain levels of radioactivity that will be harmful to humans for 250,000 years.

Major Nuclear Waste Sites in the United States

△ Hanford
△ Richland
△ Idaho Falls
○ West Valley
☐ Sheffield
○
Beatty △ △ Nevada Test Site
☐ Maxey Flats ○
Los Alamos △ △ Pantex
Sandia △
Carlsbad ★
△ Oak Ridge
△ Savannah River
△ Barnwell

0   500
Miles

△ Active
☐ Closed
○ Sea Burial Site
★ Waste Isolation Pilot Project (WIPP)

Congress finally got around to addressing this problem in 1982 with the Nuclear Waste Policy Act. This legislation requires the Department of Energy (DOE) to dispose of the nuclear power industry's radioactive waste in a deep underground repository by 1998.

In the first round of searching for a repository, the DOE was required to nominate three sites west of the Mississippi and three sites east of the Mississippi in a second round. The department's candidate sites in the West were at Deaf Smith County, Texas, Hanford, Washington, and Yucca Mountain, Nevada.

Each site had staunch opponents and good reasons why it should be crossed off the list. Deaf Smith County sits atop the Ogallala aquifer. A leaking nuclear dump there could poison at least a portion of the nation's biggest source of groundwater, a resource serving humans and agriculture from Texas to Nebraska. Hanford is just 6 miles from the Columbia River, which carries water throughout the entire Northwest and into the Pacific Ocean. In December 1987, Congress tore up the compromise that led to the 1982 law. It indefinitely shelved the search for an eastern site and narrowed the hunt in the West to Yucca Mountain. Lawmakers from Nevada were unhappy, but colleagues from Texas, Washington, and a variety of eastern states rejoiced in this classic NIMBY victory.

The action came despite warnings by Nevada officials and geologists that Yucca Mountain's location in a seismic zone and its proximity to the U.S. nuclear weapons testing grounds make it unstable and therefore unsuitable for a nuclear waste dump. A 1987 report by the U.S. Geologic Survey warned that historic fluctuations in underground water levels at Yucca Mountain indicated that the groundwater could rise to the level of the stored nuclear waste while it was still dangerously radioactive. This would, of course, contaminate the groundwater.

Even if these problems were overcome, the DOE is years away from completing tests to determine the suitability of Yucca Mountain. Even if the site is deemed safe, the department concedes it won't meet the 1998 deadline for opening the nuclear dump. And if Yucca Mountain is unsuitable, the hunt for another site—and all the political and geological questions accompanying it—must begin anew. Meanwhile, huge amounts of nuclear waste are accumulating at the power plants.

The nuclear utilities that create this waste don't want to store it themselves, not even temporarily. Storage costs them money and focuses public attention on the nuclear waste problem. The nuclear utilities have been agitating for creation of an interim federal facility where the waste could be kept accessible until somebody comes up with a permanent solution for its safe disposal. In Washington parlance, this is the "Monitored Retrievable Storage" (MRS) facility. Opponents of this approach to temporary storage say that if the MRS were created, there would always be the danger that it would become the permanent disposal facility by default.

TRANSPORTING NUCLEAR CARGOS

The storage of radioactive materials is one problem; their transportation is another. Every day trucks and trains loaded with radioactive cargos crisscross our nation virtually unnoticed by the public. This lack of knowledge is good in one sense: When shipments do come to our attention, it's because of accidents. However, should a truck carrying spent nuclear fuel have a serious accident, the public would have no warning signals, no well-organized accident contingency plans, and no emergency evacuation zones.

So far, the traffic has been mostly one way: nuclear materials going into the plants. Someday, the spent fuel rods will have to be shipped to a final resting place, exponentially increasing the chance of a serious transportation accident. If the MRS proposal is implemented, the spent fuel rods will make an extra trip to the designated site before being shipped to their radioactive grave. And if we build more nuclear generators, we will simply be increasing the chance of a transportation catastrophe.

NUCLEAR WEAPONS PLANTS

Safety, waste, and transportation problems don't begin and end with commercial nuclear power. Even if we solved these problems tomorrow, we'd still have to deal with the mess resulting from federal nuclear programs.

After Chernobyl, Congress finally began investigating the condition of our nuclear weapons plants and found an environmental horror story. Operating under the veil of national security, these plants have been relentlessly enriching plutonium and churning out warheads for four decades, sometimes with callous disregard for safety.

For instance, operators of the Hanford, Washington, plutonium complex once deliberately released a huge plume of radioactive iodine into the air simply to see if they could reduce the time it takes to process uranium into plutonium. The fallout quickly spread over an 8,000 square-mile area of Washington and Oregon, yet nobody outside the plant was alerted to its presence, even though the plume contained 200 to 300 times as much radioactive iodine as was released by the accident at Three Mile Island.

What is most frightening about the Hanford release is that it represents just one of thousands of incidents that have occurred at the 280 nuclear weapons facilities at 20 sites across the country. The private contractors who run our nuclear weapons facilities have systematically released radioactive and toxic refuse into our air, land, and water. Bob Alvarez, at the time a nuclear weapons and energy expert at the Environmental Policy Institute, says that at Hanford alone, "200 billion gallons of dilute radioactive and toxic liquids have been deliberately released to the soil and seepage basins, enough to create a lake the size of New York City and 40 feet deep."

Alvarez calls the Hanford complex "the most contaminated site in the non-Soviet world." It contains 123 defunct contaminated laboratories, processing buildings, reactors, and warehouses, as well as 149 corroding storage tanks of high-level radioactive waste. All this sits on a 570-square-mile reservation on the banks of the Columbia River.

The DOE has responsibility for overseeing the private contractors who run our nuclear weapons facilities. In 1986, the DOE appointed a panel of outside experts to examine the N reactor at Hanford because of similarities between it and the Chernobyl reactor. The DOE also asked the National Academy of Sciences (NAS) to review the entire Hanford complex. The outside experts recommended more than $50 million worth of safety improvements to the N reactor. Two panel members said it should be shut down. The NAS warned that a catastrophic hydrogen explosion was possible at Hanford. In January 1987, the DOE announced a 6-month shutdown of the N reactor; 3 months later, the Senate Armed Services Committee voted for a permanent shutdown.

Even though Hanford is the most contaminated of the DOE facilities, experts believe that the Savannah River plant, which produces tritium in South Carolina, poses the greatest risk. Many people live near the plant. It sits atop an important regional aquifer. Despite the threat of groundwater contamination, the facility dumps 200,000 gallons of dilute radioactive and toxic waste directly on the ground every day.

When DuPont operated Savannah River under a contract with the DOE, the plant had countless accidents that were kept secret from the public for more than three decades. In a 1985 memo made public in 1988, DuPont scientist G.C. Ridgely summarized the 30 worst incidents at Savannah River. Here are just a few examples: During a 1960 startup, power surged at 12 times the normal rate. The reactor was 40 seconds from the core coolant boiling. A 1957 test caused the melting of a fuel assembly. A 1970 melting of a source rod caused a major release of radiation into the plant that took 3 months to clean up.

However, such incidents are not merely history. As recently as August 1988, 3 days after DuPont began a restart of the P reactor, unexpected gases were detected in the reactor vessel, causing operators to shut the plant down. Later in the day, without determining the source of the gases, the crew began a restart. The next morning, the reactor had an alarming power surge. DuPont ignored the "power spike" and continued to increase power. The DOE was not notified about the incident until the following day. Eleven days after the erratic situation began, the reactor was finally shut down for a scheduled 30 days and then indefinitely. The Savannah River facility as a whole has set a daunting average of from 9 to 12 forced shutdowns per reactor every year since 1971.

One of the major problems with the DOE weapons program is that its facilities are antiquated. Most of them were built in the 1940s and 1950s when nuclear technology was in its infancy. Very few safety improvements have been made since then. In addition, the DOE has never had to meet the same environmental and operating standards as commercial nuclear reactors. Neither the DOE's nuclear reactors nor its waste disposal methods are monitored by the NRC.

Four of our nation's largest weapons plants, including both Hanford and Savannah River, have been either shut down or severely cut back. Even if they never produce another pound of radioactive materials, we face a very expensive and technologically challenging cleanup job. The DOE has hundreds of inactive contaminated facilities and millions of tons of high-level radioactive waste stored in temporary tanks and in hundreds of toxic dumps.

Cleanup estimates have ranged as high as $200 billion. Compare this to the $10 billion Congress earmarked for the first 10 years of cleanup under the superfund toxic waste dump abatement program. Clearly, something is drastically wrong with the way the DOE has handled these sites. While hiding behind the cloak of national security, this agency has created an environmental disaster that is without parallel in the private sector. Safety problems, radioactive waste, and a government that is overly supportive of nuclear technology are common to both nuclear power generation and nuclear weapons production. So is the cost to society. Both are exorbitantly expensive.

ADDING UP THE COST

Nuclear power has come a long way from 1954 when Lewis L. Strauss, chairman of the AEC, promised it would be a safe, clean, limitless source of electricity that would be "too cheap to meter." The cost of building a nuclear power plant has skyrocketed over the past 20 years. In 1970, construction of a nuclear power plant cost less than $200 per kilowatt—1,000 watts, or the amount of electricity needed to turn on ten 100-watt light bulbs. That jumped to $750 per kilowatt in 1980, to $1,900 per kilowatt in 1984, and to more than $3,500 per kilowatt today. These higher costs mean higher prices for consumers.

Along with escalating construction costs, the nuclear industry was rocked by energy conservation following the 1973 oil embargo and public reaction to Three Mile Island. Since 1973, 117 planned nuclear plants have been canceled, including 30 that were already in the construction phase. The last time a nuclear plant received a construction permit was 1978. Electricity that was supposed to be too cheap to meter has turned into an economic nightmare.

Forbes magazine wrote in 1985 that "the failure of the U.S. nuclear power program ranks as the largest managerial disaster in business history, a disaster on a monumental scale. The utility industry has already invested $125 billion in nuclear power, with an additional $140 billion to come before the decade is out, and only the blind, or the biased, can now think that most of the money has been well spent. . . . Without even recognizing the risks, the U.S. electric power industry undertook a commitment bigger than the space program ($100 billion) or the Vietnam War ($111 billion)."

Several factors enticed electric utilities into this expensive gamble with nuclear power. To begin with, the federal government used hundreds of millions of our tax dollars for basic research and development of nuclear power technology under the Atoms for Peace program.

After this free ride for the utilities, General Electric and Westinghouse built 21 "turnkey" plants. These plants were built at fixed prices of between $200 and $300 million each and then turned over to the purchasing utilities in ready-to-operate condition. While these plants cost General Electric and Westinghouse more to build than they had estimated, the plants did their job of proving to utilities that nuclear power could produce electricity, which led to future business for the builders.

Finally, the profit motive was a strong factor in the rush to nuclear power. The way utilities make their profits strongly influences the investments they make. Utility rates are generally set so the utility not only recovers all its day-to-day operating costs of providing electricity to customers, but also receives a guaranteed profit based on the value of its physical assets, namely, its power plants. The bigger the investment a utility has in power plants, the bigger its profits. The huge cost of nuclear plants means more profit dollars than yeilded by coal or gas plants.

With government investment in research, industry investment in loss leader plants, and the economics of utilities' own rate structure encouraging investment in high-cost facilities, the power companies' appetites were sufficiently whetted. Orders for new reactors started flooding in during the late 1960s and early 1970s. Unfortunately, this second generation of reactors was not built at fixed prices, and what was originally thought of as a new and efficient way of boiling water to crank turbines turned out to be increasingly sophisticated, complex, and expensive.

The first signs of trouble came when the nuclear utilities discovered that coal-powered electric plants, which had become larger and more efficient, remained competitive with nuclear plants. To retain their cost advantage, the new nuclear plants also had to be larger, so they were capable of producing even more electricity. This meant more design work, more labor hours, more materials, and, of course, more money. In addition, the new, larger plants were even more complex to construct than the older ones, leading to many unforeseen problems. As each problem was discovered, another component of the reactor had to be rebuilt, further escalating construction costs.

Utility companies worried very little about these mounting overruns. For 40 years, their customers had steadily increased their use of electricity. The 1960s had been the industry's most profitable decade ever. Even the energy crisis of the 1970s seemed to play right into the hands of the nuclear power industry. The Nixon administration's 1974 Project Independence envisioned nuclear power providing 40 percent of our electricity by 1990 and 50 percent by 2000. Fortunately, we are far short of that goal. In 1988, nuclear energy provided approximately 18 percent of our electricity. Renewable sources provided 14 percent, with hydropower accounting for half of the electricity produced by renewables, according to Public Citizen.

However, the energy crisis was accompanied by a recession and an increased public commitment to energy conservation. We dramatically decreased our use of electricity. Suddenly, the nuclear industry found itself planning and building plants that wouldn't be needed for 10 or 20 years. At the same time, high interest rates and rising construction costs had made nuclear power far more expensive than competing fossil fuel plants.

The first wave of nuclear plant cancellations began quickly, led by the Tennessee Valley Authority's decision to drop eight nuclear projects. Plants on the drawing board fell in domino fashion as more and more utilities realized that abandoning their projects was preferable to pushing on into an uncertain market. However, some utilities were too far along with construction to turn back. Their only hope was to complete their plants quickly so they could recoup construction costs through rate hikes. Some got their plants completed and operating. Others, like Public Service of New Hampshire, didn't. That otherwise financially healthy company ended up in bankruptcy because of its Seabrook nuclear plant.

CURRENT TRENDS IN THE NUCLEAR POWER INDUSTRY

The threat of global warming may be frightening to atmospheric scientists, but it's viewed as a golden opportunity for renaissance and growth by the moribund nuclear-power industry. Plant manufacturers are asking us not only to forget Chernobyl and Three Mile Island, but to ignore costly construction overruns, escalating electricity costs, and the nuclear waste dilemma. Instead, they're asking us to focus on global warming and buy what they claim is a new, modern generation of cheap, safe nuclear power plants that will solve all our problems with carbon dioxide emissions from fossil fuels.

Westinghouse, a major builder of nuclear plants and one of the industrial giants cashing in on the global warming threat, is using a fancy full-color brochure to hawk its new plant. The sales pitch claims the plant is "ACCEPTABLE to the American public. . . a friend to the consumer. . . SIMPLER to construct, operate and maintain. . . designed with inherently SAFE, PASSIVE systems. . . AFFORDABLE for the power producer." Later on, the nuke peddlers zero in their spiel on the environment: "As we all become more concerned about long-term potential damage to the earth and its atmosphere when we burn carbon-based fuels, we will come to appreciate the many environmental advantages of nuclear facilities."

Except for the tie-in with global warming, all this should sound familiar to anyone who was listening four decades ago when the nuclear industry first came to us with glowing promises of clean, safe, efficient power. Let's just, for argument's sake, assume that this industry can design, build, and operate a plant that is totally safe from meltdowns and accidents that poison our land, water, and atmosphere and threaten people with instant or lingering death; that such a plant can be built on time and on budget; and that it can finally fulfill the heretofore empty promise of electricity that is too cheap to meter.

Concede this to the next nuclear plant salesperson you meet and then ask: "What do we do with the radioactive waste? What about the huge piles of uranium tailings that remain from uranium mining and that are polluting communities in the West? What about contaminated concrete and steel that require safe disposal when a nuclear plant wears out and is dismantled? And what about the money spent on perpetuating nuclear power and its waste problems when we should be devoting our research dollars to developing renewable forms of energy?"

The nuclear industry didn't have the answers to these questions 40 years ago, and it still doesn't have them today.

PEOPLE MAKING A DIFFERENCE

JUANITA ELLIS

© 1989 DAVID J. SAMS

Juanita Ellis is not likely to forget her long battle with Texas Utilities (TU) over the Commanche Peak nuclear plant 80 miles from her Dallas home. The stacks of boxes of documents collected during the fight will continue to serve as a personal monument to her cause.

Ellis wasn't planning on making Commanche Peak a career when she and six other people met late in 1973 to discuss the proposed plant. From that gathering emerged CASE (Citizens Association for Sound Energy) that was to dog TU nearly every step of the way over the better part of two decades.

Unable to stop the Dallas City Council from endorsing Commanche Peak, Ellis intervened at state rate hearings "to find out the plant's true cost. It was like trying to hit a moving target." From $779 million in 1974, the estimate zoomed to about $9 billion by 1989.

CASE couldn't prevent the Nuclear Regulatory Commission (NRC) from granting a construction permit in 1974. But when TU sought an operating license in 1979, CASE intervened before the NRC's Atomic Safety and Licensing Board. By now, CASE was getting attention from news media made skeptical of nuclear power by Three Mile Island. Ellis had other allies: upwards of 50 whistleblowers reporting construction problems at the plant.

In December 1983, the licensing board noted CASE's allegations of unsafe construction and put the utility's proceedings on hold until TU could assure quality work. Ellis won a major victory early in 1985 when TU put its own hold on the proceedings after CASE alerted the NRC to new design and construction flaws.

The turning point came later in 1985 when a new management team took over TU. Ellis says the team began cooperating with CASE and worked out a correction plan, including reinspection of all construction. "The plan looked good," she says. "They had addressed our concerns." CASE no longer had major reasons to continue its challenge, according to Ellis.

The challenge was dropped in 1988 after negotiations with TU produced what Ellis calls "a unique and sweeping agreement." CASE experts would have access to the plant and all documents, including inspection reports, for at least five years. Ellis was added to a TU committee overseeing safety at Commanche Peak. TU would reimburse CASE $4.5 million for the cost of its challenge and pay CASE $750,000 over five years to hire engineers to monitor construction and operation.

Ellis walked a fine line as Commanche Peak headed for startup. "For this deal to work," she notes, "there has to be a certain amount of trust, but that doesn't mean blind trust. A lot of what we're doing is checking to confirm what we've been told by TU."

The deal brought almost constant criticism from people who wanted Commanche Peak abandoned. Ellis says her goal was never to stop the plant from operating, only to ensure that it was safe. Without the deal, CASE might have delayed licensing for a while and then been shut out of Commanche Peak, according to Ellis.

"In lots of ways, it has been a nightmare since the settlement," Ellis says. "It hurt me deeply that people would think we had sold out. When you sell out, you take the money and run. You don't sign up for another five years."

WHAT WE CAN DO

If you agree by now that we should not be substituting nuclear power for fossil plants as the answer to global warming, you will want to set our course down a better path. You may also want to help focus public attention on the problems with the nuclear plants that are now operating, especially the waste that they produce.

Some of your actions will contribute directly to these goals; other actions will help change the political climate that supports the nuclear industry; and still others will be aimed at changing the policies that have gotten us into this mess in the first place. Here are some ideas to get you started.

INDIVIDUAL ACTIONS

Asserting Your Right to Know

The first step in fighting nuclear pollution is to educate yourself on the direct risks it poses to you and your family. This means you need to know what kind of nuclear facilities are located in your area. Define your area broadly; keep in mind how far the devastation from a nuclear accident can spread. Start out by asking your electric utility what percentage of its electricity is generated by nuclear power. (Even if your own utility does not operate a nuclear power plant, it may own part of one or it may buy electricity from another company that owns one.)

The next step is to find out if there are other kinds of nuclear facilities in your area, such as nuclear weapons plants or military and research facilities operated by the federal government. Some universities also operate nuclear reactors. Good sources for information on nuclear facilities in your area include:

- The local electric power company
- The local newspaper

- The public library's reference desk
- The office of your representative at the city or county government level
- Your local environmental organization

If there is a nuclear power plant in your area, you will want to find out where the official Public Document Room is. It is usually located in a local library, and it will have all NRC documents relating to the plant. This is a treasure trove of information.

When you have located the nearest nuclear power plant, pay it a visit. Most utilities have a visitor center where they tell you how wonderful the nuclear power plant is. Wait until the question-and-answer session, and then ask some tough questions. This will do more than show the plant operators that you are concerned. It is an excellent educational tool for other people on the tour. Here are some questions for starters:

- How many tons of radioactive waste did this plant generate last year? Where do you store this waste? How long will it be until your on-site storage facilities fill up? What will you do with your radioactive wastes then?
- How often has your plant shut down? How many times did it shut down last year other than for routine maintenance? What was the longest length of time it was shut down last year? What was the longest it was ever shut down? How do you provide replacement power when the plant is shut down?
- How many safety incidents did your plant have last year? The plant must disclose such incidents to the NRC through Licensee Event Reports (LERs). Ask to see the plant's LERs. How many of these involved operator errors? Has your company had to pay fines to the NRC for safety violations?
- How many rems of radiation did plant workers receive over

the last 12 months? How about temporary workers hired to do repairs?

- What worker training programs are conducted? Do plant operators take periodic exams to test their ability to operate the plant safely? Are they passing?
- If a serious accident occurred at the facility, how would the people in the area be notified of the accident? What is the evacuation plan for the area? How is it publicized? Ask for a copy.

If the tour guide refuses to provide you with adequate answers, there are other ways to find out. You can call the public information officer at the nuclear power plant or ask your librarian to help you find some of the answers. If you still are not getting the answers, write a letter to the editors of your local and regional newspapers. Point out that your community has the right to know the answers to these questions.

For some information, you may have to resort to using your state's public records law or the federal Freedom of Information Act. As you are tracking down this information, be persistent and let people know why you are concerned. The more people who hear that you are worried, the more likely they are to become concerned themselves.

You may find it more difficult to get information from a government facility or a university that has a nuclear facility. They are less likely than a utility to need to promote a positive public image and may be more secretive about their operations. If you encounter this, attempt to get the media to ask the questions about safety and facility operation.

Public Citizen, the Washington-based consumer advocacy group, also publishes an annual review of nuclear plant safety violations called the "Nuclear Power Safety Report." Contact Public Citizen, Critical Mass Energy Project, 215 Pennsylvania Avenue, S.E., Washington, DC, 20003, (202) 546-4996.

You also have a right to know where your elected officials stand on questions of nuclear safety. Your state and federal legislators write laws that change the way regulatory agencies behave or that put new requirements on utilities. Keeping your legislators informed about your concerns is important. You should write them letters to probe their level of awareness and concern on this issue. A more direct approach is to speak up at candidate forums and, after elections, ask to visit with your representative. Here are some questions to ask:

- Do you know who generates high-level radioactive waste in your district?
- Do you know how much they generate each year?
- Do you know what they do with the waste?
- Are you concerned that we keep generating more radioactive waste each year without knowing how to dispose of it safely?
- Do you favor reducing the amount of radioactive waste we generate each year?
- If so, what steps would you take to get this waste generation reduced? In this area? In the country?

Avoid Nuclear Investments

You may be supporting nuclear power without even knowing it. If you have money invested, make sure it is in socially responsible mutual funds or in corporations that are not part of the nuclear industry in this country. Encourage your friends and relatives to do the same. If you belong to any organizations that invest money, suggest they adopt a similar policy.

The Council on Economic Priorities publishes "Shopping for a Better World—A Quick and Easy Guide to Socially Responsible Supermarket Shopping." It tells you, among other things, whether a particular manufacturer is involved with the nuclear industry.

Organizations that can give you information on socially responsible investing include The Council on Economic Priorities, 30 Irving Place, New York, NY, 10003; The Interfaith Center on Corporate Responsibility, 475 Riverside Drive, Room 566, New York, NY, 10115; The Investor Responsibility Research Center, 1755 Massachusetts Avenue, N.W., Washington, DC, 20036; The Social Investment Forum, 222 Lewis Wharf, Boston, MA, 02110; and The Working Assets Money Fund, 230 California Street, San Francisco, CA, 94111.

Becoming Energy Efficient

The same home energy-efficiency measures recommended in Chapter 4 to improve air pollution also help reduce our society's reliance on nuclear power. Because producing electricity with nuclear energy is extremely expensive, reducing our use can also produce savings on your electric bill.

GETTING POLITICAL

Getting Your State to Move in the Right Direction

While there are steps you as an individual can take to make a difference, you can make an even bigger difference if you press your state to start planning now for safe energy in the future. Although no new plants have been proposed since 1978, a new generation of nuclear plants looms on the horizon. Reactor manufacturers are busy trying to set up demonstration projects for what they like to call "inherently" safe reactors. Even if all the safety problems were to be solved with this new breed—and it is very unclear that they will—the industry is no closer to figuring out what to do with high-level radioactive waste it will generate.

Your state probably has an office of consumer counsel, consumer advocate, or public counsel to protect the interests of all ratepayers at hearings by the state agency that regulates public utilities. This office should be your friend. It can provide a lot of help in steering you through your state's regulatory process. The consumer advocate's office is also an excellent place to find out which environmental and consumer groups are involved in utility issues in your state. Your first step should be to get in touch with one of these groups.

Now that you have found a friend in the consumer advocate and located others of your persuasion, you are ready to make sure your state regulators hear your point of view. Every state has a public service commission that oversees electric and gas utilities. Most states guarantee the public a right to speak during hearings about rates and plans for new power sources. These are excellent forums where citizens can provide alternate facts and press for new approaches.

In these forums, you can become an advocate of "least-cost planning": a process that represents a dramatic change from archaic utility planning that only looked for ways to produce more power, rather than finding the most efficient way to meet consumers' needs.

Utilities look 15 to 20 years into the future to determine what electricity demand will be and then develop and implement a plan to meet that demand. Traditionally, the public and utility regulators get their chance to comment on the plan only after the utility has made its decisions. Least-cost planning allows consumers and regulators to get actively involved at the beginning of the planning process.

Utilities want to sell electricity and consumers want the electricity to operate their appliances. Least-cost planning changes the premise that utilities must continually produce more electricity to keep appliances working. The least-cost premise is that a utility can meet its future production requirements by promoting efficiency and reducing demand, rather than simply building new generating plants.

Least-cost planning encourages a utility to develop a mix of resources to meet future demand at the lowest long-run cost to its customers and itself. In developing this mix, the planners should consider all costs associated with each resource, including environmental, societal, and economic costs. Factoring in environmental and societal costs is new to the utility cost-benefit equation. For least-cost planning to work effectively, it is imperative that the cost of mining, waste disposal, air and water emissions, transportation, and refining be included in the ultimate cost of meeting future electricity demand. This allows energy efficiency and conservation to compete on an equal basis with new power plants. In head-to-head competition with a new power plant, efficiency and conservation are almost always the least-cost route.

Some states have already adopted comprehensive least-cost-planning programs. They include California, Connecticut, Delaware, Maine, Massachusetts, Nevada, New York, Washington, and Wisconsin. Many other states are considering this approach. If your state isn't among them, ask your legislators and utility regulators to get to work setting up this sensible system, which not only protects the environment, but can minimize increases in the cost of electricity. Be sure to ask your utility whether it follows the principle of least-cost planning in making its projections for future power supply and demand.

Be careful here; many utilities will say, "Of course we have been doing least-cost planning. Do you think we would buy more expensive resources than we have to!" You should respond with these specific questions to make sure the least-cost planning they are doing is the kind they should be doing:

- Does your planning model integrate demand and supply-side resources using the same cost-benefit, cost-effectiveness analysis? Does the company consider conservation and efficiency as resources with which to meet future demand?

- Are the environmental costs associated with each resource incorporated into the cost-benefit analysis?
- Does the utility have a two-year action plan for carrying out the short-run projects identified in the least-cost integrated resource plan?
- Is there public access to the long-range planning process, from the initial assessment of resources to the final selection of the least-cost integrated resource mix?

Unfortunately, many electric utilities are trying to insulate themselves from the kind of public pressure you can bring to bear. In the world of big profits, least-cost energy planning isn't always popular. In fact, utilities are trying to get out from under current regulations that allow citizen participation in the planning process.

The for-profit power industry is actively seeking to repeal the Public Utility Holding Company Act of 1935. This New Deal law has prevented the electricity industry from being monopolized by a few giant national corporations. It has kept issues such as how much you pay for electricity largely in the hands of state regulators, who are typically more accessible and accountable to citizens. Recently, these utilities have been working in Congress to amend this law in such a way that states could lose control of planning and rate making to a federal commission. That commission, the Federal Energy Regulatory Commission, already sets prices for electricity from some power plants. Its record has been pro-big power and anti-consumer. Write your representative and senators and tell them you oppose repeal or weakening of the Public Utility Holding Company Act. At the same time, take advantage of the rights you do have under the current law to help influence energy planning.

How do we meet our nation's electricity needs without using nuclear power and still solve the problems of global warming caused by fossil-fuel power plants? Energy efficiency is clearly the first step, but in the longer run, we must develop renewable energy sources. As important as efficiency is, we will not be able to meet all our electricity needs through efficiency alone. Renewable fuel sources produce energy without being permanently depleted. The sun, the wind, the ocean tides, and geothermal power are renewable sources of energy. So is biomass, the vegetable matter used for fuel. Fossil fuels, such as coal, natural gas, and oil, are not renewable; once they are burned, we cannot replace them. Wood is considered a renewable resource so long as we don't use up more trees than we replace.

In 1988, renewable energy sources, including hydropower, supplied nearly 14 percent of our nation's electricity, according to Public Citizen. But the amount could be far greater if the government encouraged research and development of renewables. In 1981, the federal government spent $1 billion on research and development of renewables. However, during the Reagan administration the money was continually decreased, falling to $115 million in Reagan's final budget. Unless we encourage our federal representatives to increase the level of funding for development of renewables, the program may wither away. And with it our hopes of alleviating the environmental impact of fossil fuels and nuclear waste.

Individual actions can make a difference. You can install a solar collector to heat hot water. If you are planning to remodel your home or build a new one, you can use passive solar methods. These can range from architectural design to simply the proper placement of shade trees around your home to reduce your air conditioning needs. And rooftop solar panels can also provide enough hot water for hospitals, hotels, and schools.

For those living in rural areas, a single-unit wind turbine can generate up to 10 kilowatts, enough power for an average household. Farmers and ranchers should consider producing

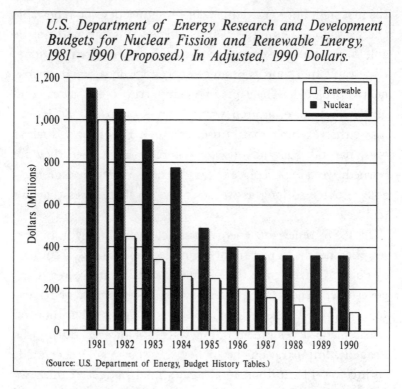

U.S. Department of Energy Research and Development Budgets for Nuclear Fission and Renewable Energy, 1981 - 1990 (Proposed), In Adjusted, 1990 Dollars.

□ Renewable
■ Nuclear

Dollars (Millions)

(Source: U.S. Department of Energy, Budget History Tables.)

biogas from manure as a renewable source of gas power. For more information on small-scale biogas technology, contact the National Center for Appropriate Technology, P.O. Box 3838, Butte, MT, 59702. In other areas, the municipal landfill is an excellent place to capture renewable methane gas. Utilizing landfill gas generates power, and burning methane instead of allowing it to escape directly into the atmosphere reduces its impact on global warming.

Here are some things you can do:

- Ask your local school board to begin using solar panels as a renewable nonpolluting energy source.
- Urge your municipal government to sponsor programs to encourage businesses to install solar power.
- Encourage your utility to use renewables to generate elec-

tricity. Wind, photovoltaics, and small-scale hydropower units are the best options.

- Encourage your local government to capture methane from its landfill and use solar-powered water heaters.

With the current price of energy not yet reflecting the growing scarcity of fossil fuels and pollution from non-renewable sources, many people will put off these investments. In order to prepare for the future, we need government leadership.

- Ask your representative and senators to support large increases in the funding for renewables.
- Ask them to vote for increased spending for research into environmentally safe alternate methods of producing electricity.
- Urge them to support financial incentives for the development of alternatives such as solar and wind power.
- Encourage them to cut the money going for nuclear power and increase it for renewables.

PEOPLE MAKING A DIFFERENCE

—————— • ——————

LISA CRAWFORD

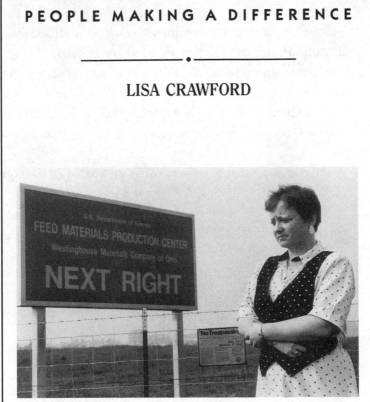

MICHAEL SNYDER

Lisa Crawford thought she was living across the street from an animal food factory—the "Feed Materials Productions Center." In late 1984, however, she learned the truth: The facility in Fernald, Ohio, was a Department of Energy (DOE) uranium plant that releases large amounts of radioactive waste in the process of making reactor rods and weapons components.

That news was bad enough, but the worst was yet to come. Uranium had contaminated the well water that the Crawford family had been drinking and bathing in for six years. The DOE said uranium levels in the water were more than 30 times what was being proposed as a safe limit. What's more, the DOE had known about the situation since 1981, but kept silent until Representative Thomas Luken of Ohio forced officials into revealing the plant's dirty secrets.

Lisa Crawford was angry. Overnight, she was transformed from an uninvolved citizen into an environmental activist. She joined the recently formed Fernald Residents for Environmental Safety and Health—FRESH. She and her husband, Ken, became the first plaintiffs in a $300 million class-action suit against National Lead of Ohio (NLO), which operated the plant under a DOE contract. The Crawfords, joined by 18 other plaintiffs, demanded damages for lost property values and mental anguish suffered by the 14,000 people living in a 5-mile radius of the plant.

Crawford became the leader of FRESH in September 1985 when the group's founder had a baby. Continuing her full-time job as a secretary, Crawford served as the FRESH spokesperson, issued press releases, and kept tabs on activities at the plant. Four months later, she made her first trip outside the Midwest and her first airplane flight to testify before Congress.

Crawford learned some sobering statistics. The DOE admitted that since the plant had opened in 1951, more than 100 tons of uranium had been pumped into the air and 74 tons had been dumped into a nearby river. Officials couldn't say what happened to another 337 tons. Crawford discovered that Hamilton County, where Fernald is located, has some of the nation's highest rates of fatal bladder, liver, and lung cancer; the death rate from breast cancer in the Cincinnati area exceeds the national average by 31 percent; and deaths from colon cancer are 21 percent higher than the national norm.

The Crawfords and other plaintiffs settled the lawsuit in 1989. The DOE agreed to pay $78 million to the Fernald residents, with some of the money earmarked for a fund to provide continual medical monitoring for people living around the plant. The $78 million comes from the U.S. Treasury because NLO's contract with DOE left taxpayers, not NLO, holding the bag in case of problems at the plant.

This victory didn't end FRESH's activities. "We're forging on," says Crawford. "We know it's going to take years, but we want this facility cleaned up. We're going to keep breathing down their necks."

Does she have any advice for someone whose normal, quiet life is suddenly filled with environmental activism? "Be persistent, ask a lot of questions, and don't believe everything you're told."

CHAPTER EIGHT

A Global Perspective

RESCUING MOTHER EARTH

Although this book has focused largely on the world's most resource-hungry, wasteful nation—our own—the United States does not have a patent on fouling the air, land, and water. Except for the relative handful of primitive peoples still living in sustainable harmony with nature, environmental destruction knows no language or political or cultural barriers.

Everything we have learned about our problems with acid

rain, air pollution, global warming, hazardous waste, nuclear energy, the ozone layer, pesticides, and toxic chemicals applies to the rest of the developed world.

The Soviet Union has a massive problem with toxic and nuclear waste. Air pollution is blamed for the deterioration of the structures built by the ancient Greeks and Romans and the soaring Gothic cathedrals of Europe. Acid rain is killing trees in Germany's Black Forest. More than 2 million tons of toxic waste was dumped into the Black Sea in 1988. Fish kills have occurred in the Adriatic Sea because of pollution. The Mediterranean is a cesspool in places because of widespread lack of sewage treatment around the Mediterranean basin. An accident at a chemical plant in Switzerland poisons the Rhine River and the drinking water in the Netherlands. And the Netherlands worries about what global warming and rising oceans levels mean for the elaborate system of dikes that protect its low-lying terrain.

In Northern England, the Sellafield nuclear complex routinely vents radioactivity into the air on a magnitude many times greater than what was released in the accident at Three Mile Island. In Seascale, the village nearest Sellafield, 1 child in 60 dies of cancer.

In the Third World, these same types of problems are growing daily as poorer nations struggle to gain a share of the international economy. At the same time, the developed world is exporting its pollution to the Third World in such forms as transboundary air pollution and dumping of hazardous waste in poor nations that need any money Western nations offer them. It costs up to $350 a ton to dispose of hazardous waste in the United States. The job can be done for as little as $40 a ton in the Third World. In March 1988 the African nation of Guinea received a shipment of 15,000 tons of what was labeled "raw material for bricks." Within two months, vegetation was dying around the stored material, which turned out to be toxic ash from Philadelphia's trash incinerators.

Not all the Third World's troubles are imported. As the Third World develops, it often adopts the industrial processes that pollute the developed countries. Mexico City has some of the worst air pollution on the planet. And when it comes to two extremely serious environmental problems — global warming and destruction of arable land — the Third World is fast becoming a co-equal partner with the major industrialized countries.

DESTROYING OUR RAIN FORESTS

Our Earth once had an estimated 6 million square miles of tropical rain forests — a relatively small 3 percent of the planet's area, but a very important part of global ecology. Today, only 3.5 million square miles remain, an area roughly the size of the United States, including Alaska and Hawaii. The United Nations Food and Agriculture Organization estimates that the planet loses up to 45,000 square miles of rain forest every year to agriculture, ranching, and timbering in places such as Southeast Asia, Africa, and Central and South America. Other sources, like the Zero Population Growth organization in Washington, estimate a much higher loss — nearly 61,000 square miles a year.

The Amazon basin, 3.1 million square miles of it, has the world's largest and most biologically diverse tropical forest. It contains anywhere from one-tenth to one-half of the planet's plant, insect, and animal species, depending on who is making the estimate. Edward Wilson of Harvard University calculates that forest destruction worldwide causes the extinction of about 10,000 species every year. In addition, one-quarter of all our medicinal drugs are derived from tropical forest plants. These include medicines that treat heart disease and childhood leukemia. We will never know how many other valuable drugs have been lost by forest destruction.

The World Bank says the Amazon region supplies one-fifth of the fresh water on the planet, and because of deforestation, the Amazon basin is responsible for one-tenth of the carbon dioxide rising into our atmosphere. The World Bank should know. It is one of the many forces responsible for the destruction of an estimated 372,000 square miles of Amazon rain forest through 1988, with an estimated additional 30,000 square miles being ravaged every year.

Two-thirds of this forest lies in Brazil, the biggest single forest destroyer in the world. In the early 1900s, Brazil built a railroad into a portion of its vast forest in an effort to encourage settlement there. More than 11,000 square miles of Amazonia were stripped of forest in an effort to grow crops. The experiment didn't work, and today the area remains a desolate scrubland.

However, Brazil did not learn from its mistake. In 1969, it enacted a National Integration Program aimed at populating Amazonia with hundreds of thousands of landless people and unemployed poor from other parts of the nation. Some of the people targeted for resettlement were small farmers from the south of Brazil who had been displaced from the land by the advent of capital-intensive agribusiness.

Another goal of the program was to get large investors—including multinational corporations—to clear the forest lands and raise cattle for export to the industrialized world. At the heart of this ambitious effort was construction of a 3,500-mile highway across Amazonia, along with subsidiary roads.

The program has been a disaster for Brazil and the rest of the world. The richness of the once-vast Amazon forest is in its trees, not its soil. Land cleared by slash-and-burn techniques supports a farmer for a year or two before the soil is dead and the farmer is forced to relocate elsewhere in Amazonia to repeat the destructive process. A pasture carved from the forest is soon barren, each year supporting fewer cattle, some of them destined to feed fast-food appetites in the United States. Amazonia imports more beef than it exports. Some of the big ranchers don't care. They make profits anyway from cushy tax deals, government subsidies, and land speculation.

Satellite photos of just one Brazilian state, Rondonia, record 170,000 or more fires that were ignited to clear the land for the 500,000 colonists who poured into Rondonia in the early 1980s. In 1984, 4,000 square miles of forest were leveled in Rondonia—a rate that at least one study estimated would cut Rondonia's forestland in half by the early 1990s and reduce all of this once-vital acreage to a clearcut disaster area sometime around the turn of the century. As the main road pushed through Rondonia into the adjacent state of Acre, a new wave of colonists moved deeper into Amazonia. They were joined by farmers and small ranchers whose dreams of a new life in Rondonia were dashed by the quick life-and-death cycle of the cleared land.

Caught in the Amazonia land rush were Indians and the rubber tappers who were living in sustainable harmony with the forest. For decades, the rubber tappers had been exploited by the rubber companies, who paid low prices for latex and charged high prices for supplies from company stores. Economic oppression gave way to violence after the ranchers began clearing the forest, often using hired gunmen to evict rubber tappers whose families had been working the same forest trails for generations. In fact, the opening of Amazonia has been compared in its violence to the settling of the American West in the last century.

The destruction of the forest is made even more incomprehensible by data gathered by Steve Schwartzman of the Environmental Defense Fund: A family of rubber tappers, who also gathered Brazil nuts from the forest, made $1,333 a year income in sustainable harmony with its environment; a family working a small farm in Amazonia made $800; a family with a small ranch made $710.

The destruction of the forest clearly has not brought prosperity to Brazil, which continues to be one of the world's largest debtor nations. It has not solved Brazil's unemployment problem, only shifted a portion of it to Amazonia. It has not brought sustainable agriculture to a nation where 5 percent of the population owns 80 percent of the arable land. The Worldwatch Institute says the ravaging of the Amazon forest could hurt agriculture in other portions of Brazil, because the forests of the Amazon basin produce and export much of the water vapor for the entire country. Less forestland means less rainfall elsewhere in the huge nation.

There is collective responsibility for what has occurred in Brazil. Multinational lending agencies, who get their funds from industrialized countries, put up a large chunk of the money to finance the road building that opened up Amazonia. The World Bank was first on the scene until protests by environmentalists, U.S. Senator Robert Kasten of Wisconsin, and Chico Mendes, leader of the rubber tappers, led it to suspend financing. The Inter-American Development Bank moved into the breach until it too reacted to continued protests and stopped bankrolling the main highway through Acre.

But Japan has moved into the financing void with plans to continue the highway all the way to Lima, Peru, on the Pacific coast of South America. This will make it easier for Japan, one of the world's largest consumers of timber, to obtain Amazon hardwoods. They are needed to augment the supply of wood that nation already gets from tropical forests in Indonesia and from North America's premier rain forest—the Tongass National Forest in Alaska.

DEGRADING OUR FERTILE LAND

As we saw in Chapter 2, destruction of tropical forests is a major source of increasing levels of carbon dioxide in our atmosphere and a major contributor to our global warming problems. But the escalating loss of the forests is just one component in another mounting global problem—the degradation of our Earth's land. The Worldwatch Institute lists the three other principal causes as overgrazing of rangelands; overcultivation of croplands; and waterlogging and salinization of irrigated lands.

According to the United Nations, some 23,000 square miles of land worldwide—about the size of Belgium—become irreversibly desertified every year. The United Nations says another 77,000 square miles are degraded annually to the point where they can no longer be farmed or grazed profitably. In 1984, the international organization said that desertification threatened 35 percent of our Earth's land area, with moderate degradation already affecting land that provides a living for 20 percent of the world's population.

A major factor in land degradation is soil erosion, by which the rich organic matter and nutrients in the upper layers of the soil are washed or blown away because of poor agricultural practices and droughts. The Worldwatch Institute estimates that at least 20.3 billion tons of topsoil are carried to the sea by rivers and streams each year. That figure does not include the huge amount of soil sediment that collects behind irrigation and flood-control dams. Once lost, topsoil is not quickly replaced. It takes from 200 to 1,000 years for just 1 inch to form.

To replace the natural nutrients of topsoil, farmers turn to increased fertilization, which only adds to environmental degradation.

But the loss of topsoil is not exclusively a Third World problem. Following the drought-ridden summer of 1988, wind erosion damaged 22,300 acres of our Great Plains in an 8-month period—the worst such soil loss in our prime grain region since record keeping began in 1954, according to Zero Population Growth. What makes this soil loss dramatic is the fact that the United States is one of the few food-producing nations with a conservation program aimed at reducing excessive erosion of topsoil.

There are an estimated 3 billion cattle, sheep, goats, and camels living on the pasturelands of our planet. More than half the world's pastoralists live in Africa, but the perennial grasses on Africa's rangelands are being trampled and devoured by ever-increasing livestock herds. Overgrazing eventually leaves the ground barren, and a crusty top layer of dirt prevents plant roots from penetrating into the soil. Severe erosion follows, and the land quickly turns to desert. Nomadic pastoralists then move on, and the degradation is repeated elsewhere. This is not only the case in Africa, but all over the world as humans try to reconcile the destructively synergistic forces of increasing population and decreasing food production.

OUR DECREASING FOOD SUPPLY

The years after World War II were very good ones for the world's granaries. Grain production worldwide climbed from 624 million tons in 1950 to 1.64 billion tons in 1984, a 40 percent increase in the amount of grain available around the planet on a per capita basis. There were success stories everywhere, according to Worldwatch Institute. Between 1970 and 1984, Indonesia doubled its harvests of grain, almost all of it rice. Mexico raised its grain production fourfold between 1950 and 1984. China, our Earth's most populated nation, used a variety of agricultural technologies to increase its grain production by nearly 50 percent from 1976 to 1984.

But in the four years following 1984, the world's total harvest declined 14 percent. Some of the decrease was attributed to natural disasters, like the 1987 monsoons in India and the serious droughts that struck Canada, China, and the United States the following year. World harvests in 1987 were 85 million tons below 1986. The falloff in 1988 amounted to 76 million tons of grains that provide half of all the calories to humans when consumed directly and some of the rest when consumed in grain-fed cattle and poultry.

When the 1987 harvests began, the world's storehouses contained enough grain to feed everyone for 101 days. Yet, we entered the 1989 planting season with an estimated 54 days' supply—the lowest point since 57 days' supply at the beginning of 1973.

In 1950, only Western Europe and Asia imported more grain than they produced themselves. Net exporters were Australia, Latin America, North America, and New Zealand. Africa, Eastern Europe, and the Soviet Union were self-sustaining.

By 1988, Western Europe was a net exporter of grain, but Africa, Eastern Europe, Latin America, and the Soviet Union were net importers. So was Asia, where imports totaled 12 times what they were in 1950.

The world's food growing area increased by some 24 percent between 1950 and 1981, when it reached an all-time high. It has since fallen by about 7 percent. Some lands have been taken out of production to preserve and rejuvenate them. However, others have been degraded by poor and nonsustainable growing practices. For instance, prolonged irrigation causes a buildup in the soil of salts that are toxic to many food plants. This unsustainable practice is also lowering underground water tables around the world. And these aquifers cannot be quickly replenished. The Worldwatch Institute says that if the estimated 57 million tons of grain produced by unsustainable irrigation in the United States were subtracted from global grain production, worldwide demand would exceed worldwide production.

POLLUTING OUR OCEANS

We cannot rely on the oceans to fill the nourishment gap. The waters that comprise 71 percent of our Earth's surface area are being overfished and assaulted by air pollution, direct dumping of hazardous waste, and impure runoffs from our farmlands and coastal cities.

In 1950, the oceans supplied 21 million tons of fish to feed us. The sea harvest jumped to 70 million tons in 1970 and today hovers around 84 million tons. Many experts warn that we cannot expect the tonnage to increase very much over the next few decades. Six fisheries in the Atlantic Ocean and five in the Pacific have become so depleted that commercial fishing is no longer practical in those areas. The United Nations Food and Agriculture Organization estimates that 42 other fisheries are either overexploited or severely depleted.

The fishing industry is trying to combat decreasing catches with more efficient fishing techniques. In the northern Pacific, Japanese, South Korean, and Taiwanese boats are destroying entire populations of marine life with drift nets. Each night, upward of 700 boats deploy these vast nets over an area of sea the size of Ohio. They vacuum the waters, taking in many forms of marine life, the edible and the inedible. In 1988, the pink salmon fishery in Alaska expected to harvest 122 million fish. It brought only 40 million back to port. Many marine scientists believe these and similar statistics for other commercial fisheries are a direct result of drift-net fishing.

Fish are very important to the grain-importing countries in the Third World. Fish account for 40 percent of the developing world's total consumption of animal protein. For the world as a whole, fish supply about one-fourth of our animal protein intake. Globally, about 100 million people depend directly on the oceans for a livelihood. Many of them work in the chronically depressed Third World.

The United Nations has attempted to control the pollution and overexploitation of the marine environment. In 1970, it convened the Third Law of the Sea Conference to study marine issues and set international regulations governing the use of the oceans. Of the 150 nations attending the conference, 125 signed the draft agreement. Today, only nine have actually ratified it. It has been rejected by ratifying authorities in 35 nations, including three of the world's major maritime nations: the United Kingdom, the United States, and West Germany.

OVERPOPULATING OUR PLANET

We're now ready for our Earth's most challenging environmental problem: population growth. The late Margaret Mead, an anthropologist who spent many years studying Third World cultures, once wrote that "every human society is faced with not one population problem but two: how to beget and rear enough children and how not to beget and rear too many."

At the start of the industrial revolution, when we began

infusing our atmosphere with the steady upswing of carbon dioxide emissions that are warming it, approximately 500 million people populated the planet. Today, the head count stands at 5.2 billion and is growing at an alarming rate. The Population Institute in Washington says that 23 humans are born every 5 seconds, 397,440 every day, about 145 million a year, leaving our planet with a net annual population gain of some 93 million people. Experts on overpopulation say that unless there is a change in our current birth and death rates, the number of people contending for the world's diminishing resources will double to 10.4 billion by 2029. The birth rate could grow even more because 3 billion young people—equal to the world's census in 1960—will enter their reproductive years in the coming three decades.

Our population explosion is not happening equally around the world. Areas with more grain than they consume—the United States and Western Europe—have lower birth rates. Population growth is occurring where it can least be afforded in economic, social, health, and nutritional terms. Forty percent of the developing world's population is under the age of 15 and approaching their most reproductive years. Ninety countries, virtually all of them in the Third World, will double their populations in the next generation. It would be difficult enough for the industrialized world—with its per capita gross national product of $12,000—to double its food production, jobs, public and social services over 30 years.

Consider the immensity of the problem in the developing world with its per-person gross national product averaging $610 and its already high rates of poverty, unemployment, hunger, and illiteracy. To accommodate their growing populations, the nations of the Southern Hemisphere alone must create 800 million new jobs by 2000. Many of the people who will be born in the Third World in the next generation will be crammed into urban slums. In 1950, the developing world had only one city with a population exceeding 5 million. The Population Institute projects 46 such teeming urban areas by 2000.

The combination of overpopulation and poverty can produce political unrest in both rural areas and cities as the land gets overcrowded and less productive. Central America is already a relatively unstable area politically. There are now more than 100 million people living off the land between the Rio Grande and the Isthmus of Panama. Their numbers are expected to rise to 225 million by 2025.

The world must soon answer two very basic questions raised by our global population explosion and our declining rate of food production. Where are all the human beings going to live? And what are they going to eat?

PEOPLE MAKING A DIFFERENCE

•

MECHAI VIRAVAIDYA

When someone buys a condom in Thailand, they usually ask for a "mechai." And when they talk about one of the Third World's most successful family planning advocates, they use the same word.

Meet master showman Mechai Viravaidya, the P.T. Barnum of birth control. Since founding the nonprofit Population and Community Development Association (PDA) in 1974, he's been a glitzy, yet serious superstar who has helped cut Thailand's population growth dramatically.

His methods? Balloon-blowing contests with condoms; brightly hued condoms attached to his business cards; distribution of birth-control key chains—a condom encased in clear plastic with the legend, "In Case of Emergency, Break Glass." PDA advertises birth-control methods on television and through T-shirts that read "A Condom a Day Keeps the Doctor Away," "Stop at Two," and "Too Many Children Make You Poor."

In the early days, Mechai distributed condoms in traffic jams and at movie theaters, boxing matches and religious festivals. On New Year's Eve, traffic policemen are given condoms to distribute in Mechai's "cops and rubbers" operation. He's installed vending machines in bus terminals that sell a full range of birth-control devices. Taxi drivers who sell a quota of condoms get car insurance paid by the PDA.

There's a reason for all the hoopla. "If one can get people to laugh together about the topic of family planning, the battle is half over," says Mechai, who was educated as an economist and has worked as a development official for the government, written newspaper columns, acted in a Thai TV soap opera, and had a nightly radio show with a trademark sign-off: "Don't Forget Your Pill."

Behind the showmanship is a national network of thousands of family planning centers encouraged by the government. Thailand's dominant religion, Theraveda Buddhism, carries no taboo against family planning. Thailand's population growth rate fell from 3.2 percent in 1970 to 1.7 percent in 1988. Birth control is as prevalent in rural areas as it is in teeming, urban Bangkok.

Mechai believes that population control in the Third World must accompany economic growth, rather than follow it. "Most developing countries have separate fertility and development programs," he told author Pranay Gupte. "But if you couple them, the chances are greater that you will have increased economic growth and decreased population growth. One just has to link population control with development."

A case in point is Mahasarakham, Thailand's second poorest province. At the urging of Mechai and the PDA, the provincial governor linked aid for farmers to the recipients' agreement to limit family size. A single office dispenses birth control devices and agricultural assistance. This, Mechai says, is not coercion. "It is just that if you agree to practice family planning, you get the first crack at low-interest loans and technical expertise. We want to achieve the twin goals of a better life and reduced population growth."

WHAT WE CAN DO

What can we do to help put our Earth and its population in balance? We can start by recognizing that the United States consumes far more energy and raw materials per person than almost any other nation. The more we can reduce the amount of energy and resources each one of us consumes, the more we can put our resource base and our population in balance—and the less we will consume resources from other parts of the world that are essential to their resource balance.

The phrase "think globally, act locally" cannot be repeated too often. The same measures that we have discussed to help solve environmental problems at home will also help improve the world resource balance.

Organizational pressure can be brought to bear: The environmental community has already forced the World Bank to stop making development loans that lead to destruction of rain forests.

Beyond what we can do as individuals, we need to be aware of how U.S. policies affect the world's resource base. We must examine requests to assist development projects that, on first blush, look like lifesavers, but then turn sour. For instance, as a nation, we have learned that damming rivers to allow widespread irrigation has created unarable land due to salinization. So our policies should not encourage irrigation dams in other countries.

Similarly, we should be cautious about exporting our agricultural techniques. The hope of the Green Revolution got mired down in the expense and pollution from massive doses of pesticides and fertilizers. We must recognize that some of the most serious environmental destruction on our Earth is directly traceable to the ingenuity of American inventors and research scientists. In a sense, we invented hazardous and nuclear waste.

When it comes to disposing of these wastes, we must remember that the world is our backyard. We can't solve our waste problems by exporting them. When we choose household cleaning products that are not hazardous, we decrease pressure to export wastes to the other side of the globe. And when we choose alternatives to building nuclear power plants, we make it less likely that our country will fail to find an acceptable waste site here and begin looking overseas. It would be a sad day, indeed, if we were to even consider asking a starving nation to take our nuclear waste or to decide whether a continuing supply of our surplus wheat is worth the price of spending 250,000 years living with some of the most vile byproducts of our civilization.

The process of healing our Earth's wounds begins with the individual and the belief that one person's actions in the United States contribute either to the cleaning of our Earth or to its continued fouling. Where we set our thermostats has a direct bearing not only on the levels of air pollution around our own homes but on acid-rain levels in Canada and the amount of carbon dioxide in our planet's atmosphere. So do our decisions about whether to buy a fuel-hungry car to use for solitary commuting or whether to car-pool, take public transportation, or ride a bicycle to work.

Our individual actions and environmental advocacy are forces for demonstrable change when they are shared by enough people. For instance, the U.S. ban on the use of chlorofluorocarbons in spray cans began at the grassroots, not at the top. The global lesson here is not that most of the rest of the world has failed to follow our lead. It is that we as individuals and a nation have avoided loading our atmosphere with tons of CFCs that would now, had we not acted, be helping to destroy our Earth's ozone layer.

We have learned—or should have—from misadventures like

South Vietnam, Nicaragua, and Lebanon that we cannot be the military policeman of the world. Neither can we become its environmental policeman. It is incumbent on us—not as the world's model for democracy, but as the world's biggest polluter—to set the example for all nations in curing our Earth's environmental sickness.

We have no right, for example, to complain to Mexico about the fallout in Arizona from its copper smelters as long as coal-fired generators in the Midwest are helping to destroy Canadian forests. We cannot protest when Latin American sends us produce laden with pesticides banned in this country as long as our chemical factories are making and exporting these poisons to Latin America. We may deplore the destruction of tropical rain forests and its impact on global warming. But we cannot preach to a Third World that is trying to feed its hungry and resettle its poor so long as we refuse to force our automakers to produce cars that are far more energy efficient and far less destructive to the climate of our planet. We cannot condemn China for basing its industrial development on its coal reserves when we continue to burn coal without spending the money required to develop safe, clean renewable forms of energy that the entire community of nations would be able to use.

As a nation, we are the composite of our individual actions. If we all live in harmony with nature and follow the path of environmental sustainability in our daily lives, it is more likely that our government will follow suit. A step as simple as composting our garbage is but one of the individual strides we can take along the path to sustainable development. This is a path that our nation and all nations must begin following if we are to save our Earth from ourselves and leave our children a better legacy than they now face.

PEOPLE MAKING A DIFFERENCE

———————— • ————————

CHICO MENDES

© MIRANDA SMITH PRODUCTIONS, INC., 1988

Environmental destruction has many victims but few martyrs. The 2,500 or more people killed by the poison gas leak in Bhopal, India, were victims. Chico Mendes, who died defending Brazil's rain forest and way of life, was a martyr.

Amnesty International says Amazonian land disputes e. ded in more than 1,000 murders in the 1980s. When Mendes was gunned down three days before Christmas 1988, the shot echoed worldwide.

Mendes was a *seringueiro*, a rubber tapper who led his forest-dwelling colleagues in the fight against the ecological massacre of Amazonia. By the late 1980s, 372,000 square miles of the world's biggest and most biologically diverse tropical forest had been destroyed—one-eighth of Amazonia, equal in area to California, Washington, and Montana combined—and at the rate of one football field every 5 seconds.

A third-generation *seringueiro*, Mendes learned to tap rubber trees at age 7. A decade later, he learned reading and politics from a dissident Army officer hiding in the forest. Like tens of thousands of other solitary *seringueiros*, Mendes gathered renewables, latex, and brazil nuts for a living.

For decades, *seringueiros* were exploited by the rubber barons, companies that pay low prices for latex and charge high ones for supplies. In the 1970s, Brazil began building roads into Amazonia, bringing in poor homesteaders and big ranchers whose chopping and burning displaced rubber tappers and Indians.

Ranchers soon controlled about two-thirds of the remote state where Mendes and other rubber tappers practiced their environmentally sustainable trade. Ranchers, often obtaining land titles by bribery, hired gunmen to evict *seringueiros*. As co-founder of the rubber tappers' association, Mendes saved 3 million acres of rainforest by rallying scores of *seringueiro* families to form a human blockade against bulldozers and chainsaws. In 1979, Mendes was kidnapped and beaten almost senseless. When the association president was slain in 1980, Mendes took over.

Protests, arrests, organizing, death threats, hiding out, and long absences from his wife and two children became a way of life for Mendes. In place of *seringueiros*, he saw homesteaders working infertile land for a year or two before moving on to repeat the "farm-and-fail" process. He saw huge ranches supporting increasingly fewer head of cattle and Amazonia importing more beef than it exported.

Mendes also ignited the fury of deforestation foes outside Brazil. Pressure from Mendes, environmentalists, and members of Congress forced the World Bank and the Inter-American Development Bank to withdraw loans for Amazon road building. However, Japan, the world's largest buyer of tropical hardwoods, agreed to finance the project.

Mendes's most tangible legacy was to convince Brazil to create "extractive reserves"—5 million acres set aside for environmentally sound development. "Our goal," he said, "is not to preserve the forest like some untouchable sanctuary but to develop rational uses. Cattle ranching and agriculture are irrational uses. They create a factory of misery."

A friend, Steve Schwartzman of the Environmental Defense Fund, says Mendes's fight to save the forest taught the world that "environmental protection in the Amazon and the developing world in general can't be separated from social justice for the people who live there."

CHAPTER NINE

A Call To Action

·

BECOMING AN ENVIRONMENTAL ACTIVIST

BY RUTH CAPLAN

The previous chapters clearly demonstrate that we are headed down a path we cannot sustain. The good news is that we can choose to walk another path. Our first step in this new direction is understanding how each of us is part of the problem and how we can become a part of the solution.

In each chapter you have read about ways to alter daily habits so that you can lead a more environmentally conscious life. Not only do these suggestions help us have a positive impact as individuals, they encourage us to think about how our individual actions are connected to larger problems and how possible solutions can affect not just our own lives but those of our neighbors and larger communities.

The behavior of individuals must change, but so must that of corporations and all levels of government. How can we eat pesticide-free fruits and vegetables if our supermarket doesn't carry them? How can we breathe clean air if our neighbor is a polluting chemical plant? How can we cut down on driving if we have inadequate public transportation? There needs to be a shift in the locus of power. Citizens should have power over investment decisions in their community; workers power over environmental conditions at their workplace; consumers power over the products and packaging available on supermarket shelves.

This requires that each of us as consumers stand up for our rights to purchase products that don't pollute our world or strip it of nonrenewable resources. It requires that each of us encourage businesses to choose this path and support such efforts in the marketplace. It requires that we get organized.

In each chapter, you have read stories of people who went beyond individual actions to organize in their community or workplace. Their actions *made a difference*. The purpose of this chapter is to provide you with some of the tools for effective action—tools that you can use to make a difference in your own community.

ONE PATH TO ENVIRONMENTALISM

Not many of us start out intending to become an environmental activist. I know, I didn't. But as I struggled to understand and respond to environmental problems in my own backyard, I learned that there was much more I could do to bring about change than I ever dreamed possible.

My first tentative steps down the environmental path came on Earth Day 1970. Hearing the drums of environmental activism across the country, I joined with others in my community who walked the shoreline of Lake Ontario in upstate New York picking up bottles and cans. Nothing more came from that walk, at least not right away. I did, however, keep in touch with the latest developments in the environmental movement through *Environmental Action*, a magazine published in Washington by the organizers of the first Earth Day.

About a year later, a few friends got together to talk about the environmental problems we had been reading about and discuss what we could do about them. Most of us had young children, and we wanted them to have healthy food and a safe environment. So we started meeting together informally, sharing ideas and encouraging each other. We began to recycle our glass bottles and aluminum cans, and those of us with babies switched from the new disposable diapers to reusable cloth. Wherever possible, we began to use our bikes instead of hopping into the car, and we bought bike seats to carry our toddlers.

As others heard about our meetings, they wanted to join. Our small group of friends evolved into a larger, more serious organization. We began to look beyond our individual actions on the home front to what we could do to improve our town's environment. Ecology Action of Oswego was born.

And then into our world of young children and vegetable gardens came a local strawberry farmer. Inviting himself to one of our meetings, he arrived with a tape recorder in hand and a message to share. On the tape, Dr. Arthur Tamplin, a nuclear chemist from Lawrence Livermore Laboratory, talked about plutonium. We all listened intently as he described how plutonium is created by nuclear fission; how it is radioactive and very dangerous if it gets into human lungs; and how it decays very slowly, retaining half its potency after 24,000 years; and how our country was building its energy supply around nuclear power plants and fast moving toward a "plutonium economy."

The strawberry farmer's interest in nuclear power was more than academic. His farm was next door to a nuclear power plant that Niagara Mohawk, our upstate New York utility, had started to operate in 1969 at Nine Mile Point. He told us that the New York State Power Authority was building another one out there, 9 miles from the center of our town. He left us with a challenge: "What are you going to do about it?"

With this challenge and Dr. Tamplin's words echoing in our ears, we vowed to educate ourselves on nuclear power. For almost a year we read everything we could get our hands on, sharing every word of information with each other. We learned about leaking nuclear waste storage tanks in Hanford, Washington, and contaminated streams at a waste site in Maxey Flats, Kentucky. We learned of the government's plans to build "breeder reactors" fueled with plutonium. And we discovered there already was a "reprocessing" plant in West Valley, New York, where plutonium was separated from other nuclear waste and where workers were being exposed to radiation.

The more we learned, the more convinced we became that there were far safer ways to boil water for steam generators than with nuclear plants. It wasn't just our backyard we were concerned about—nuclear power was already causing problems in many parts of the country.

We heard that the federal government wanted to build nuclear plants all along the coast, since Lake Ontario was seen as a massive source of water perfect for cooling the reactors. We also heard that the governor of New York was trying to get the federal government's experimental breeder reactor located in upstate New York, making use of the West Valley reprocessing plant to separate out the uranium fuel that could be resued. All this was going on with no input from the very citizens who would be the neighbors of the nuclear plants.

Then a public notice appeared in our local newspaper. The U.S. Atomic Energy Commission notified us that the Power Authority wanted permission to operate the reactor they had been building. Then a second notice appeared and that was the real shocker: Niagara Mohawk wanted permission to construct a third nuclear plant at Nine Mile Point. The notices told us in small print that there would be hearings and that interested parties could petition to intervene.

The day of reckoning had arrived. Would we continue to be a study group, or had we learned enough to know we didn't want another nuclear plant in our backyard? Our group met to plan our response to these notices. It was a very long meeting that night, and in the end we didn't all agree. But about half of us decided it was time for action. It felt like my first jump off a diving board—scary, but exhilarating.

Our next step involved learning about what it meant to intervene. We had to find a lawyer willing to represent us. This was a big challenge, particularly because we had no money. But this was the only way we could present our concerns at the required hearings.

If we had any doubt that we were making the right decision, it was instantly dispelled by our first public meeting on the proposed plant, which we held at the local high school. We invited Niagara Mohawk to make a presentation. Having studied nuclear power for a whole year, we were well-prepared to ask a wide range of questions. Niagara Mohawk presented a simplistic slide show portraying the "wonders" of nuclear power. Three slides were used to show us how the AEC would protect us. One slide was of a red book. One of a green book. And one of a blue book. With these three books of federal regulations we need not worry, said our utility.

What about the leaking tanks at Hanford? The contaminated water in Maxey Flats? The leaking storage pits in West Valley, New York? Where was the AEC? From everything I'd read, they weren't doing anything, except saying there were no problems. The more detailed our questions, the more uninformative were their answers. We left the meeting angry and more convinced than ever that we had to get involved.

Fortunately, we found a lawyer at a nearby law school. We became intervenors, and we worked closely with our lawyer to prepare for the hearings. We tracked down expert witnesses. I still remember mustering my courage and calling Cornell University to ask an economist to provide expert testimony about electricity demand projections. And, we helped finance our efforts by selling tacos at the town fair.

Well, we didn't stop those two reactors, but we certainly made a difference. We forced the AEC to look at energy efficiency and renewables as alternatives to building a nuclear plant—a precedent for the country. And by submitting our own testimony on how much electricity people would need in future years, we showed the state, which was just beginning to require utilities to make 15-year projections, that these projections were way off base. And our projections would prove invaluable to us in future fights.

We had learned you just can't win against the AEC. No one had won, and there were intervenors like us all across the country. But all our interventions had been very important in educating people about the problems with nuclear power. As a result, more and more people began questioning the nuclear future being touted by the AEC and the electric utilities. No longer did we feel like we were a voice crying out in the wilderness.

And thanks to our lawyer, a teacher of law in the truest sense, we learned how to bring our case before the AEC. This legal knowledge came in handy. Even before we received the final decision on the new plant, known as "Nine Mile Two," another utility announced its plans to build a nuclear plant with four other utilities on the other side of town. Out of money, but not out of spirit, we spent the next 5 years serving as our own lawyers fighting the Sterling nuclear plant.

This time we made our presence known beyond the hearing room. We found support from environmental and peace groups in nearby cities—Ithaca, Rochester, and Syracuse. And we discovered that farmers didn't want the high-voltage transmission lines running across their land, lines that would have to be built to bring the electricity from the nuclear plant. Together, we formed the Lakeshore Alliance. Together, we educated, demonstrated, and sent out a resounding message—"No More Nukes." Together, we won.

We kept organizing after the Nuclear Regulatory Commission gave the go-ahead to Sterling. We kept organizing after the newly formed state siting board gave its approval. We kept organizing while we appealed both decisions. Finally, with the facts behind us so we could argue convincingly that the electricity from this plant was simply not needed, we got the state siting board to reverse its approval. Most importantly, the *local* member of the siting board changed his vote! I'll never forget sitting in the back of that hearing room in Albany with one of the two other women who had carried on the legal work with me and watching the front row of utility lawyers turn around and file out, looking neither right nor left. Once they had smirked at our participation. Now we had defeated five electric utilities in the state along with their bevies of lawyers, who earned more than $5 million. We hadn't earned a penny, but we went home knowing we had made a difference.

And it wasn't just the legal work that made the difference. The fact that so many people were involved convinced the siting board to reconsider its decision. The marches, the rallies, the TV coverage had not gone unnoticed. And we won because people in upstate New York had begun to take conservation seriously and use less electricity. The combination of organizing, individual actions, and legal strategies added up to the final victory.

GETTING ORGANIZED

WORLD HUNGER EDUCATION SERVICE

The best way to become an environmental activist is to join a group. In the Appendix, we list a wide range of environmental organizations. Some national organizations have local groups and chapters. Others have resources you can use locally.

If you want to work on a local environmental problem, you will often find it is best to start a group in your own community. This gives you flexibility to structure the group to meet your community's specific needs and to assure a sense of local control. But whether you join an existing group or form your own, the following discussion of the dynamics of how to build a group will help assure that your group works together productively.

This chapter helps you go beyond individual efforts to a real community movement. But first you may ask: Why organize?

When you begin to work with a group, you will have the support of shared goals and shared work. You will also be able to draw on the special talents of people in your community so that you can become experts on the problems you care about the most.

It is critically important to get other people involved—and to *keep them involved.*

PREPARING TO ORGANIZE

The first step of imagining yourself as an organizer is always the hardest. Your first reaction is likely to be: "I've never organized anything in my life!" But good organizing is just good common sense. Much of what you do every day involves the use of basic organizing skills. Have you ever organized a business meeting, a church picnic, a neighborhood garage sale, a PTA bake sale, a school carnival, or even a friend's birthday party? If so, you have already learned the basic tenets of successful organizing:

- Find a lot of people to help
- Share tasks
- Keep up group morale
- Keep people oriented toward the tasks ahead
- Acknowledge people for their role
- Celebrate group successes

Many groups begin like ours did in Oswego—a group of friends with similar concerns meeting together. But if you are to be effective, you will need to broaden your efforts. The next sections provide guideposts for organizing a successful group.

DECIDING ON GOALS

By the time you are ready to work with a group, you have already done a lot of thinking about the problems you see in your community. But if you are going to have a successful group, the group first has to agree on the problem or problems it will work on. Unless there is an immediate threat to the community, such as a hazardous waste dump oozing into drinking water wells, most groups begin with an exploratory phase.

Stating the problem is only the prelude to turning *problems* into *issues*. Having a clear issue statement assists the group in at least three ways. It identifies those responsible for the problem. It guides the group toward a solution. It also makes planning tactics easier.

First, state the problem in crisp, concrete, specific terms. Second, pinpoint the group's "target." The target might be the company that was responsible for causing the problem. Or the target might be the officials who have the power to respond to the problem. Sometimes, the same target that caused the problem also has the power to provide a solution.

The group also needs to express clearly what remedies it seeks to address the problem. Then you will be ready to set down a list of steps you will need to take. But before you can do this, you may need to research the problem further. You will also find that your priorities will change as you learn more about the problem.

Often, a new group tends to think in grand terms. But by making its goals too broad, a group will soon feel powerlessness; the problem seems simply too big to solve. Take the example of a small community where runoff from a rocket production plant has contaminated drinking water.

Approach A

Problem: "Industry in our town is polluting us!"

Solution: "Stop all toxic waste now!"

Likely result:

If you use this approach to get other people to join you, success is unlikely. The first statement does not define the problem in a specific way that people can grasp. And the proposed solution is unmanageable. While everyone might agree about the problem, no one will stay involved in an effort that is so diffused and difficult to tackle.

Approach B

Issue:

Giant Rocket Company, under chairman of the board Michael Gerardi, has dumped three cancer-causing chemicals near our drinking water wells and has made our families sick.

Solution:

The Neighbors Action Group (NAG) believes better health will result if Gerardi agrees to:

1. Meet with NAG members and state and federal officials.
2. Provide us with bottled water immediately.
3. Agree with the state to stop discharges into the Foamy Creek Valley.
4. Adopt an alternate source reduction and recycling plan for Giant Rocket Company.
5. Compensate the victims of Giant's dumping practices.

Likely result:

People will want to join the group. They can understand the specific issue, and the group has proposed definite solutions to meet people's concerns. Individuals can see how they can help the group keep pressure on Giant.

Setting realistic goals prevents later disappointment. It even allows citizen groups and organizers to give themselves credit when they accomplish a goal. Good morale makes for a better group. Whether you are forming a new group or pulling together a coalition of groups to work on a problem, the name you choose will send an important message about your group's goals. Many groups choose names with initials that form an acronym like "STOP"—Stop Torrent of Pollutants.

GETTING OTHERS TO PARTICIPATE

The easiest way to begin organizing is with your own friends, the organizations you work with, and other friendly organizations. Beyond this, you need to think about whom you want to help you take action on the environmental problem or problems you care about the most. Who will share your views? Who will bring the expertise you need?

Usually, two types of people join local environmental groups. One is people who are directly affected by the problem. The other includes people or organizations that, for a variety of reasons, might support the goals of the people whom the problem affects directly. Organizers often set out to persuade people in the first category to join. After all, this is their issue. In communities with a well-identified toxic dumpsite, for instance, this means talking to the people who live closest to the dump. Possibilities for later contact include neighbors, sympathetic clergy, a local environmental group, and a local union. Local colleges can provide experts on environmental problems.

How do you recruit new members to the group? Knocking on doors is the most direct way to begin. You should have a simple leaflet that gives very basic information about the cause for concern, along with a proposed statement of the group's purpose and a telephone number of a contact person. The leaflet can also ask neighborhood residents to attend a meeting.

Door-to-door canvassing takes more time than simply dropping off some literature, because you will want to spend time talking with people. But the process can produce valuable one-on-one dialogue and new members for your organization. Canvassing can help you better understand the opinions of people who may not agree with your position and give you insight in how to address these people in future educational efforts. If nobody is home when you do your canvassing, leave some information anyway.

A petition directed at city or county government officials gives you names for followup at the same time you are building public pressure. This is a good way to meet neighbors and talk about the issue as part of a door-knocking campaign.

A public meeting draws attention from neighborhood residents and the press. This gives new people a chance to see what you are about, before they may feel comfortable attending a small meeting in someone's home. Be sure to have a signup sheet at the door and to follow up by contacting all the people who sign your sheet by phone or mail within the next week. Explore with them their interest and what they might want to contribute—time, talent, money. Whatever approach you take, remember that people are most likely to turn out if they make a commitment to do so.

KEEPING PEOPLE INVOLVED

Once you have gotten people to attend one meeting, you want to keep them coming back. The best way to hold their interest is to make sure people feel they are making a real contribution and each person is recognized for the work they have done. This can be as simple as a pat on the back or acknowledging a person's contribution at a group meeting. Also keep in mind that people are attracted to a group that projects an upbeat attitude; they want to feel their time will be well-spent.

Holding Meetings
As any group organizes, it will have to handle many items of business. New matters will always arise. The group will need to become familiar with three tasks. These are: managing information, setting priorities for activities, and making decisions to move the group forward.

Meetings should be fun and sociable without seeming silly or frivolous, orderly but not stiff, and everyone should be able to have their say without launching into long-winded speeches. To make meetings more productive and accomplishments more likely, activists should never underestimate the importance of clearly defining a meeting's agenda and strategically selecting a meeting time.

Developing an Agenda

Every group needs an "agenda" — a list of topics to be addressed at a meeting. The agenda should be neatly typed or written, but it need not be fancy. Agendas can present topics in order of importance or in the preferred order of discussion. At the beginning of the meeting, ask if there are any additions to the agenda, and assign each item a set amount of time so the meeting keeps moving and all points are covered. Agree in advance when the meeting will end, and try to stick to that deadline. Make sure you allow for input from participants so everyone feels involved. Be willing to discuss and adapt the original strategy to keep the action moving.

The phone calls or letters that go out to inform members about the meeting should mention the agenda. For example, "We're having a meeting on Monday night at the school to discuss a plan to ask the Mayor to meet with us."

One person should keep the meeting on track. As the group discusses each item on the agenda, this person — often called the "chair" or "facilitator" — makes sure that the group has decided what action to take (if any) and that everyone understands what the decisions are. The meeting's leader should also take note of who will do what tasks and how. At the end of the meeting, the leader can quickly summarize the decisions, the task assignments, the goals connected to the tasks, and the arrangements for the next meeting.

BROADENING THE GROUP TO
NEW MEMBERS

As your organization develops an identity and a track record, more people will want to get involved. Groups must have a clear-cut plan for how to reach out and involve new members. Group leaders and members alike should be aware that new members will take some time to get "up to speed" on more complicated issues. At the same time, the group should help new members feel there are very real ways to get involved immediately. Too often, new people come to a group meeting where no one pays attention to them. New people arrive and depart without introduction or recognition. Sometimes, the group does not make an effort to "catch them up" on its activities. Here are some suggestions on how groups can help new members feel comfortable:

- Form a "new members" committee. This committee can develop outreach plans for new members. The committee can also tell new members about group history and current activities.
- Develop an information packet. A simple packet of information sheets allows people to "brief" themselves at home, at their own pace. The sheets should address the issues and how the group approaches specific problems.
- Leaders of meetings must avoid using jargon. Even a group of people familiar with the issues has trouble following a statement like this: "Giant Corp. has violated its NPDES permit. We're going to meet with the EPA, DEQ, and CDC to check into using CERCLA and RCRA to find out about all the TCE, TCA, and PCE in our alluvial aquifer." In fact, this kind of language will send new people out the door, never to return.

Good leaders are good teachers. By remembering they had

to learn from scratch, leaders can help the rest of the group become knowledgeable. Leaders who operate on the principle, "Everything I know you can know, and I'll teach you," are likely to meet with success. Leaders who say, "Oh, leave that up to me. . . . You don't need to know that," will not foster group spirit. People will not join the group if they feel stupid or too far behind to catch up.

Information is a tool people and groups can use to obtain power. Providing the whole group with information and knowing how to use that information, places power in each member's hands. Together, a well-informed group will be more powerful and more successful.

KEEPING AN ORGANIZATION TOGETHER

All members should understand the normal procedures of the organization. Who calls meetings? Do committees exist? Which members serve on which committees? Does the group make decisions by majority rule? By consensus? Who speaks for the group in public? How does the group ensure that its spokespeople make statements to the public and press that accurately reflect group policy? Who manages the group finances and how? What posts must the group fill to keep functioning?

Deciding on answers to these questions will help the group avoid conflicts and mistakes. In addition, each group needs to decide how to rotate, communicate, recreate, evaluate, and celebrate!

HOW TO ROTATE

"Mary's the only person who ever goes on TV!". . . "I do all the work on the mailings!". . . Such statements will come from unhappy members of a group that need to take a second look at the organization. It is especially important that the group rotate the least favorite tasks or have everyone get together to do these tasks quickly. Does Sandy always address the mailings and take them to the post office? Next time, the group should hold a mailing party, and treat Sandy to the extra piece of pizza.

HOW TO COMMUNICATE

How does the group spread new information among its members and the community? No matter how simple or low-budget a group is, it should establish a way to communicate regularly with its members and the community. A newsletter is a good way to inform people, to give notice about upcoming events, and to recruit new people for the effort. Newsletter writing is easy. Writers should use simple, nontechnical language. Each issue should offer an invitation for new people to get involved. Also, each issue should let readers know what the group has accomplished. Remember that big victories come as the result of many small steps.

THE NEED TO RECREATE

The group should allow for "time-out" periods. These periods allow members to recharge their batteries by taking their minds off the issue and to pay attention to family needs. Of course, sharing the load among a wider circle of people reduces the chance that a few people will get burned out.

Admitting the tensions that exist within a group and having a sense of humor about them are two good ways to face problems, along with taking time out. "We're forming a social group of women in our area who are fighting toxics, just to find a time to laugh and support each other," says Penny Newman of California's Concerned Neighbors in Action. "If we can't laugh at ourselves and the experiences we've been through, we'd go crazy."

The group also needs to involve the spouses and children of leaders in some way, so families feel more united. In some families, only one partner participates in the group, but the spouse may still want to come to public meetings or victory parties, especially if the group designs the events to make everyone feel included.

HOW TO EVALUATE

Each success or failure a group experiences must undergo evaluation. This helps build a stronger group as well as increase its chances for success. Two yardsticks exist to measure and evaluate a group's plans and activities:

- Has the activity helped build the group, involving more people in more substantial tasks?
- Has the activity/plan/campaign brought the group closer toward its goals?

If the evaluation process produces a "no" answer to either of these questions, the group needs to adjust its focus or its activities.

THE NEED TO CELEBRATE

It may seem obvious, but in the heat of battle, groups often forget to stop and celebrate their victories. Celebrations are a chance for members to recognize each others' work and remember that life exists outside "the issue." What's more, celebrations remind the group that it is winning along the way in the struggle to achieve its long-term goals.

KEEPING UNITED

Community groups must be aware of the varying opinions and needs of their members. They must be open to including all types of people, and be able to use their differences to the group's advantage. It is important for organizers to remember that people from different religious backgrounds can bring a wide variety of institutional supports to the cause. In addition, one issue can unite people of different races and economic backgrounds.

Every member of the group must take care to preserve group unity. To avoid the in-group syndrome, make a special effort to hold your meetings in different neighborhoods and at different kinds of local institutions. If your meetings are always in the same neighborhood, home, or church, not everyone in a diverse group will feel equally comfortable, and you will miss an important opportunity to get to know each other better.

Be sure to include new members: Bringing a new person into a project that is already in the works provides a chance to show the new member the ropes and bring that person into the group in a more concrete way.

Having a "star" in your midst may be very destructive to good group dynamics. When newspapers, television, radio stations, and magazines are all looking for one person to talk to—a star or leader—they encourage this dynamic.

These are only a few examples of possible sources of conflict within groups. With some foresight, diplomacy, and an honest recognition of normal group dynamics, these types of problems can easily be resolved.

LEARNING ABOUT THE ISSUE

JOHN C. EVANS

Before you are ready to select the action that is most appropriate for the problem and your community, you need to spend some time learning about the issue. Defining an issue may require research by group members—talking to experts, looking for information in libraries, and contacting other activists concerned about similar problems.

The two main sources of information you will want to pursue are government and private industry. In learning about your issue, be sure to take advantage of local resources. Your local library and nearby college libraries will be invaluable. Read your local newspapers regularly, and be sure to clip and file pertinent information. Newspapers file clippings of stories in rooms called "morgues." A researcher with access to a morgue can quickly find information about a firm or subject, because the newspaper is likely to have a file of clippings on the subject. If the newspaper refuses access to its morgue, the local library may have clipping files, microfilm copies of the newspaper, and an index to guide the search.

GOVERNMENT RESOURCES

While sometimes you will find yourself fighting lax enforcement by public agencies, you would be very foolish to write them off as a source of information. Depending on the nature of your problem, you will want to pursue local, state, or federal government agencies.

It is important to understand that you can call anybody you want in government and ask them anything you need to know in their area of jurisdiction. Many state and federal officials are more than willing to help you find your way around the resources of their agency. Your first step is to determine which agencies at which levels have jurisdiction over the problem you are working on.

Local Government

Local government offices collect information every day from private citizens and businesses. Depending on a researcher's concerns, local offices may provide a great deal of information about public health and what the government has done to protect health. The offices can also trace land ownership and some business practices that they regulate.

- For health records, a researcher can start at a city or county health department office. If the office has a library, it should contain documents that track the rate at which certain diseases or health conditions appear—the "incidence"—in that area. Some coroners' offices will have similar health information on file. This information will explain the more common causes of death in an area. Death records can be misleading! Sometimes the coroner or attending physician lists only the *immediate* cause of death, not the disease that led to the final stage.

- Other local government offices regulate the use and disposal of potentially toxic materials. All these public offices should open their records to the public for inspection and photocopying. Some offices even offer free photocopies.

- Sanitation departments do more than pick up garbage. They may know where firms have located special toxic dumpsites. And they will know the regulations governing waste disposal. Water treatment authorities constantly monitor the quality of the water people use and keep records of substances they find in the water. Air quality control boards monitor, and some regulate, pollution in a city's air.

- In a rural area, the officials of the agricultural extension services should know what toxic substances farmers are using. Fire marshals and chiefs have to keep a record of substances used or stored in the community their departments serve in order to fight fires effectively.

- Tracing the ownership of a parcel of land or a business is not difficult when the resources of local government offices are handy. The local tax assessment office will have a record of land ownership and value. A city or county planning and zoning commission may have the same information on file. The commission also maintains up-to-date zoning maps that explain what type of business or residence is allowed on each space in the area. Lawyers and researchers may use the office of the county recorder of deeds' to conduct title searches to determine the true ownership of land or property. The resources of this office are especially useful when the researcher narrows the focus to include a specific area of the city or town.

- A good place to start looking for information is under the county or city government listing in the telephone directory. Check out agencies with such titles as Environmental Protection, Public Health, Sanitary Commission, Solid Waste, Water Management, and Water Resources.

- If you are concerned about losing environmentally sensitive areas, you will want to know what local planning and zoning boards do and how they do it. What is citizen involvement in the planning and zoning process? Do special zoning exceptions have specific development criteria that citizens can veto? Are there master plans? What are they based on?

As you begin your research, take advantage of opportunities to get acquainted with the agency staffs—both planners and enforcers. You will find that bureaucrats who are willing to go out of their way to help you get the information you need will prove invaluable.

During the first stages of informing yourself, it's a good idea to attend every meeting that is in any way related to the issue you're interested in. Many meetings don't allow citizens to participate in discussions—but you can still monitor what is going on.

State Agencies

State governments have larger versions of some local offices. For instance, a researcher concerned about toxics may compare information obtained from a county health department with statewide information from the state health department's environmental health section, library, or public information office.

Some sources of help include the state's energy office; the environmental agency; pest control authorities, often in the department of agriculture; the office of the state insurance commissioner or regulator, which often has health data filed by insurance companies; unemployment offices for data on payments made to people who have suffered occupational injuries because of toxics; the utility regulation office; and water resources boards.

Federal Agencies

While the federal government and its agencies may seem very complex, these too provide valuable resources for researchers and community groups. Earlier chapters have given you a good start in identifying federal agencies involved in environmental regulation. Your local regulators can also be helpful in directing you to state and federal regulators who have jurisdiction in the area you are concerned about.

Since toxic pollution is of widespread concern, we will use this as an example. When conducting research on toxic substances, the first place to stop for information in the federal system is the agency responsible for regulating toxics — the Environmental Protection Agency. The EPA maintains regional offices throughout the United States (see Appendix for regional office addresses).

If the movement of toxic substances in groundwater is a concern, these offices can supply information about the state or local agency that is responsible for monitoring the water supply a utility company provides. The public or private utility may monitor its own supply; the state health department may conduct tests; the U.S. Army Corps of Engineers may track water content; or a private company may observe changes in the water. Your regional EPA office is also the place to look for records of public notices of violations and enforcement actions the EPA or another agency has taken in response to bad water quality. The EPA may even have a record of complaints about water quality.

The next step is to approach the firm or agency monitoring

the water, each of which has records. Ask to see the records and photocopy them. Although a researcher may not understand the records, it is important to obtain at least 2 year's worth not only for the group and for the scientists who will review them. Another kind of information to ask for are the data analysis sheets on which the agency bases its records.

Several other federal agencies can provide helpful information to a toxics' researcher:

- To supplement brief local records about industry, or to learn more about an industry nationwide, the researcher should examine the *U.S. Survey of Manufacturers,* a publication of the U.S. Department of Commerce.
- For more information about the effects of erosion on water quality or about soil contamination, the researcher should contact the local office of the Soil Conservation Service, which is part of the Department of Agriculture.
- The local Veterans Administration (VA) office or a nearby VA hospital may collect health and toxics information for the veteran population.
- The Centers for Disease Control (CDC) contain the national epidemiological laboratories. The CDC may already have conducted tests of the substances under examination by the researcher.
- Finally, the National Center for Health Statistics within the Department of Health and Human Services assembles national data on most health problems. Collections of data from the National Center also explain the rate of disease in the United States by area of the country, type of population, race, and so on.

PRIVATE INDUSTRY RESOURCES

Throughout the information-gathering process, good subjects for inquiry are companies that produce, transport, treat, and store hazardous waste or those with plans to develop in sensitive environmental areas. A good place to start is the local Chamber of Commerce, which keeps track of the size of its member businesses. The chamber may even have a printed document that explains the dollar amount of annual sales, profits, and assets of industries in the area, as well as the number of people the firms employ and the products they sell.

The Thomas Register of American Manufacturers describes businesses that operate in an area and gives their addresses and principal products. It also gives addresses of both corporate offices and the manufacturing plants, divisions, and so forth for each company across the country.

For a local area, the Yellow Pages of the telephone directory may include listings for certain types of companies, such as waste operations. In addition, publishing firms also supply many cities with City Directories that tell who owns, operates a business, or lives at each address in the city. Some publishing firms put out state industrial directories that list the industrial sites within certain geographical areas. Other firms publish manufacturers' directories for large regions of the United States. Some of the important directories to look for in a library include:

- *U.S. Industrial Directory*
- *MacRae's Industrial Directory*
- *Walker's Manual of Western Corporations*
- *Gulf Coast Industrial Handbook*
- *Directory of New England Manufacturers*

A researcher may obtain other sources of information about corporations from the firms themselves. An office of corporate communications at a firm's headquarters can provide any member of the public with copies of its annual reports and 10-K forms, which contain the firm's complete financial information. These documents, distributed to shareholders and filed with the federal Securities and Exchange Commission, also provide information about company operations and officers. Comparing old annual reports with newer ones may yield a list of former or retired employees of the firm. If they live in the area, retired or former employees are a good source of information about corporate practices and are also easy to reach. Union offices may also know the names and addresses of former or retired workers at a certain plant.

A little research opens the way for a lot of sunshine to reach musty records and hidden secrets. Depending on the problem and the knowledge among members of your group, you can expect this phase to last anywhere up to a year.

USING THE FREEDOM OF INFORMATION ACT (FOIA)

Whatever problem you are pursuing, the federal Freedom of Information Act (FOIA) is an invaluable tool in gaining access to information. This act provides a way for citizens to see tens of thousands of executive branch documents. Citizens may also obtain correspondence between government officials and corporate executives by using the FOIA. All these documents can be helpful to researchers. The documents often provide hints about who lobbied whom and how laws and policies took shape. Many states also have freedom of information laws that grant citizens the right to obtain state government documents. Learn how to use the laws. Your public library and librarian can be the best sources of more specific information on state freedom-of-information laws.

The federal law gives an agency 10 days to respond to a FOIA request. However, many agencies rarely meet this deadline and require prodding. Citizens filing FOIA requests must first contact the agency that has the documents and ask who should receive the request. Citizens must make their requests as clear and specific as possible. For example, a citizen could ask the EPA for "all 1985 correspondence between Paul Oreffice, president of Dirty Deeds Chemical Company, and Lee Thomas, Administrator of the Environmental Protection Agency."

However, just because you ask for a document doesn't mean you will get it. All FOIAs set forth specific categories of information, such as individual personnel data and details of a criminal investigation, that can be denied to the public. Federal files are loaded with formally classified documents that can be withheld by officials. Don't take the first "no" for an answer. For example, if an official says you can't have a document because it contains a nondisclosable trade secret, ask the official to "black out" the nondisclosable information and provide a copy of the rest of the document. Even with blackouts, a document can provide valuable information not readily available elsewhere.

Any citizen conducting research "in the public interest" may ask the agency to waive the photocopying or search fees. But the agency itself decides who must pay. Citizens whose FOIA requests go unanswered after filing and appealing may consult an attorney for advice. They may even sue the government agency in court to release the documents.

Below are sample letters for making a federal FOIA request and for appealing to a higher level in an agency if the agency denies the request. If an appeal is denied, citizens may go to court to ask for documents. If the case goes to court, the law provides no deadline for the final response by the government agency. The procedure is likely to be the same for state documents.

Sample Request Letter

Freedom of Information Unit   Date

(Name and Address of Government Agency)

Re: Freedom of Information Request

Dear Sir or Madam:

Pursuant to the Freedom of Information Act, 5 U.S.C. 552, I hereby request access to (or a copy of) *{describe the document containing the information that you want}*_____.

If any expenses in excess of $_____ are incurred in connection with this request, please inform me of all such charges prior to their being incurred, for my approval. [*Or*: I ask that you waive any expenses incurred in connection with this request, in accordance with 5 U.S.C. 552 (a)(4)(A). Disclosure of the records I seek will primarily benefit the general public.]

If you do not grant my request within 10 working days, I will deem my request denied. If you deny any portion of my request, please provide me with the reason(s) for the denial. Thank you for your prompt attention to this matter.

Very truly yours,

_____/s/_____

(your telephone number)

Sample Appeal Letter

(Name and Address of Head of Government Agency)   Date

Re: Freedom of Information Appeal Number — — — — — —

Dear Secretary — — — — — — — — — — — — — — — :

By letter dated (month) (day), (year), I requested access to **(use same description as in request letter)**. By letter dated (month) (day), (year), Mr./Ms. _____ of the Office of Public Information (usually) of your agency denied my request. Pursuant to the Freedom of Information Act, 5 U.S.C. 552, I hereby appeal that denial. I have enclosed a copy of my request letter and the denial that I have received.

I consider the denial invalid for at least (give 2-3 reasons). If you do not act upon my appeal within 20 working days I will deem my request denied.

Very truly yours,
_____/s/_____
(your telephone number)

(Source: "Freedom of Information Act: A User's Guide," Freedom of Information Clearinghouse, P.O. Box 19367, Washington, D.C., 20036; the Clearinghouse also provides more FOIA information to citizens who send a self-addressed stamped envelope.)

SELECTING THE ACTION

MARK SCHAEFFER

If this is your first big campaign on an issue you care deeply about, you need to be careful about how you select your specific actions. Two words of caution: First, don't bite off more than you can chew. It is far better to start with an action that you can plan and carry out well than with a big event that could overtax your members just when the group is getting started. Plan well in advance for large actions; there are always myriad details to take care of, and you will need the time you can get. Second, recognize that most problems do not get solved overnight. You will be better able to keep your group energized if you pace yourselves.

Actions can range from a demonstration, meetings with public officials, or participating in your local planning process, or a petition drive. Once your overall goals are clear and you have done your initial research, the type of action you should initiate will be easier to determine. But you will still need to give this very careful thought. You want to be sure that the action or actions you select are part of a strategic plan that bring you closer to the group's main goal.

In some circumstances, legislative action may be the only way to push change. If you want to know more about lobbying, you should read "Making an Issue of It: The Campaign Handbook," Publication No. 613, League of Women Voters, 1730 M Street, N. W., Washington, DC, 20036 (75 cents per single copy; 50 cents for handling).

But no matter what action you choose, the first thing you should do is buy a notebook and keep a complete record of everything you do. Write down all the names, dates, phone numbers, and information you get. Every time you have a conversation with an official on the subject of interest, log it. In selecting your action, think about the resources you will need and whether you can realistically obtain them. This is especially true if you are considering legal action.

FINDING THE RESOURCES

THE EXPERTS

While you can obtain a great deal of information on your own, you are likely to reach a point where you need expert advice. You may need help understanding the toxicity of certain chemicals or how regulations apply; you may want to use an expert in a public hearing to add credibility to your arguments; you may find you need an expert to counter misleading stories in your local paper based on information supplied by the polluters; and you may need experts to go to court.

One of the best places to look for experts is at a nearby college or university. Not only can professors provide you with expert assistance, they may also be able to identify students who can help, such as the Cornell student who received her Master's degree conducting a study that was used in our testimony at Nine Mile Point.

FUNDRAISING

Even if you are fortunate and find experts who will give you free advice because they care about the issue, you will need to raise funds for your activities.

Members usually finance newly formed toxics groups out of their own pockets. As a group grows, it will soon need to raise funds to support its work. Mailing lists get longer, postage and photocopying costs increase, members have to make trips to the capital to talk with officials—all these events mean higher costs. Two good sources of funding exist: donated services, supplies, and in-kind gifts and grassroots fundraisers.

The first rule of thumb is, "Never buy anything that someone can donate." This means a group should stop before it buys a typewriter and make a request in the group's newsletter for a supporter to donate one. If the group needs office space a couple of days a week, someone should ask a local church if it will loan the space. If the group needs to print 1,000 copies of a leaflet, someone else should ask a local union if it will donate the job. Keeping to this policy will obviously help further stretch limited dollars. It will also provide a way for supporters in the community to help. That broadens the group's base of support. It also improves the hope for a successful campaign.

Local fundraising events are the best way to widen a group's net of support in the community while also raising cash. Such events are also a lot of fun. Groups have used bake sales, benefit concerts, carnivals, film screenings, raffles, and walk-a-thons to raise money. The best chance for fundraising success comes when the group designs an event that requires a low initial investment. The event should also take as little planning and execution time as possible and involve many people. Again, the group's yield from the event will increase if members get upfront costs of the event donated or discounted.

Here's an example of a typical fundraising event. The Stop Giant Corp. Dumping Committee needed to send a member to Washington to arrange a congressional hearing on the issue of water contamination near military sites. The committee decided to hold a pancake breakfast and car wash on a Saturday morning in 3 weeks. Group members got a local church to donate its meeting hall for the breakfast. Others asked the truckdrivers' local to print flyers announcing the breakfast. Still others persuaded the neighborhood Boy Scout troop to leaflet the area—and receive a public service badge in the process! The high school choir found volunteers to wash cars. Two local grocers donated all the food for the breakfast. Senior citizens from the local senior center helped with food preparation. A popular local musician donated her talent for the morning's entertainment.

The group charged $5 for the breakfast and $2 for a car wash during breakfast. The group had to spend $8 for plastic forks and paper napkins and $20 to rent a microphone and speakers. Eighty people attended the breakfast; 32 of them had their cars washed. The group netted $436—enough to sponsor the trip to Washington *and* pay for mailing the next two newsletters. Everybody had a great time, only two people complained that the pancakes weren't hot enough, and 12 new members joined the group!

BRINGING PUBLIC ATTENTION TO YOUR ISSUE

PUBLIC HEARINGS

There are many ways to educate the larger community on your concerns. One of the most effective is a public hearing. Either you can either hold your own public hearing, as we did in Oswego, or you can use official public hearings to educate the public by asking pertinent questions or making informative statements. I've seen many a public official squirm uncomfortably when issues they had tried to ignore were brought into such public forums!

My own experience is not unique. After studying local environmental protection campaigns in North Carolina, the

Institute for Southern Studies concluded: The public hearing became the most important educational tool in the particular campaigns surveyed. Whether they were called by government officials or by the citizens leading the opposition, these forums provided:

1. A focus for organizing mass turnout.
2. A convenient way for the press to cover the issues in the controversy.
3. An almost mandatory platform for politicians.
4. An arena that easily puts the sponsor of an environmentally risky business on the defensive.
5. An educational event on neutral turf (school auditorium or city hall) that attracts interested, but undecided people.
6. A chance for the environmental group to develop its media, outreach, planning, public education, speaking, and research skills.

With good organizing, these events gave environmentalists an excellent opportunity to:

1. Put themselves on an equal footing to challenge the company and/or regulators.
2. Impress politicians with mass opposition to the project.
3. Demonstrate to the uncommitted who come to the event the contradictions of the proposals.
4. Renew the commitment of the already convinced and allow them to enjoy the power of their collective voices.

Here are a few pointers in preparing for a public meeting:
- Do your homework. The more you have learned about the issue, the more effective you will be. But do not present yourself as more qualified than you are. Your credentials are your commitment, your knowledge (acquired the hard

way), and the fact that you speak for other concerned citizens.

- Don't assume officials know more than you do. They will assume you don't know much, and you may have a big surprise in store for them.
- Write down your questions so you can refer to them if you get nervous when it's your turn to speak.
- Ask your questions in a way that will educate other people in the audience. This means using understandable terms. Make the officials explain what they are talking about; don't let them hide behind big words.
- Make sure the news media knows when and where the meeting will be and what the issues are. This means issuing a brief news release. If this is a new issue, you may want to give the press background material ahead of time. Make sure someone in your group is available to be interviewed about your reaction to the meeting.

Most major new projects and many public planning processes require a public hearing. You need to check your local newspaper on a regular basis for a notice, invariably in small print, of such hearings. If an issue is localized, there may be notices only in community newspapers that circulate in the immediately affected area. You can also request that an agency put you on its "service list," which means you will be notified of all their hearings.

Keep in mind that there are two types of hearings. One is for public comment. This is important for public education and for regulators to judge public opinion, but it will not become part of a formal decision-making process. The second kind is an adjudicatory hearing, which is conducted in a manner similar to court cases with opportunities to present witnesses and crossexamine. The NRC hearings described at the beginning of this chapter is an example of such a hearing.

The hearing notice will tell you where you can obtain or examine the material supporting the proposal. It will also give you the date and place of the hearing. If you want to participate in any of these hearings, you may have to notify the hearing officer in advance. Sometimes, because of interest in a particular issue, participation is limited to a certain number of minutes per person or group.

If the notice is for a legal hearing, you will have to follow a much more formal proceeding to get permission to participate. You will have to show that you have "standing," which just means that you will be personally affected by the proposed action. Be sure to find out what rules different agencies must follow for giving notice. If these rules have been violated, you may have grounds to challenge the hearing, giving you added time to rally your forces.

SPEAKING AT MEETINGS

Many local organizations are looking for speakers—church organizations, fraternal orders, and garden clubs. Once you have learned the issue and have some idea of the kind of solutions you want to see, you are ready to speak to others. If you have no experience with public speaking, you will want to start out by taking turns making presentations at your own group meetings. It won't be long before you will have the confidence to go out and speak to others. If there is more of a demand for your presentation than you can fill, start a speaker's bureau. You can offer single speakers or a panel. This is a good way to involve more people in your organization.

WORKSHOPS AND TEACH-INS

Workshops are an opportunity to educate members of your own group and other potential members in your community. Workshops need to be carefully planned well in advance, with workshop leaders who know their topics very well. This is a good opportunity to invite members of other environmental groups or local experts to be workshop leaders. Soon, you will be ready to be a workshop leader yourself.

Workshops usually have two purposes: to educate people about the issues and to teach people tools they can use to take action. The best way to run your first workshop is to find people in your region who have experience. They will help you plan length of sessions, breaks, and recreational relief so that even an all-day session will be productive and fun.

Teachins in cooperation with a secondary school, college, or university can also be useful. These tend to be more subject-oriented, rather than including techniques for action. While they allow you to reach larger audiences, they lack the dynamic of smaller, more intense workshops. Be sure of the level of interest in your community before committing yourself to a teachin. Always remember to have a signup sheet for interested citizens to list name, address, and phone number.

HOW TO USE THE MEDIA

As a way of spreading your message, you will want to tell your story to the media — the newspapers, radio and television stations in your town or city. When the media cover a story, they spread the word to your community and beyond. State legislative and other government staffs take note of the stories that appear in hometown newspapers. Congresspeople and senators in Washington keep track of local media reports, as do reporters for national media such as news magazines. This section will help you use the media effectively to advance your goals.

WHAT'S THE MESSAGE?

The first and most important question about any contact with the press is: What message do you want to send and how? You can answer this question best by discussing it at a meeting. Making a press statement that only a few people in the group approve of may lead to a loss of members or interest.

There are three basic ways you can get press coverage: You can tell the press something, you can show the press something, and you can respond to what what others have said or done.

Most of this section tells you how to make statements to the press, but creating an event that the press will want to cover should also be a high priority. You want to make your event so that it is easy for the media to cover. For example, if you are planning a march, arrange handouts for media people and call them in advance. Furnish the name of the person serving as the official spokesperson for the group, so reporters can credit their information to a source. For newspapers not attending, arrange with a professional photographer (maybe someone in your group) to take pictures and deliver a picture and a press release in time for publication.

You can also get coverage by being ready to respond to other events the media is covering. Once spokespeople from your group become recognized as providing reliable information and quotable responses, the media will come back to you time and again. Many are the times I found out about breaking news because a reporter called me for my reaction!

HOW TO RELEASE THE MESSAGE

Since some media outlets only cover certain stories, the group must decide what media to use for the release. In general, electronic media cover the news that is breaking and prefer a story with action. Their stories are presented in short bursts. While it is harder to get covered on a TV news broadcast, you should pursue radio and TV talks shows. Both are very popular and will also give you more opportunity to talk about the issues. No matter what the media, good communication with a reporter over a period of time establishes trust and produces more coverage.

The type of media you select partly depends on how newsworthy the story appears to be. "Newsworthiness," a judgment about how interesting and *new* a story is, rules most media decisions. Some reporters and editors use this rule of thumb: The more people a story affects and involves and the more timely the story, the more newsworthy the story is. You must decide when your group's interest lies in being in the news. Remember you don't have to comment on a news story if you don't think it will help achieve your goal.

If you live in a small city or town, your group may have only one TV station or newspaper with which to work. In this case, you could face frustrating refusals to pay attention to your issue, especially if your target is a major employer or economic force in the community. If you find yourself in this situation, you should work through a county or state newspaper or a media outlet in a nearby town.

NEWS RELEASES AND NEWS CONFERENCES

The question of how to release a message also needs to be answered. Groups must decide whether to spread their news through a news conference or a news release. In general, news conferences work best when the issue or news at hand is controversial and very timely. The release of a report, for instance, rarely warrants more than a press release; but if your report is on a controversial issue, like showing pollution from a major local corporation, it might qualify.

Using visual aids makes any press conference far more appealing to TV reporters. If you decide to use them, spend the money to have them professionally prepared. For example, if you are detailing toxic sites in your area, an enlarged map could be used to pinpoint them. A large bar graph could also illustrate the data you have collected about these sites.

WRITING A NEWS RELEASE

The most common way for a group to get its message out to the media is through a news release, which is a brief written statement that gives key details of the story the group wants to tell, along with quotes that interpret the story.

The best news releases have a first paragraph that reads like the first paragraph, or lead, of a newspaper story. A good lead rarely exceeds 40 words. It is punchy and seeks to grab the reader's attention and make that person want to continue reading. The lead of your release can contain any of the "5 Ws & H" elements that comprise the traditional newspaper style of constructing a first paragraph. Rarely will your lead contain all six elements. But all should be presented within the first few paragraphs. The six elements are:

- Who is releasing the statement, or who has done this?
- What claims is the group making, what has someone done or found out, or what does the group propose a polluter or the government do?
- When did the event take place, or when will it take place?
- Where is the group based, where did the event take place, or where will it take place?
- Why is the data or event important?
- How was the data gathered? How will it be presented?

A few quotes from a spokesperson for the group should follow the first paragraph. Quotes should be short and punchy; one sentence is best. Effective quotes attract attention and indicate that the speaker holds a firm position. News releases should never make charges the facts do not support. If your group ever makes factual errors or misrepresents facts, your credibility could be permanently damaged.

You have the option of placing an embargo on news releases. The embargo instructs journalists to hold back the news until a certain time. For instance, an embargo time of 12 noon asks journalists not to print or report stories before noon. Journalists may write their stories, but they are on their honor not to let the news out. So if a group plans an event at noon, the group can place an embargo on news until after noon, but still distribute the release before the event to assure that the press will attend. If there is no embargo, the release should say "For Immediate Release."

The day you select to send out a news release or hold a news conference is important. Friday is rarely a good day. Fewer people read Saturday papers, so the release has less impact. Holding a news conference on a weekend or a holiday generally is not a good idea. News staffs are usually smaller on those days, so unless yours is the only event in town that day, it might be passed over in favor of another event. The advance notice that Monday releases require might mean reporters could forget a release or news conference on that day. But Monday has a distinct advantage: With government offices closed over the weekend, your release has far less competition for space in the news media. Successful Monday releases can draw attention for the week to come.

The release should always contain the name of at least one person in your organization who a reporter can contact for further information and answers to questions. Always give the business and home phone numbers of contact people. Put this information at the end of the news release.

Sample News Release

UPTONVILLE HEALTH ACTION GROUP
323 Center Street, Uptonville, North State 09999

FOR RELEASE: Jan. 2, 1990
EMBARGO UNTIL 10 a.m.

HEALTH ACTION GROUP RELEASES ILLNESS DATA

People living in one-fifth of the households in two neighborhoods near the Giant Chemical Corp. plant have reported serious health problems, the Uptonville Health Action Group said today.

The Group said its preliminary survey of the Cleary and Woodlawn neighborhoods showed that people in 20 percent of the households there have reported miscarriages, serious respiratory conditions, and urinary tract diseases.

The group announced that it would request a review of the data by local, state, and federal public health authorities.

"This survey confirms what is already common knowledge in Uptonville: Many people here have uncommon health problems," said Sally Spokesperson, chair of the Health Action Group.

"Now assistance from state and federal government scientists is what we need most," she said. "The scientists can help us find out if Giant Corp.'s wastes have caused these persistent health problems."

"This early survey indicates that a public health problem exists in Uptonville," said Dr. Helen Troichus, chair of the Department of Epidemiology at North Tech University. "The situation calls for urgent review."

Dr. Troichus supervised a team of North Tech epidemiologists and statisticians who trained and assisted 15 citizens in public health surveying.

The citizens gathered the data by interviewing adults at 134 homes in the two neighborhoods during the past 4 weeks.

The Health Action Group, whose membership is open to all, was formed in September 1984 to study pollution-related health problems in Uptonville.

For Further Information
Contact:

Sally Spokesperson
885-2222 or (h) 885-3945
Dr. Helen Troichus
887-4242 or (h) 886-1432

Be sure that after you have released your press statement a spokesperson for the group will be available to answer press calls!

THE NEWS ADVISORY

The news advisory is similar to a news release, only shorter. An advisory can be used to inform editors, reporters, and news directors in advance of a group's plans to hold a news conference. It should contain a general description of the subject of the news conference and who will be attending. It should be mailed far enough ahead so that it arrives several days before a planned news conference.

In writing the advisory, as with a release, the elemental 5 Ws & H will provide enough information. One guideline to remember is to give enough information to attract reporters, but not so much that the reporters know all the information in advance and won't bother to attend! If a reporter calls looking for further information, generally provide it on a background and embargoed basis. If you tell a reporter that they have to come to the news conference to find out what your group is going to say, then what you have to say should be important and dramatic enough to justify the mystery.

The advisory usually only needs to be one paragraph long. You should deliver advisories addressed to the editor (find out the person's name in advance by telephoning) in an envelope clearly marked "advisory." Then phone editors to make certain they received the advisories. An example of a news advisory follows:

Sample News Advisory

UPTONVILLE HEALTH ACTION GROUP
323 Center Street, Uptonville, North State 09999

NEWS ADVISORY

Dec. 31, 1989

On Monday, January 2, 1990, at 10 a.m., the Uptonville Health Action Group will release the results of a community health survey at a news conference in the Green Room of the Holiday Inn, 242 Main Street, Uptonville. Dr. Helen Troichus, chair of the Department of Epidemiology at North Tech University, will speak.

For more information, contact Sally Spokesperson, chair of the citizens' organization, at 885-2222.

HOLDING A NEWS CONFERENCE

A news conference is a meeting between reporters and people who have information that the rest of the community needs to know. News conferences can be the occasion to reveal findings, to inform the public about plans, to brief the media about a course of action, and in a conflict situation, to state a bargaining position. The best press conferences also allow reporters to ask questions, so that they can write and report longer and better stories about issues. This section explains how you can plan and hold a news conference.

A few members of your group should form a committee to plan and carry out the conference. First, the committee must decide where and when the group will hold a news conference. You should schedule a news conference at a place and time convenient for reporters. That means groups will usually hold news conferences in a public place—outside a government building, in a hotel meeting room, in the your group's conference room or one borrowed from a local public interest group. At the chosen site, be sure to post signs directing reporters to the proper place. Sometimes an on-the-spot news conference is the best approach. Holding one at a toxic waste site provides visual material for photographers and TV cameras.

There is no best time for a news conference. Different media outlets have different deadlines. Don't expect a 5:30 p.m. event to make the 6 o'clock news. A 2 p.m. news conference is too late if you want a story to make that day's afternoon newspaper. Find out what the particular deadline needs are for the newspapers and radio and TV stations you are trying to reach. Schedule your news conference for a time that allows the media to write the story and edit the videotape.

After you mail out your news release or advisory, it is important to make followup telephone calls to assignment editors. This reminds editors and reporters about the conference and encourages greater attendance. Also, after you make the calls, you will have at least some idea of how many reporters to expect. The most important followup calls should go to the editors of the wire service "daybooks," which provide daily schedules of press conferences and events. Wire services, such as the Associated Press (AP) and United Press International (UPI), provide this information to many media outlets through their daybooks. It's particularly important to send news advisories to them.

Speakers participating in the news conference should get

together to rehearse their opening statements and answers to the questions they expect at the news conference. This practice will also come in handy for radio interviews. Make sure you know all the facts about your opposition's side and decide in advance how you're going to handle "iffy" issues.

As reporters arrive at the news conference, they should be politely asked to sign in, with name, organization, mailing address, and telephone number. Give each one a press packet with the press release, other pertinent background material, and contact names and numbers.

Many groups make the mistake of choosing too large a meeting area. Select one large enough to accommodate your guests, but not so large that it gives the impression that the event was not well-attended.

Remember that members of the media are very busy and work on tight deadlines. Make every effort to start the press conference on time. Reporters hate having to wait.

To begin the press conference, your organization's representative or host should introduce himself or herself and thank the media for coming. The host should give a brief introductory statement about why the group has called the conference and read a list of speakers.

Speakers should be short, sweet, and to the point. Keeping remarks short and punchy will hold reporters' interest and force speakers to get their points across as clearly as possible without going off on tangents.

Not all speakers need to write out their speeches word for word, but speakers must be careful. It is true that "anything you say can and will be used against you." Therefore, speakers should think about how to phrase their main points and write down those words in advance. Speakers should never distort the truth or exaggerate. If several people speak at a news conference, they must make sure their presentations are not repetitive and do not contradict each other. Instead, the presentations should express several perspectives or different aspects of the same issue. For example, one person could speak about the extent of toxic contamination in a neighborhood, another person about health effects, and a third about the group's immediate goals. The speakers should also be available after the news conference to answer further questions from reporters.

A well-known or well-qualified person makes a good news conference speaker. For instance, having a local professor or former EPA official give an expert opinion helps the overall group presentation. As with any other speaker, groups should be sure they know what the expert is going to say. You need to ask the expert ahead of time under what circumstances he or she would give a negative answer or one that might be harmful to the group's position.

Having too many speakers with varied views doesn't make for a good news conference. Limit the number of speakers to three or four. At the most, the conference should include a half hour of presentations.

The host should not interrupt a speaker who makes a mistake, but instead he or she can clarify points between speakers or ask the speaker to clarify what was said. After the statements, the host should invite reporters to ask questions and preside over the question-and-answer period. Reporters should be encouraged to ask questions until all have had a chance. Or the host can end the conference and leave the floor open for questions to the speakers from reporters desiring more information.

Placing a large sign or symbol of the organization behind the speaker's platform is a good idea. It makes the presentation more interesting and provides a good background for photographs and videotaping. Some groups have shown real creativity in designing props for news conferences. For instance, one group placed a toothpaste tube on a piece of poster board. To demonstrate how a clay cover on a toxic dump works, a member pressed the tube until it burst. The message: When someone applies pressure to a closed toothpaste tube, the toothpaste finds another way out. Just think what would happen at a toxic dump!

All speakers should know they may receive hostile questions. A reporter may want to test a speaker. Or a public relations official representing a polluter may ask a question that challenges a speaker. If you think your opponents are likely to attend, the host can ask questioners to identify themselves before they ask questions. You do not have to answer a polluter's questions at your press conference. Whatever happens, remember one rule: Never blow your cool.

If a reporter from a newspaper or TV station does not attend, group members can drop extra releases at media offices after the news conference. Be sure to provide copies of the press packet.

You can also call news directors at radio stations that did not attend and ask whether they want to conduct a phone interview. You could say, for instance, "We just held a news conference documenting health damage in two Uptonville neighborhoods and calling for further investigation. Would you like to do a short interview?" The statements in the news release will probably be sufficient for the shorter news reports done by most radio stations.

Media skills are an important part of your organizing work. Remember that good press relations go a long way and are very important to cultivate. If you are timely, reliable, informed, and trustworthy, reporters and editors will come to depend on you. After all, controversy sells papers.

NETWORKING

As you get your own group on its feet or work with an existing group, you will want to involve as broad a spectrum of supporters as possible. You will also want to learn from the experiences of other organizations that have worked on similar problems. This process of reaching out to include and learn from others is called "networking."

When we formed the Lakeshore Alliance in upstate New York, we were networking. Representatives from each group in the coalition would meet once a month to plan rallies and workshops, to coordinate our efforts, to get good ideas from each other, like silk screening T-shirts, and to give each other mutual support. In between, we would keep in touch by phone. For events where we had to mobilize quickly, we would use a telephone tree, with one person calling five others, who would then call five more until everyone was reached.

Many of the local groups produced their own newsletters. A newsletter is a good networking tool if it is sent to other organizations and also provided free in public places, such as libraries and stores.

Networking with other environmental groups will help you find the resources you need, whether they are speakers, workshop leaders, written materials, or a chance to discuss strategies. The National Wildlife Federation publishes a Conservation Directory that lists conservation and environmental organizations by state, with the specific areas in which each group works. Also, watch the newspapers for names of other groups, or ask your state or local environmental office for names. Once you have a few names, they will put you in touch with others. When you realize you are part of a larger movement, you will not feel so overwhelmed by the campaign you have taken on locally.

As you build your network, you will want to reach out to other types of organizations. Consumer groups are especially important, because many environmental problems have an economic impact on communities. When you work with consumers, you demonstrate your concern about people's economic welfare — pocketbook issues — which will also help insulate you from accusations by industry that your efforts to protect the environment are selfishly narrow and ignore factors like higher prices and job losses. Names of statewide citizen action organizations are listed in the Appendix.

Depending on your issue, churches and civic groups, hunting and fishing groups, labor unions, medical and scientific associations, PTAs, and the scouts are all potential allies. Before approaching these groups, it is worth taking the time to think through why your issue would be of concern to them. The best networks are built when you can identify common goals, rather than asking others to adopt your goals. The broader your base, the more political clout you will have and the more expertise you will be able to draw on without cost.

Earlier, we talked about speaking at meetings of other organizations. If you find an organization sympathetic to your cause, you can then follow up by inviting them to work with you. This may be the time to think about creating a more formal coalition of groups committed to working on the issue. Some may want to have a more informal association, giving support from time to time. These groups should be constantly reinforced as part of your network.

EMPOWERMENT

When our small group first began meeting in Oswego, we never dreamed we would win a major victory against huge utility companies. But we did. Each step of the way we gained confidence as we began to learn how the system works and how we could become players in changing the way decisions were made.

This concept of "empowerment" is central to organizing. It recognizes that the people who want to create change, whether it is to save the environment or foster social justice, are not usually in positions of power that enable them to make a significant difference on their own. But by working with other people—organizing—they can begin to develop political clout that will get the attention of decision makers. All the techniques that have been discussed in this chapter will help you achieve this clout. Once you see that you can make a difference in the ways corporations and regulators behave, you have created power for yourself that you did not have originally. And that is what empowerment is all about.

Empowerment also means sharing, helping others to gain power. We cannot win these battles on our own. Certainly, when we look at some of the major environmental problems facing us in the next decade, we know that while our individual groups can make a difference, it will take all of us working together in a united effort to gain the power to keep our Earth green in the decades to come.

We are not promising you that it will be easy. It's hard work getting information, getting support, getting results. But it can be done. You will not win every skirmish, but keep your eyes on your final goal. Persistence pays off, as we learned in our utility fight. And as with many goals that require hard work, your victories will be very rewarding. You will know that you have made a difference for the future of our Earth and ourselves.

APPENDIX A:
ENVIRONMENTAL DIRECTORY

(Many of these organizations as well as additional listings of federal, state and local agencies can be found in *The Conservation Directory*, published annually by The National Wildlife Federation.)

GOVERNMENT AGENCIES:
CONSUMER PRODUCT SAFETY COMMISSION
Regional Offices:

Eastern Regional Center
6 World Trade Center
New York, NY 10048
(212) 264-1125

Central Regional Center
230 South Dearborn Street
Room 2944
Chicago, IL 60604
(312) 353-8260

Western Regional Office
555 Battery Street
Room 415
San Francisco, CA 94111
(415) 705-1816

DEPARTMENT OF ENERGY
Forrestal Building
1000 Independene Avenue, S.W.
Washington, DC 20585
(202) 586-5000

DEPARTMENT OF
TRANSPORTATION
400 7th Street, S.W.
Washington, DC 20590
(202) 366-4000
(800) 424-9393

U.S. ENVIRONMENTAL PROTECTION AGENCY (EPA)
401 M Street, S.W.
Washington, DC 20460
General: (202) 382-2090
Toxic Substances Control Act Hotline: (202) 554-1404
RCRA Hotline: (202) 382-3000

Regional Offices:
Region I (ME, NH, VT, MA, CT, RI)
Room 2203, John F. Kennedy Federal Building
Boston, MA 02203
(617) 223-2100

Region II (NJ, NY, PR)
Room 906, 26 Federal Plaza
New York, NY 10278
(212) 264-2525

Region III (DC, DE, MD, PA, VA, WV)
841 Chestnut Building
Philadelphia, PA 19107
(215) 597-9814

Region IV (AL, FL, GA, KY, MS, NC, SC, TN)
345 Courtland Street, N.E.
Atlanta, GA 30365
(404) 874-0607

Region V (IL, IN, MI, MN, OH, WI)
230 South Dearborn Street
Chicago, IL 60604
(312) 353-2000

Region VI (AR, LA, NM, OK, TX)
1445 Ross Avenue
Dallas, TX 75202
(214) 767-2600

Region VII (IA, KS, MO, NE)
726 Minnesota Avenue
Kansas City, MO 66101
(913) 236-2800

Region VIII (CO, MT, ND, SD, UT, WY)
999 18th Street, Suite 500
Denver, CO 80202-2405
(303) 293-1603

Region IX (AZ, CA, NV)
215 Fremont Street
San Francisco, CA 94105
(415) 974-8135

Region X (AK, ID, OR, WA)
1200 Sixth Avenue
Seattle, WA 98101
(206) 442-5810

FEDERAL ENERGY REGULATORY COMMISSION
825 North Capitol Street, N.E.
Washington, DC 20426
(202) 357-8200

U.S. FISH AND WILDLIFE SERVICE
Department of Interior
Interior Building
18th-C Street, N.W.
Washington, DC 20240
(202) 343-1100

FOOD AND DRUG ADMINISTRATION
5600 Fishers Lane
Rockville, MD 20857
(301) 443-1544

NATIONAL PARK SERVICE
Interior Building
Box 37127
Washington, DC 20013-7127
(202) 343-6843

U.S. NUCLEAR REGULATORY COMMISSION
Washington, DC 20555
(301) 492-7000

UNITED NATIONS ENVIRONMENT PROGRAMME
United Nations Plaza

Room DC2-0803
New York, NY 10017
(212) 963-8138

Established by the UN general assembly to encourage and help coordinate global environmental efforts. Reports regularly on environmental problems and helps develop new approaches to better management of our resources.

NATIONAL GROUPS WITH REGIONAL AND LOCAL AFFILIATES:

AMERICAN LUNG ASSOCIATION
1740 Broadway
New York, NY 10019
(212) 315-8700

A voluntary agency concerned with prevention and control of lung disease and aggravating factors, including air pollution. Works with citizens and other groups for effective air pollution control.

CITIZEN'S CLEARINGHOUSE FOR HAZARDOUS WASTES
Box 926
Arlington, VA 22216
(703) 276-7070

Provides assistance to citizens and grassroots groups
working to promote responsible hazardous and solid waste management.

CLEAN WATER ACTION PROJECT
317 Pennsylvania Avenue, S.E.
Washington, DC 20003
(202) 547-1196

National citizen organization working for clean and safe water at an affordable cost, control of toxic chemicals, and the protection of our nation's natural resources.

ENVIRONMENTAL DEFENSE FUND
257 Park Avenue South
New York, NY 10010
(212) 505-2100

Lawyers, scientists and economists working to protect and improve environmental quality and public health in the fields of energy and resource conservation, toxic chemicals, water resources, air quality, land use, wildlife.

GREENPEACE, USA
1436 U Street, N.W.
Washington, DC 20009
(202) 462-1177

Employs nonviolent direct action to confront environmental abuse. Campaigns address decimation of marine mammal populations, ocean disposal of toxic and radioactive wastes, preservation of Antarctica, acid rain, and nuclear weapons testing.

LEAGUE OF AMERICAN WHEELMEN
6707 Whitestone Road
Suite 209
Baltimore, MD 21207
(301) 944-3399

National organization of bicyclists founded in 1880 to advance and defend the rights and interests of bicyclers. 500 affiliated local clubs.

LEAGUE OF WOMEN VOTERS
1730 M Street, N.W.
Washington, DC 20036
(202) 429-1965

Non-partisan organizations working to promote poltical responsibility through informed and active participation of citizens in government. Takes political action on water and air quality, solid and hazardous waste management, land use and energy.

NATIONAL AUDUBON SOCIETY
950 Third Avenue
New York, NY 10022
(212) 832-3200

Our stewardship of natural resources includes management of nature sanctuaries, production of educational television specials on conservation issues and scientific research to save endangered species.

NATIONAL TOXICS CAMPAIGN
37 Temple Place
4th floor
Boston, MA 02111
(617) 482-1477

National grassroots membership organization that helps communities and citizens fight toxics in their areas. Provides organizing, technical and legal assistance.

NATIONAL WILDLIFE FEDERATION
1400 16th Street, N.W.
Washington, DC 20036-2266
(202) 797-6800

Over 5 million members nationwide. Through education and research, supports judicious use of resources for people and wildlife.

NATURAL RESOURCES DEFENSE COUNCIL
40 West 20th Street
New York, NY 10011
(212) 727-2700

Combines legal action, scientific research and citizen education to protect America's natural resources and improve the quality of the human environment.

THE NATURE CONSERVANCY
1815 North Lynn Street
Arlington, VA 22209
(703) 841-5300

Private sector leader in protecting and maintaining the best examples of endangered species, natural communities and ecosystems in the world. Manages over 1,000 nature preserves.

PLANNED PARENTHOOD FEDERATION OF AMERICA
810 7th Avenue
New York, NY 10019
(212) 541-7800

Non-profit health and advocacy organization joining affiliates nationwide that operate medically supervised clinics providing family planning services and information.

RAILS TO TRAILS CONSERVANCY
1400 16th Street, N.W.
Suite 300
Washington, DC 20036
(202) 797-5400

Works with local recreation and conservation associations to convert thousands of miles of abandoned railroad corridors to public trails for walking, bicycling, horse-back riding, cross-country skiing, wildlife habitat and nature appreciation.

SIERRA CLUB
730 Polk Street
San Francisco, CA 94109
(415) 776-2211

To explore, enjoy and protect wild places of the earth; to practice and promote the responsible use of the earth's ecosystems and resources; to educate and enlist humanity to protect and restore the quality of the natural and human environment, and to use all lawful means to carry out these objectives.

U.S. PUBLIC INTEREST RESEARCH GROUP
215 Pennsylvania Avenue, S.E.
Washington, DC 20003
(202) 546-9707

Environmental and consumer advocacy organization representing the public interest in areas of environmental protection, energy policy, and government and corporate reform.

TROUT UNLIMITED
501 Church Street, N.E.
Vienna, VA 22180
(703) 281-1100

International conservation organization dedicated to the protection of clean water and the enhancement of trout and salmon fishery resources.

THE WILDERNESS SOCIETY
1400 Eye Street, N.W.
Washington, DC 20005
(202) 842-3400

Works to preserve wilderness and wildlife, protect America's forest, parks, rivers, and shorelands and broaden awareness of human relationship with the natural environment.

WORK ON WASTE
Dr. Paul Connett and Ellen Connett
82 Judson Street
Canton, NY 13617
(315) 379-9200

National grassroots citizens' organization working to provide the public with a source of information concerning resource management alternatives to landfilling and mass-burn incineration. Promotes re-use, recycling, composting and waste reduction.

OTHER NATIONAL GROUPS:

AMERICAN COUNCIL FOR AN ENERGY-EFFICIENT ECONOMY (ACEEE)
1001 Connecticut Avenue, N.W.
Suite 535
Washington, DC 20036
(202) 429-8873

Non-profit research group conducting research and development on efficiency technologies. Also promotes efficiency policy.

AMERICAN FORESTRY ASSOCIATION
P.O. Box 2000
Washington, DC 20013
(202) 667-3300

Citizens' organization for conservation of trees and forests. Local and national education and action promoting stewardship of national, state, private and urban forests.

AMERICAN RIVERS
801 Pennsylvania Avenue, S.E.
Suite 303
Washington, DC 20003
(202) 547-6900

National organization dedicated to the preservation of the nation's remaining freeflowing rivers and their landscapes for fishing, boating, hiking, scenery and wildlife. Measures results in river miles and streamside acres protected.

AMERICANS FOR THE ENVIRONMENT
1400 16th Street, N.W.
Washington, DC 20036
(202) 797-6665

National non-profit, non-partisan educational institution, serves as a political skills training arm for the environmental community.

ASSOCIATION FOR COMMUTER TRANSPORTATION (ACT)
1776 Massachusetts Avenue, N.W.
Suite 521
Washington, DC 20036
(202) 659-0600

ACT works to increase mobility by making commuting more convenient and less costly. Solves commute-related problems through ride-sharing and other transportation supply and demand management actions.

BICYCLE CENTENNIAL
P.O. Box 8308
Missoula, MT 59807
(406) 721-1776

A non-profit, recreational cycling organization. Developed cyclist maps for over 16,000 miles of bicycling routes.

BIO INTEGRAL RESOURCE CENTER
P.O. Box 8267
Berkeley, CA 94707
(415) 524-2567

Non-profit organization that provides practical information on least toxic pest management methods. You can receive BIRC's catalog of publications by sending $1.

CENTER FOR MARINE CONSERVATION
1725 DeSales Street, N.W.
Suite 500
Washington, DC 20036
(202) 429-5609

Dedicated to the conservation of endangered and threatened species and their marine habitats, with focus on research, policy analysis, education, and public information and involvement.

CENTER FOR SCIENCE IN THE PUBLIC INTEREST
1501 16th Street, N.W.
Washington, DC 20036
(202) 332-9110

Investigates consumer, food and nutrition issues, publishes reports, and initiates legal action.

CONSERVATION AND RENEWABLE ENERGY
INQUIRY AND REFERRAL SERVICE
P.O. Box 8900
Silver Spring, MD 20907
(800) 523-2929

Source of information on home energy conservation and renewable energy.

THE CONSERVATION FOUNDATION/WORLD WILDLIFE FUND
1250 24th Street, N.W.
Washington, DC 20037
(202) 293-4800

Performs research and public education on land use, toxic substances, water resources, environmental dispute resolution, and air pollution control.

THE CONSUMER PESTICIDE PROJECT
425 Mississippi Street
San Francisco, CA 94131
(415) 826-6314

Provides organizing assistance for citizens to persuade supermarket managers and chains to adopt a pesticide reduction program.

COUNCIL ON ECONOMIC PRIORITIES (CEP)
30 Irving Place
New York, NY 10003
(212) 420-1133
(800) 822-6435

A non-profit research organization devoted to impartial analysis of crucial public interest issues.

DEFENDERS OF WILDLIFE
1244 19th Street, N.W.
Washington, DC 20036
(202) 659-9510

Protects wild animals and plants, especially endangered species; preserves habitats on land and sea; prevents wildlife deaths from poisons, pollutants, marine entanglement; promotes wildlife education.

EARTH ISLAND INSTITUTE
300 Broadway
Suite 28
San Francisco, CA 94133
(415) 788-3666

Initiates and supports internationally-oriented action projects for the protection and restoration of the environment.

ENERGY CONSERVATION COALITION
1525 New Hampshire Avenue, N.W.
Washington, DC 20036
(202) 745-4874

A project of Environmental Action Foundation. Members of the 20-member coalition include national, consumer, environmental, church and scientific organizations. Promotes federal and state efficiency policies.

ENVIRONMENTAL ACTION FOUNDATION
1525 New Hampshire Avenue, N.W.
Washington, DC 20036
(202) 745-4879

Promotes a healthy and sustainable environment focusing on toxic pollutions, energy, solid waste, recycling, and energy conservation. Activities include research, education, grassroots organizing and legal action.

ENVIRONMENTAL LAW INSTITUTE
1616 P Street, N.W.
Suite 200
Washington, DC 20036
(202) 328-5150

A national environmental law research and education center which provides technical assistance, public information, training and creative research.

ENVIRONMENTAL POLICY INSTITUTE/FRIENDS OF THE EARTH/OCEANIC SOCIETY
(EPI/FOE/OS)
218 D Street, S.E.
Washington, DC 20003
(202) 544-2600

Devoted to helping citizens have a voice in shaping the environmental policy which affects all of us—our public health, cost of living and quality of life.

GLOBAL GREENHOUSE NETWORK
c/o Jeremy Rifkin
1130 17th Street, N.W.
Suite 630
Washington, DC 20036
(202) 466-2823

Informal network of progressive activists in 35 countries. Aims to share information and foster political action.

GLOBAL TOMORROW COALITION
1325 G Street, N.W.
Suite 915
Washington, DC 20005-3104
(202) 628-4016

Alliance of organizations and individuals dedicated to fostering broader public understanding in the United States of the long term significance of interrelated global trends in population, resources, environment and development.

HUMAN ENVIRONMENT CENTER
1001 Connecticut Avenue, N.W.
Suite 827
Washington, DC 20036
(202) 331-8387

Provides education, information and services to encourage common effort by environmental, minority, human resources and urban groups.

INFORM
381 Park Avenue South
Suite 1201
New York, NY 10016
(212) 689-4040

Research and public education to identify and report on practical actions for the conservation and preservation of natural resources.

INSTITUTE FOR LOCAL SELF RELIANCE
2425 18th Street, N.W.
Washington, DC 20009
(202) 232-4108

An educational and research organization that promotes environmentally sound economic development. Provides technical assistance to citizens, government officials and small businesses.

IZAAK WALTON LEAGUE OF AMERICA
1401 Wilson Boulevard
Level B
Arlington, VA 22209
(703) 528-1818

Promotes means and opportunities for educating the public to conserve, maintain, protect and restore the soil, forest, water, air and other natural resources of the United States.

LEAGUE OF CONSERVATION VOTERS
1150 Connecticut, N.W.

Suite 201
Washington, DC 20036
(202) 785-8683

Non-partisan, national political campaign committee to promote the election of public officials who will work for a healthy environment. Evaluates environmental records of members of congress and presidential candidates.

MOBILE AIR CONDITIONING SOCIETY
7425 Westchester Pike
Upper Darby, PA 19082
(215) 352-6080

Source of information on recycling car air conditioner refrigerant.

NATIONAL ASSOCIATION OF RAILROAD PASSENGERS
236 Massachusetts Avenue, N.E.
Washington, DC 20002
(202) 546-1550

Alliance of citizens concerned with promoting rail use and protecting the environment.

NATIONAL CENTER FOR POLICY ALTERNATIVES
2000 Florida Avenue, N.W.
Suite 400
Washington, DC 20009
(202) 387-6030

Provides information on innovative state approaches to solving environmental problems.

NATIONAL COALITION AGAINST THE MISUSE OF PESTICIDES
530 7th Street, S.E.
Washington, DC 20003
(202) 543-5450

Assists individuals, organizations and communities with useful information on pesticides and their alternatives.

NATIONAL PARKS AND CONSERVATION ASSOCIATION
1015 31st Street, N.W.

Washington, DC 20007

(202) 944-8530

A national organization dedicated solely to protecting and enhancing our park system. Offers public education and research programs.

NUCLEAR INFORMATION & RESOURCE SERVICE (NIRS)

1424 16th Street, N.W.

Suite 601

Washington, DC 20036

(202) 328-0002

Non-profit, national information center and clearinghouse for individuals and groups concerned about nuclear energy. Provides information, resources and networking assistance.

POPULATION CRISIS COMMITTEE

1120 19th Street, N.W.

Suite 550

Washington, DC 20036

(202) 659-1833

Develops worldwide support for international population and family planning programs through public education, policy analysis and liaison with international leaders and organizations.

THE POPULATION INSTITUTE

110 Maryland Avenue, N.E.

Suite 207

Washington, DC 20002

(202) 544-3300

Works to enlist and motivate key leadership groups to participate in the effort to bring population growth into balance with human dignity and freedom.

PUBLIC CITIZEN/CRITICAL MASS ENERGY PROJECT

215 Pennsylvania Avenue, S.E.

Washington, DC 20003

(202) 546-4996

Non-profit research and advocacy organization founded to oppose nuclear power and promote safer energy alternatives such as energy efficiency and renewable energy technologies. Serves as a technical and informational clearinghouse.

PUBLIC CITIZEN/FREEDOM OF INFORMATION CLEARINGHOUSE
P.O. Box 19367
Washington, DC 20036
(202) 785-3704

Provides technical and legal assistance to the public to seek access to information held by government agencies. Litigates cases to protect the public's right of access to such information.

RADIOACTIVE WASTE CAMPAIGN
625 Broadway, Second Floor
New York, NY 10012
(212) 473-7390

An environmental advocacy and public interest organization focusing on radioactive waste issues. Conducts research, information dissemination and public education activities.

RAINFOREST ACTION NETWORK
301 Broadway, Suite A
San Francisco, CA 94133
(415) 398-4404

International organization working to protect the world's tropical rainforests.

RESOURCES FOR THE FUTURE
1616 P Street, N.W.
Washington, DC 20036
(202) 328-5000

Works to advance research and education in the development, conservation, and use of natural resources including the quality of the environment.

RENEW AMERICA
1400 16th Street, N.W.
Suite 710
Washington, DC 20036

(202) 232-2252

Promotes increased natural resource efficiency, including renewable energy, sustainable agriculture, water conservation, and the recycling of refined materials.

ROCKY MOUNTAIN INSTITUTE
Amory and Hunter Lovins
1739 Snowmass Creek Road
Drawer 248
Old Snowmass, CO 81654
(303) 927-3851

The leading national advocates for energy efficient technologies.

SAFE ENERGY COMMUNICATION COUNCIL (SECC)
1717 Massachusetts Avenue, N.W.
L.L. 215
Washington, DC 20036
(202) 483-8491

A coalition of national environmental, safe energy, and public interest media groups. Produces broadcast and print ads to respond to the nuclear industry and utility campaigns and helps groups develop media skills.

SCENIC AMERICA
216 7th Street, S.E.
Washington, DC 20003
(202) 546-1100

Works to fight billboard pollution and other forms of visual pollution, preserve scenic beauty, and promote scenic highways.

SEA SHEPHERD CONSERVATION SOCIETY
P.O. Box 7000
South Redondo Beach, CA 90277
(213) 373-6979

International marine conservation action organization, directed toward the conservation and protection of marine wildlife.

SIERRA CLUB LEGAL DEFENSE FUND
2044 Fillmore Street

San Francisco, CA 94115
(415) 567-6100

Wilderness, wildlife, parks, forests—often only legal action saves them. Toxics, acid rain, pollution—sometimes only litigation stops them. Represents environmental groups nationwide.

SOCIAL INVESTMENT FORUM
C.E.R.E.S. Project
711 Atlantic Avenue
Boston, MA 02111
(617) 451-3252

National association of professionals and investors seeking to promote and facilitate the socially responsible investment movement.

TREEPEOPLE
12601 Mulholland Drive
Beverly Hills, CA 90210
(213) 273-8733

A non-profit tree-planting organization. Trains citizen foresters and educates people about local and global forest issues.

THE TRUST FOR PUBLIC LAND
116 New Montgomery Street, 4th Floor
San Francisco, CA 94105
(415) 495-4014

Acquires and protects open spaces for people to use and enjoy as urban parks, neighborhood gardens and recreational wilderness areas.

UNION OF CONCERNED SCIENTISTS (UCS)
26 Church Street
Cambridge, MA 02238
(617) 547-5552

Serving the American people through programs involving nuclear power safety, energy policy, the greenhouse effect, nuclear arms control and other impacts of science and technology.

WORLD RESOURCES INSTITUTE
1709 New York Avenue, N.W.

Suite 700
Washington, DC 20006
(202) 638-6300

A policy research center created in late 1983 to help governments, international organizations, the private sector and others to address vital issues concerning environmental integrity, natural resource management, and international security.

WORLDWATCH INSTITUTE
1776 Massachusetts Avenue, N.W.
Washington, DC 20036
(202) 452-1999

Research organization concerned with identifying and analyzing emerging global problems and trends and bringing them to the attention of opinion leaders and the general public.

ZERO POPULATION GROWTH
1400 16th Street, N.W.
Suite 320
Washington, DC 20036
(202) 332-2200

Works to achieve a balance among people, resources and environment by advocating population stabilization in the United States and worldwide.

REGIONAL GROUPS:
CONSERVATION LAW FOUNDATION OF NEW ENGLAND
3 Joy Street
Boston, MA 02108
(617) 742-2540

Environmental law organization dedicated to the preservation of New England's natural resources. Works on energy conservation and utility regulation; environmental health; groundwater protection; public and private land preservation.

GULF COAST TENANTS LEADERSHIP DEVELOPMENT PROJECT
Box 56101
New Orleans, LA 70156
(504) 949-4919

Trains local leaders to mobilize their neighbors to demand social justice and better living conditions. Also works on toxics issues.

PEOPLE AGAINST HAZARDOUS LANDFILL SITES (PAHLS)
P.O. Box 37
608 Highway 130
Wheeler, IN 46393
(219) 465-7466

A statewide alliance of grassroots organizations working on various pollution problems. Serves as a national and international clearinghouse for information on a range of pollution issues.

SILICON VALLEY TOXICS COALITION
760 North 1st Street
2nd Floor
San Jose, CA 95112
(408) 287-6707

Focuses, although not exclusively, on toxics contamination in high-tech industries. Groundwater clean-up and pollution and accident prevention.

SOUTHWEST RESEARCH AND INFORMATION CENTER
P.O. Box 4524
Albuquerque, NM 87106
(505) 262-1862

A multi-racial, multi-issue grassroots membership community organization fighting for basic rights to land and resources, growth and preservation of diverse cultures and self-determination. Sees safe environment as a fundamental human right.

TOXICS COORDINATING PROJECT
942 Market Street, #502
San Francisco, CA 94102
(415) 781-2745

A statewide coalition of organizations and activists working to protect California's health, environment and economy from toxic chemicals.

APPENDIX B:
RECOMMENDED READINGS

GLOBAL WARMING

The Challenge of Global Warming. Washington: Natural Resources Defense Council, 1989.

Flavin, Christopher. "Slowing Global Warming: A Worldwide Strategy." Worldwatch Paper No. 91. Washington: Worldwatch Institute, 1989.

Schneider, Stephen H. *Global Warming.* San Francisco: Sierra Club Books, 1989.

OZONE DESTRUCTION

"Atmosphere." (A quarterly journal focusing on ozone protection published by Friends of the Earth International, Washington, D.C.)

Roan, Sharon L. *Ozone Crisis.* New York: John Wiley & Sons, Inc., 1989.

Shea, Cynthia Pollock. "Protecting Life on Earth: Steps to Save the Ozone Layer." Worldwatch Paper No. 87. Washington: Worldwatch Institute, 1988.

AIR POLLUTION

"Darkening Skies: The Mounting Air Pollution Crisis in the United States." Sierra Club Report. San Francisco, 1989.

Public Citizen's Guide to Radon Home Test Kits. Washington: Public Citizen, 1989.

Renner, Michael. "Rethinking the Role of the Automobile." Worldwatch Paper No. 84. Washington: Worldwatch Institute, 1988.

TOXICS

Cutting Chemical Wastes: What 29 Organic Chemical Plants are Doing to Reduce Hazardous Wastes. New York: Inform, 1985.

The Dynamic Duo: RCRA and SARA Title III: A Citizen's Handbook on the Nation's Hazardous Waste Law. Washington: Environmental Action Foundation, 1989.

Epstein, Samuel S., M.D., Lester O. Brown and Carl Pope. *Hazardous Waste in America.* San Francisco: Sierra Club Books, 1982.

Serious Reduction of Hazardous Waste: For Pollution Prevention and Industrial Efficiency. Washington: Congressional Office of Technology Assessment, 1986.

WASTE REDUCTION AND RECYCLING

Coming Full Circle: Successful Recycling Today. New York: Environmental Defense Fund, 1988.

"Garbage: The Practical Journal for the Environment." (A bi-monthly magazine published by Old-House Journal Corporation, Brooklyn, New York.)

Robinson, William D., ed. *The Solid Waste Handbook: A Practical Guide.* New York: John Wiley & Sons, Inc., 1986.

Shea, Cynthia Pollock. "Mining Urban Wastes: The Potential for Recycling." Worldwatch Paper No. 76. Washington: Worldwatch Institute, 1987.

Wirka, Jeanne. *Wrapped in Plastics: The Environmental Case for Reducing Plastics Packaging.* Washington: Environmental Action Foundation, 1990.

Yepson, Jr., R.B., ed. *The Encyclopedia of Natural Insect and Disease Control.* Emmaus: Rodale Press, 1984.

PESTICIDES

For Our Kids' Sake: How to Protect Your Child Against Pesticides in Food. Mothers and Others for Pesticide Limits. Washington: Natural Resources Defense Council, 1989.

Intolerable Risk: Pesticides in Our Children's Food. New York: Natural Resources Defense Council, 1989.

Mott, Lawrie and Karen Snyder. *Pesticide Alert: A Guide to Pesticides in Fruits and Vegetables.* San Francisco: Sierra Club Books, 1988.

NUCLEAR ENERGY
Deadly Defense: Military Radioactive Landfills. A Citizen Guide by the Radioactive Waste Campaign. New York, 1988.

Safety Second: The NRC and America's Nuclear Power Plants. Union of Concerned Scientists. Bloomington: Indiana University Press, 1987.

Tomain, Joseph P. *Nuclear Power Transformation.* Bloomington: Indiana University Press, 1987.

ENERGY EFFICIENCY
The Energy Savers Handbook: For Town and City People. Emmaus: Rodale Press, 1982.

Sant, Roger, Dennis Bakke and Roger Naill. *Creating Abundance: America's Least-Cost Energy Strategy.* New York: McGraw-Hill, 1984.

World Resources 1988-1989. New York: Basic Books, 1988.

GLOBAL ENVIRONMENT
Caulfield, Catherine. *In the Rain Forest: Report from a Strange, Beautiful, Imperiled World.* New York: Alfred Knopf, 1984.

Ehrlich, Paul R. and Anne. *Population Explosion.* New York: Simon & Schuster, 1990.

State of the World 1990. Worldwatch Institute. New York: W.W. Norton & Co., 1990.

ORGANIZING
Hall, Bob, ed. *Environmental Politics: Lessons from the Grassroots.* Durham: Institute for Southern Studies, 1988.

Moore, Andrew Owens. *Making Polluters Pay.* Washington: Environmental Action Foundation, 1987.

INDEX

EARTH DAY 2000 IS COMING!

Formed by the organizers of the first Earth Day held on April 22, 1970, Environmental Action looks ahead to the next decade with a full commitment to the spirit of citizen awareness and activism on behalf of the environment. And now, we invite you to join the action to make the 1990's our environmental decade.

This book, *Our Earth, Ourselves,* is the opening chapter on the road to Earth Day 2000. As you read this book, you learned of many ways you and your community can make a difference. But, to attain our goals, to make our gains real, we are asking every concerned citizen to take the next step by becoming a member of Environmental Action.

Through membership in EA, you can join forces with environmentalists across the country. We will keep you abreast of new environmental threats and the ways you and others can make a difference. EA will serve as your advocate before Congress to get strong environmental laws.

We invite you to join the Action. Please, take time today to fill out the coupon below and send your $25 membership contribution. Earth Day 2000 is coming. Help us all make this decade one for the world.

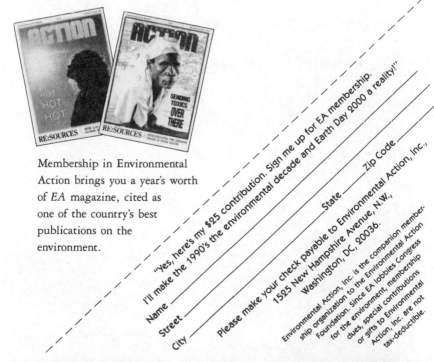

Membership in Environmental Action brings you a year's worth of *EA* magazine, cited as one of the country's best publications on the environment.

"Yes, here's my $25 contribution. Sign me up for EA membership. I'll make the 1990's the environmental decade and Earth Day 2000 a reality!"

Name _____

Street _____

City _____ State _____ Zip Code _____

Please make your check payable to Environmental Action, Inc., 1525 New Hampshire Avenue, N.W., Washington, DC, 20036.

Environmental Action, Inc. is the companion member-ship organization to the Environmental Action Foundation. Since EA lobbies Congress for the environment, membership dues, special contributions or gifts to Environmental Action, Inc. are not tax-deductible.